25 FUN-TO-BUILD PROJECTS FOR LEARNING ELECTRONICS THEORY

EDITORS OF ELEMENTARY ELECTRONICS

 TAB BOOKS Inc.

Blue Ridge Summit, PA

FIRST EDITION

SECOND PRINTING

Copyright © 1987 by Davis Publications, Inc. Material in this book is reprinted
by permission of Davis Publications, Inc. and before revision was
Copyright © 1981, 1979, 1978, 1977, 1975, 1971, 1968, and 1967
by Davis Publications, Inc.
Printed in the United States of America

Library of Congress Cataloging in Publication Data

25 fun-to-build projects for learning electronics theory.

Includes index.
1. Electronics—Amateurs' manuals. I. Elementary
electronics. II. Title: Twenty-five fun-to-build
projects for learning electronics theory.
TK9965.A113 1987   621.381   87-1918
ISBN 0-8306-0239-9
ISBN 0-8306-2839-8 (pbk.)

TAB BOOKS Inc. offers software for
sale. For information and a catalog,
please contact TAB Software Department,
Blue Ridge Summit, PA 17294-0850.

Questions regarding the content of this book
should be addressed to:

Reader Inquiry Branch
TAB BOOKS Inc.
Blue Ridge Summit, PA 17294-0214

Contents

Preface

This is the fourth in a series of books by the editors of *Elementary Electronics* magazine. The first three books in the series are *GIANT Book of Easy-to-Build Electronics Projects* (TAB Book No. 1599), the *Second Book of Easy-to-Build Electronics Projects* (TAB Book No. 1679), and *55 Easy-to-Build Electronics Projects* (TAB Book No. 1999). All of these exciting electronics project books are published by TAB BOOKS, Inc., of Blue Ridge Summit, Pennsylvania. If you don't have copies of the first three books, you can order them from your local bookstore or directly from TAB BOOKS Inc.

This book is a little different from the other books in the series. The projects in each of the following chapters were specifically chosen and organized to help you learn about electronics and electricity. Not only will you find many exciting projects to build, but you will also find sections that explain the theory of various aspects of electronics to you. This book will bring you hours of pleasurable hobby time.

List of Project Sources

25 FUN-TO-BUILD PROJECTS FOR LEARNING ELECTRONICS THEORY

Chapter 1

Basic Electronics

BASICS OF ELECTRICITY

One of the most thought-provoking discoveries of modern physics is the fact that matter and energy are interchangeable. Centuries of scientific head-scratching about the nature of matter, the mystery of fire, and the once-terrifying crack of lightning have all come to focus on the smallest particle that is the building block of any given substance: the atom. An atom is necessarily matter and yet this atom of matter can undergo nuclear fission and release quantities of energy that are beyond the imagination. In the atom lies the secret of all phenomena. One theory of the universe, hypothesized by Georges Lemaitre, even regards the present universe as resulting from the radioactive disintegration of one primeval atom!

By the beginning of the 19th century, the atomic theory of matter—which actually originated in 5th century Greece when the atom was named— was firmly established. It was due primarily to the efforts of 17th century scientists who—actually working in the tradition of medieval alchemy—

sought the prime constituent of all matter. Mainly through the work of John Dalton, whose investigations as to how various elements combine to form chemical compounds, it came to be regarded that an atom was the indivisible and indestructible unit of matter.

This viable and working view of the indestructible atom served science until 1897 when the atom itself was found to be destructible! To anyone concerned with electricity or electronics, the year 1897 is a memorable one: it was the year J. J. Thomson, the English physicist, identified and experimentally revealed the existence of the first subatomic particle—the electron!

The First "Electronic" Experiment

We blithely speak of electricity as the flow of electrons yet, often, we are little aware of the great body of research that went into elucidating this fundamental of basic electricity. In fact, before the discovery of the electron, convention held that the flow of electric current was in the direction that a posi-

1

tive charge moved. This convention of positive current, being the flow of positive charges and opposite to the direction of electron flow, is still found to be useful in circuit analysis and is used even today.

Thomson's experiment established that a particle much lighter than the lightest atom did indeed exist. The electron, as it was named, was the first subatomic particle to be defined.

The experiment was conducted utilizing a rudimentary version of a cathode ray tube—the modern version of which is in almost every home today in the form of the television picture tube. Before Thomson's experiment, it was discovered that when electric current was passed through a gas in a discharge tube, a beam of unknown nature traveled through the tube from the negative to positive terminal (opposite to the direction conventionally held as the direction of the flow of current).

This "cathode ray" beam also traveled in a straight line and was deflected by electric or magnetic forces applied perpendicular to the beam. What Thomson did was to use these facts to determine for one of the mysterious particles comprising the beam of cathode rays the relationship of its mass, m, to its electric charge, e. By deflecting the beam with a known electric force (Fig. 1-1) and then measuring what magnetic force applied in the opposite direction would bring the beam back to its original undeflected position, he could determine the relationship of e to m. He established a definite value for e/m and thereby "discovered" the electron which, as we now know, is 1,837 times

smaller in mass than the lightest atom, the hydrogen atom. It also carries the smallest charge that occurs in nature; every electric charge is actually an integral multiple of the charge of the electron.

From Minus to Plus

With the discovery of the electron, it was still over a dozen years into the 20th century before a graphic conception of the atom evolved. Since the atom is electrically neutral and electrons are negatively charged, the existence of positively charged particles was a necessity, and the existence of a proton was postulated. Eventually the nuclear model of the atom was evolved. Each atom was conceived to resemble a solar system in miniature. The nucleus—positively charged—is surrounded by a number of electrons revolving around it; the charges balance and the atom is electrically neutral (Fig. 1-2). Further research in the 20th century has gone on to reveal more elementary particles than you can shake a stick at: neutrons, positrons, neutrinos, mesons, and more. The number continues to grow and yet the ultimate nature of matter remains a riddle. But, in a discussion of basic electricity, only the electron and proton need concern us.

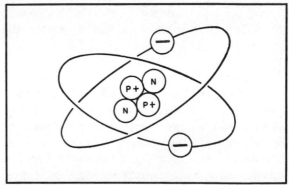

Fig. 1-2. The charge of each electron balances that of a proton. Other particles affect atomic mass but can be ignored in study of electronics.

Electrons in Orbit

An atom of matter has a number of electrons orbiting around its nucleus. A hydrogen atom, for example, has a single electron; carbon on the other

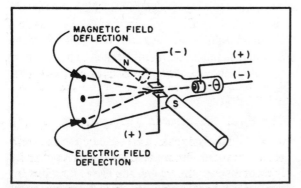

Fig. 1-1. An electron beam, like that in a TV picture tube (CRT), can be deflected magnetically or by an electric field. Force needed "measured" the electron.

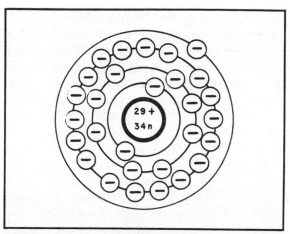

Fig. 1-3. The number of electrons to each ring are limited—2 in first; 8 in second; 18 for the third; and a total of 32 in fourth orbital ring.

hand has 6. These electrons are arranged in rings or shells around the central nucleus—each ring having a definite maximum capacity of electrons which it can retain. For example, in the copper atom shown in Fig. 1-3 the maximum number of electrons that can exist in the first ring (the ring nearest the nucleus) is two. The next ring can have a maximum of eight, the third ring a maximum of 18, and the fourth ring a maximum of 32. However, the outer ring or shell of electrons for any atom cannot exceed eight electrons. However, heavier atoms may have more than four rings.

The Outer Orbit

The ring of electrons furthest from the atom's nucleus is known as the valence ring and the electrons orbiting in this ring are known as valence electrons. These valence electrons, being further from the nucleus, are not held as tightly in their orbits as electrons in the inner rings and can therefore be fairly easily dislodged by an external force such as heat, light, friction, and electrical potential. The fewer electrons in the valence ring of an atom, the less these electrons are bound to the central nucleus. As an example, the copper atom has only one electron in its valence ring. Consequently, it can be easily removed by the application of only the slightest amount of external energy. Ordinary room tem-

perature is sufficient to dislodge large numbers of electrons from copper atoms; these electrons circulate about as free electrons. It is because of these large numbers of free electrons that copper is such a good electrical conductor. There could be no electrical or electronics industry as we know it today if it were not for the fact that electrons can fairly easily escape, or be stripped from the valence ring of certain elements.

Electronic Charges

If an electron is stripped from an atom, the atom will assume a positive charge because the number of positively charged protons in its nucleus now exceeds the number of negatively charged orbiting electrons. If, on the other hand, the atom should gain an electron, it will become negatively charged as the number of electrons now exceeds the protons in its nucleus. The atom with the deficiency of electrons is known as a positive ion, while an atom with a surplus of electrons is known as a negative ion.

Presence of an electrical charge on a body can be illustrated by use of an electroscope (Fig. 1-4).

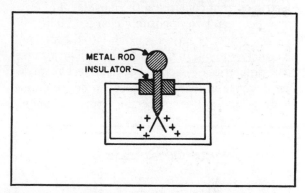

Fig. 1-4. An electroscope is a simple device to indicate electrical charges that are too weak to be measured with standard meters.

Two leaves of aluminum or gold foil hang from a metal rod inside a glass case so they're free from air disturbances. When the metal rod is touched by a charged body, the leaves acquire static electricity of the same polarity and, since like charges repel, they stand apart. The greater the charge, the further apart the leaves spread.

3

Electron Flow

When an electrical conductor is placed between these two oppositely charged bodies, free electrons are attracted by the positive body—free electrons will move through the wire. This movement of free electrons will continue only until the excess of electrons is equally divided between the two bodies. Under these conditions, the charges on both bodies will be equal and the electron flow will end.

In Fig. 1-5 are a battery, lamp, and connecting leads between the battery and lamp. In this instance, the battery serves as an electric charge pump—free electrons continually developed at its negative terminal by chemical action flow through the connecting leads and lamp back to the positive terminal of the battery by the attraction of oppositely charged bodies. The battery, connecting leads, and lamp form an electrical circuit which must be complete before the free electrons can flow from the battery's negative terminal to its positive terminal via the lamp. Thus, the battery serves as a source of potential difference or voltage by continually supplying a surplus of electrons at its negative terminal. Summing up, we can say a flow of electric current consists of the movement of electrons between two oppositely charged bodies.

We cannot progress very far into the study of electricity without first becoming familiar with the basic properties of electrical circuits. Just as we define distance in feet and inches, so do we define electrical properties in specific terms and units.

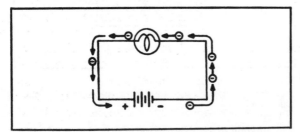

Fig. 1-5. Electron flow in any circuit is from negative to positive.

Potential

Earlier, we saw that an electric charge difference has to exist between the ends of an electrical conductor in order to cause a flow of free electrons through the conductor. This flow of electrons constitutes the electric current. The electric charge difference, or potential difference, exerts a force on the flow of free electrons, forcing them through the conductor. This electric force or pressure is referred to as electromotive force, abbreviated EMF.

The greater the charge or potential difference, the greater will be the movement of free electrons (current) through the conductor as there will be more "push and pull" on the free electrons. The symbol used to designate electrical potential is the letter E which stands for electromotive force. The quantity of EMF is measured by a unit called the volt. Hence, the common name most often used in place of EMF is voltage.

Current Intensity

We have learned that an electric current consists of a flow of charge carriers (generally free electrons) between two points of different electrical potential. The rate of flow of these charges determines the intensity or strength of this current flow. Current strength is expressed in units known as amperes. One ampere of current flows in a circuit when 6,240,000,000,000,000,000 electrons flow out of a negative terminal, through a conductor, and back into a positive terminal in one second. The symbol for the ampere is the letter I which stands for intensity.

Resistance

The flow of electric current through a conductor is caused by the movement of free electrons present in the atoms of the conductor. A bit of thought then indicates that the greater the number of free electrons present in the atoms of a particular conductor, the greater will be its electrical conductivity. Gold, silver, and copper rank as excellent electrical conductors, as their atoms readily release free electrons. On the other hand, the atoms of such elements as sulphur have almost on free electrons available and they are thus very poor electrical conductors. Such materials are known as electrical insulators. Between these extremes lie elements such as carbon whose atoms have a moderate number of free electrons available and thus are moderately good electrical conductors.

Even the best electrical conductors offer some opposition to the passage of free electrons. This opposition is called resistance. You might consider electrical resistance similar to mechanical friction. As in the case of mechanical friction, electrical resistance generates heat. When current flows through a resistance, heat is generated; the greater the current flow, the greater the heat. Also, for a given current flow, the greater the resistance, the greater the heat produced.

Electrical resistance can be both beneficial and undesirable. Toasters, electric irons, etc. all make use of the heat generated by current flowing through wire coils. Resistance is also often intentionally added to an electrical circuit to limit the flow of current. This type of resistance is generally lumped together in a single unit known as a resistor.

There are also instances where resistance is undesirable. Excessive resistance in the connecting leads of an electrical circuit can cause both heating and electrical loss. The heating, if sufficient, can cause a fire hazard, particularly in house wiring, and the circuit losses are a waste of electrical power.

Electrical resistance is expressed by a unit known as the ohm, indicated by the letter R. An electrical conductor has a resistance of one ohm when an applied EMF of one volt causes a current of one ampere to flow through it.

Resistance Factors

There are other factors beside the composition of the material that determine its resistance. For example, temperature has an effect on the resistance of a conductor. As the temperature of copper increases, for example, its resistance increases. The increase in temperature causes the electrons in the outer ring of the atom to resist release to the free electron state. This increase in resistance is known as a positive temperature coefficient. Not all conductors show this increase in resistance with an increase in temperature; their resistance decreases with an increase in temperature. Such materials are said to have a negative temperature

coefficient. Certain metallic alloys have been developed which exhibit a zero temperature coefficient: their resistance does not change with changes in temperature.

As you might suspect, the length of a conductor has an effect upon its resistance. Doubling the length of a conductor will double its resistance. By the same token, halving the length of a conductor will cut its resistance in half. Just remember that the resistance of a conductor is directly proportional to its length.

The cross-sectional area of a conductor also determines its resistance. As you double the cross-section of a conductor, you halve its resistance; halving its cross-section doubles its resistance. Here again, the "why" of this is pretty easy to see: there are more current carrying electrons available in a large cross-section conductor than in a small cross-section conductor of the same length. Therefore, the resistance of a conductor is inversely proportional to its cross-sectional area.

Circuit Relationship

Now that we have a basic understanding of voltage, current, and resistance, let's take a look at just how they interact under circuit conditions.

Figure 1-6A shows a battery, ammeter (a device to indicate current strength), and resistor connected in series. Notice that the ammeter indicates that 4 amperes are flowing in the circuit.

Figure 1-6B shows the identical setup with the exception that the battery voltage has now been doubled. The ammeter now shows that twice the original current, or 8 amperes, is now flowing in the circuit. Therefore, we can see that doubling the voltage applied to the circuit will double the current flowing in the circuit.

In Fig. 1-6C the same circuit appears again; this time, however, the battery voltage is one half its original value. The ammeter shows that one half of the original current, or 2 amperes, is now flowing in the circuit. This shows us that halving the voltage applied to the circuit will halve the current flowing through the circuit.

All this boils down to the fact that, assuming the same circuit resistance in all cases, the current

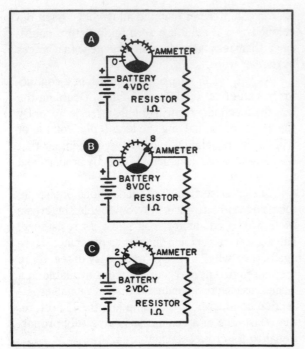

Fig. 1-6. In A, B, and C, the value of the resistor remains constant while the supply voltage is altered with a resulting current change.

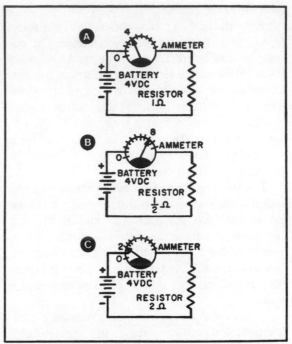

Fig. 1-7. Battery voltage A, B, and C is held constant while resistor is halved and doubled in value. Resulting current changes are basis for Ohm's law.

flowing in a circuit will be directly proportional to the applied voltage—increasing as the voltage is increased, and decreasing as the applied voltage is decreased.

In Fig. 1-7A we again see the circuit consisting of the battery, ammeter, and resistance. Notice that the ammeter indicates that 4 amperes are flowing through the circuit.

In Fig. 1-7B we see that the value of resistance has been cut in half as a result, the ammeter indicates that twice the original current, or 8 amperes, is now flowing in the circuit. This leads us to the correct assumption that for a given supply voltage, halving the circuit resistance will double the current flowing in the circuit.

Figure 1-7C again shows our basic circuit, but with the resistance now doubled from its original value. The ammeter indicates that the current in the circuit is now one half of its original value.

Summing things up: for a given supply voltage, the current flowing in a circuit will be inversely proportional to the resistance in the circuit.

Ohm's Law

From what you have seen so far, you are probably getting the idea that you can determine the current flowing in a circuit if you know the voltage and resistance present in the circuit, and the voltage if you know the current and resistance, or the resistance if the voltage and current are known.

All this is quite current, and is formally stated by Ohm's law as follows:

$$I = \frac{E}{R}$$

Where:

E = voltage
I = current
R = resistance

Now, let's take a look at how this formula is used: To find voltage:

6

$$E = I \times R$$

To find current:

$$I = \frac{E}{R}$$

To find resistance:

$$R = \frac{E}{I}$$

A handy way to remember Ohm's law is by means of the triangle shown in Fig. 1-8. Simply cover the quantity (voltage, current, or resistance) that you want to determine, and read the correct relationship of the remaining two quantities. For example, if you want to know the correct current (I), put your finger over I and read E/R.

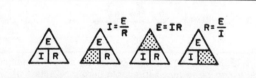

Fig. 1-8. Shaded portion of triangle indicates unknown quantity in the formula. Visible factors appear in their proper mathematical relation. Just fill in the known values and go on with multiplication or division.

Ohm's Law to Determine Voltage

Let's delve a bit more deeply into Ohm's law by applying it to a few cases where we want to determine the unknown voltage in an electrical circuit. Take a look at Fig. 1-9, which shows a simple series circuit consisting of a battery and resistor. The value of this resistor is given as 200 ohms, and 0.5 ampere of current is flowing through the circuit. We want to find the value of battery voltage. This is easily done by applying Ohm's law for voltage as follows:

$$E = I \times R$$

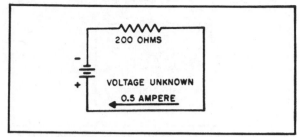

Fig. 1-9. Unknown quantity, voltage, found easily by applying Ohm's law.

Let's go through this again, this time using a practical illustration. Figure 1-10 shows a string of light bulbs, the total resistance of which is 400 ohms. You find that the bulbs draw 0.3 amperes when lighted. Let's say you would like to operate this string of bulbs from the standard 120-volt house current, but you don't know the voltage rating of the individual bulbs. By using Ohm's law for voltage, you can easily determine the voltage to light the bulbs as follows: (unknown voltage) = 0.3 (amperes) × 400 (bulb resistance) = 120 volts.

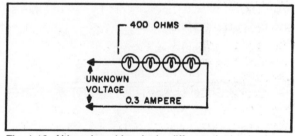

Fig. 1-10. Although problem looks different the basic circuit is same as that for Fig. 1-9.

Ohm's Law to Determine Current

Now, let's take a look at a few examples of how to determine the value of unknown current in a circuit in which both the voltage and resistance are known.

Figure 1-11 shows a series circuit with a battery and resistor. The battery voltage is 20 volts dc and the value of resistance is 5 ohms. How much current is flowing through the circuit?

$$I = \frac{E}{R}$$

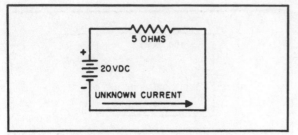

Fig. 1-11. Formula needed here is different since current is unknown. Just look for triangle in Fig. 1-8 that has I shaded.

$$I = \frac{20 \text{ (battery voltage)}}{5 \text{ (resistance in ohms)}}$$

$$I = 4 \text{ amperes}$$

Again, to get a bit more practical, let's take a look at Fig. 1-12. Here we see an electric heater element connected to the 120-volt house line. We know that this particular heater element has a resistance of 20 ohms. The house current line is fused with a 15-ampere fuse. We want to know whether the heater will draw sufficient current to blow the fuse. Here's how to find this out by use of Ohm's law for current.

$$I \text{ (unknown current)} =$$

$$\frac{120 \text{ (line voltage)}}{20 \text{ (Heater resistance in ohms)}}$$

$$1 = 6 \text{ amperes}$$

We find from the above use of Ohm's law for current that the heater draws 6 amperes, so it can be safely used on the line fused with the 15-ampere fuse. In fact, a 10-ampere fused line can also do the job.

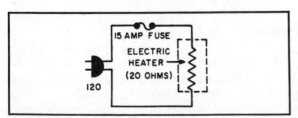

Fig. 1-12. Basic circuit is same as that in Fig. 1-11. Although three factors are given, current is unknown quantity.

Ohm's Law to Determine Resistance

Ohm's law for resistance enables us to determine the unknown value of resistance in a circuit. Figure 1-13 again shows a simple series circuit with the battery voltage given as 20 volts and the current flowing through the circuit as 0.5 ampere. The unknown resistance value in this circuit is found as follows:

Ohm's law for resistance: $R = \dfrac{E}{I}$

$$R \text{ (unknown resistance)} = \frac{20 \text{ (battery voltage)}}{0.5 \text{ (current in amperes)}}$$

$$R = 40 \text{ ohms}$$

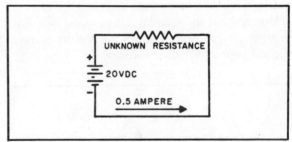

Fig. 1-13. Most Ohm's law problems are simple series circuits or can be reduced to simple series circuits.

Figure 1-14 is a practical example of how to determine unknown resistance. Here, we want to operate a 6-volt light bulb from the 120-volt house line. What value of series dropping resistor do we

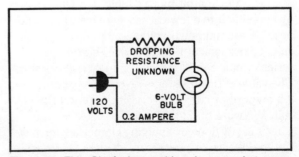

Fig. 1-14. This Ohm's law problem is somewhat more complex.

need to drop the 120-volt house current down to 6 volts? The bulb draws 0.2 ampere.

We must first determine the voltage which must be dropped across the series dropping resistor. This is done by subtracting the line voltage (120) from the bulb's voltage (6). This gives us a value of 114 volts which we use in conjunction with Ohm's law for resistance as follows:

$$R \text{ (unknown resistance)} = \frac{114 \text{ (voltage dropped by resistor)}}{0.2 \text{ (bulb current in amperes}}$$

$$R = 570 \text{ ohms}$$

Resistance in Series

Many practical electrical and electronic circuits use two or more resistances connected in series. The point to remember in this case is that the total resistance is the sum of the individual resistances. This is expressed by the formula:

$$R \text{ (total resistance)} = R1 + R2 + R3 + \text{ etc.}$$

where R1, R2, R3, etc. are the individual resistances. Thus, in Fig. 1-15 the total of the individual resistances is R (total) = 40 + 6 + 10 + 5 = 61 ohms.

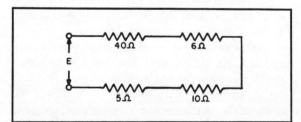

Fig. 1-15. Resistance in series is added. As far as voltage applied and current flow is concerned the individual resistors are only one.

Resistances may also be connected in parallel in a circuit as in Fig. 1-16. In this case the current flowing in the circuit will divide between the

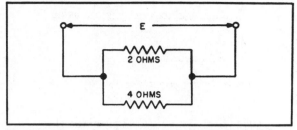

Fig. 1-16. Resistors in parallel are added algebraically—the result will always be a value less than that of the lowest in the circuit.

resistances, the greater current flowing through the lowest resistance. Also, the total resistance in the circuit will always be less than the smallest resistance since the total current is greater than the current in any of the individual resistors. The formula for determining the combined resistance of the two resistors is:

$$R \text{ (total)} = \frac{R1 \times R2}{R1 + R2}$$

Thus, in Fig. 1-16 the effective resistance of R1 and R2 is:

$$R \text{ (total)} = \frac{2 \times 4}{2 + 4} = \frac{8}{6} \text{ or } 1.33 \text{ ohms.}$$

In a circuit containing more than two parallel resistors as in Fig. 1-17, the easiest way to determine the total circuit resistance is as follows: first, assume that a 6-volt battery is connected across the resistor network. Pick a value that will make your computations simple. Then determine the current

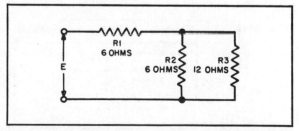

Fig. 1-17. Ohm's law can be used to determine the equivalent resistance of two or more resistors in parallel. Total current—then solve for ohms.

flowing through each of the resistors using Ohm's law:

$$I = \frac{E}{R1} = \frac{6}{2} = 3 \text{ amperes}$$

$$I = \frac{E}{R2} = \frac{6}{3} = 2 \text{ amperes}$$

$$I = \frac{E}{R3} = \frac{6}{6} = 1 \text{ ampere}$$

Next, add the individual currents flowing through the circuit:

$$2 \text{ amperes} + 3 \text{ amperes} + 1 \text{ ampere}$$
$$I = 6 \text{ amperes}$$

Inserting this 6 amperes in Ohm's law, the total circuit resistance is found to be:

$$R = \frac{6}{6} = 1 \text{ ohm}$$

The combined equation for determining the total resistance of n number of resistances would be:

$$\frac{1}{R} = \frac{1}{R1} + \frac{1}{R2} + \frac{1}{R3} + \ldots \frac{1}{Rn}$$

Quite often an electronic circuit will contain a combination of series and parallel resistances as in Fig. 1-18. To solve this type of problem, first determine the combined resistance of R2 and R3:

$$R \text{ (total)} \frac{6 \times 12}{6 + 12} = \frac{72}{18} = 4 \text{ ohms}$$

This total value of R2 and R3 may be considered a single resistance which is in series with R1, and forms a simple series circuit. This simple series circuit is solved as follows:

$$R \text{ (total)} = 6 + 4 \text{ or a total of 10 ohms.}$$

Power

The amount of work done by electricity is termed the watt and one watt is equal to one volt multiplied by one ampere. This may be expressed as: $P = E \times I$ where E = voltage in volts, I = the current in amperes. Also:

$$P = \frac{E^2}{R} \text{ and } P = I^2R$$

As an example, assume that a toaster draws 5 amperes at an applied voltage of 115 volts. Its wattage would then be:

$$P = 115 \times 5 \text{ or 575 watts.}$$

MAGNETISM AND THE ELECTRON

The atom and a concept of its structure were a necessary preface to our discussion of basic electricity. By the same token, both are necessary to understanding basic magnetism.

As we've mentioned, electrons are in continual motion about the nucleus. The orbit is, in fact, a small loop of current and has a magnetic field that's associated with a current loop. In addition, experimental and theoretical investigation seems to indicate that the electron itself has a spin. Each electron, having its own axis, is a spinning sphere of electric charge. Electron spin, like the quantum and wave theories of light, is not so much a literal interpretation of a phenomenon as a useful concept that holds water when applied to the phenomenon of magnetism.

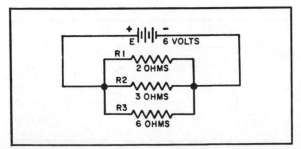

Fig. 1-18. Series-parallel circuit is not really difficult. Add R2 and R3 algebraically. Add effective resistance to R1 for total resistance.

When the electron spins, the charge that is in motion produces a magnetic field. And, to briefly state the electronic explanation of magnetism, it seems that the magnetic properties of matter can be attributed to the orbital and spinning motion of the electrons comprising the atoms of the matter.

Millennia of Magnetism

Some of the basic principles and effects of magnetism have been known for centuries. The Greeks are credited as the ones who first discovered magnetism. They noted that a certain type of rock had the ability of attracting iron. The Chinese noted that an elongated piece of this rock had the useful property of always pointing in a north-south direction when suspended by a string. This was the beginning of our compass.

This strange stone which intrigued people over the centuries is actually a form of iron ore known as magnetite. Not all magnetite shows magnetic properties. Another name for the magnetic variety of magnetite is lodestone—the term lodestone being derived from two separate words, lode and stone. The term "lode" stands for guide, hence lodestone means "guide stone."

All magnets, whether natural or man-made, possess magnetic poles, which are commonly known as the magnet's north and south poles. As is the case of the electrical charges (which we studied earlier) between unlike magnetic poles and repulsion between like poles, it has been found that this magnetic attraction and repulsion force varies inversely as the square of the distance from the magnetic poles.

The Magnetic Field

We all know how a magnet exerts a force of attraction on a piece of magnetic material such as iron or steel. Also, when the north poles of two magnets are brought close together, they will try to repel each other, while there will be attraction between the north and south poles of two magnets. Although it is not clearly understood just what this force of magnetic attraction and repulsion is, it is convenient to visualize magnetic lines of force

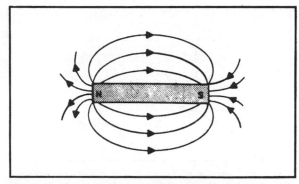

Fig. 1-19. Lines of force around bar magnet can be made visible by sprinkling iron filings onto white paper over magnet.

which extend outward from one magnetic pole to the other as illustrated in Fig. 1-19.

Permeability

Magnetic lines of force can pass through various materials with varying ease. Iron and steel, for example, offer little resistance to magnetic lines of force. It is because of this that these materials are so readily attracted by magnets. On the other hand, materials such as wood, aluminum and brass do not concentrate or encourage the passage of magnetic lines of force, and as a consequence are not attracted by magnets.

The amount of attraction a material offers to magnetic lines of force is known as its permeability. Iron and steel, for example, possess high permeability since they offer little resistance to magnetic lines of force. Nonmagnetic materials have low permeability. For practical purposes, we can say that reluctance is to magnetic lines of force what resistance is to an electrical current.

Electromagnetism

Any electrical conductor through which flows an electrical current will generate a magnetic field about it which is perpendicular to its axis as shown in Fig. 1-20. The direction of this field is dependent upon the direction of current flow, and the magnetic field strength proportional to the current strength. If this current-carrying conductor is wound into a coil, forming a solenoid, the magnetic field will be

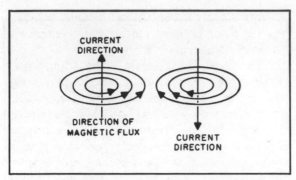

Fig. 1-20. Direction of flux lines is changed by direction of the current. Heavy current is needed to make flux lines visible with sprinkled filings.

increased by each individual turn that is added. If an iron core is inserted in this current-carrying coil, the generated field will be increased still further. This is because the lines of force are concentrated within the iron core which has considerably less reluctance than the surrounding air.

The magnetic power of a multi-turn current-carrying coil through which a core is inserted is proportional to the current flowing through the coil as well as the number of turns in the coil. The current through the coil is termed ampere turns. As an example, if a coil consisting of 200 turns is carrying 2 amperes, its ampere turns equal:

Ampere turns = 200 turns ×
2 amperes or 400 ampere turns

Similarly a coil of 100 turns through which a current of four amperes flows also has 400 ampere turns.

Electromagnetic Induction

We saw earlier how a current-carrying conductor will generate a magnetic field which is perpendicular to the conductor's axis. Conversely, a current will be induced in a conductor when the conductor is passed through a magnetic field. The strength of this induced current is proportional to both the speed at which it passes through the field and the strength of the field. One of the basic laws pertaining to electromagnetic induction is Lenz's law which states: "The magnetic action of an in-

duced current is of such a direction as to resist the motion by which it is produced."

Figure 1-21 illustrates two coils, A and B, which are placed in close proximity to each other. Coil A is connected in series with a switch and battery so that a current may be sent through it when the switch is closed, and coil B is connected with a current-indicating dc meter. When the switch is closed, current will flow through coil A, causing a magnetic field to be built up around it. In the brief instant that the field is building up to maximum, it will "cut" the turns of coil B, including a current in it, as indicated by a momentary flick of the indicating meter. When the switch is opened, breaking the current flow through coil A, the field around coil A will collapse, and in so doing will again induce a current in coil B. This time, however, the flow of current will be in the opposite direction. The meter will now flick in the direction opposite to when the switch was closed. The important thing to remember is that the conductor must be in motion with respect to the magnetic field or vice versa in order to induce a current flow. You can perform this simple experiment using two coils made of bell wire wrapped around large nails, a few dry cells in series, and a dc zero-center scale meter.

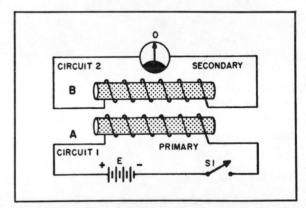

Fig. 1-21. Two-core transformer is inefficient since an air gap at either end does not have permeability of a ferrous metal and some flux lines do not go through core of secondary winding (B)—their effect is lost.

Self Induction

As mentioned a short while ago, a magnetic field is built up around a coil at the application of current through the coil. As this field is building up, its moving lines of flux will cut the turns of the coil inducing a counter-electromotive force or counter-EMF which opposes the current flowing into the coil.

The amount of counter-EMF generated depends upon the rate of change in amplitude of the applied current as well as the inductance of the coil. This value of inductance is dependent upon the number of turns in the coil; a coil with many turns will have greater inductance than a coil with few turns. Also, if an iron core is inserted into the coil, the inductance of the coil will increase sharply. The unit of inductance is known as the henry.

The Transformer

One of the most important and widely used applications of magnetic induction is the transformer.

Figure 1-22 shows the basic construction of a typical transformer. While two separate windings are shown here, some transformers can have as many as five or six windings.

A transformer consists of two or more separate windings, electrically insulated from each other. One winding, known as the primary winding, is fed from a source of alternating current.

The alternating currents flowing through the primary induce a current in the secondary winding by virtue of magnetic induction. The transformer core is constructed from a relatively high perme-ability material such as iron which readily conducts magnetic flux between the primary winding and secondary winding.

The alternating current flowing in the primary of the transformer produces a variation in the magnetic flux circulation in the transformer core which tends to oppose the current flowing in the primary winding by virtue of self-induction. The counter-EMF is just about equal to the voltage applied to the primary winding when no load is connected to the transformer's secondary winding. This accounts for the fact that very little current flows through the primary winding when no load is connected to the secondary. The negligible current that does flow under this no-load condition is known as the transformer magnetizing current. As the current drawn from the secondary winding increases, the primary current will increase proportionately due to the reduction in the counter-EMF developed in the primary winding of the transformer.

In any transformer the ratio of the primary to secondary voltage is equal to the ratio of the number of turns in the primary and secondary windings. This is expressed mathematically as follows:

$$\frac{Ep}{Es} = \frac{Np}{Ns}$$

where

Ep = primary supply voltage
Es = voltage developed across secondary
Np = number of primary turns
Ns = number of secondary turns

The above formula assumes that there are no losses in the transformer. Actually, all transformers possess some losses which must be taken into account.

Transformer Losses

No transformer can be 100 percent efficient due to losses in the magnetic flux coupling the primary and secondary windings, eddy current losses in the transformer core, and copper losses due to the re-

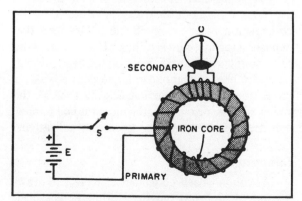

Fig. 1-22. Toroidal core is highly efficient but is very difficult to manufacture. Familiar C- and E-shape core has less waste and windings are slipped over the core. Efficiency is good—about 90 percent for most designs.

sistance of the windings.

Loss of magnetic flux leakage occurs when not all the flux generated by current flowing in the primary reaches the secondary winding. The proper choice of core material and physical core design can reduce flux leakage to a negligible value.

Practical transformers have a certain amount of power loss which is due to power being absorbed in the resistance of the primary and secondary windings. This power loss, known as the copper loss, appears as heating of the primary and secondary windings.

There are several forms of core loss—hysteresis and eddy current losses. Hysteresis losses are the result of the energy required to continually realign the magnetic domain of the core material. Eddy current loss results from circulating currents induced in the transformer core by current flowing in the primary winding. These eddy currents cause heating of the core.

Eddy current loss can be greatly reduced by forming the core from a stack of individual sheets, known as laminations, rather than from a single solid piece of steel. Since eddy current losses are proportional to the square of core thickness, it is easy to see that the individual thin laminations will have much less eddy current loss as compared with a single thick core.

Another factor which effects eddy current loss is the operating frequency for which the transformer is designed to operate. As the operating frequency is increased, the eddy current losses increase. It is for this reason that transformers designed to operate at radio frequencies often have air cores and are void of ferrous metals.

Theory and Practice

We've come a long way from our initial discussion of the atom and its importance for an understanding of electricity and magnetism. And there's still a long way to travel to understand all about the subatomic nucleus and its satellites and how they are being harnessed in an ever-expanding electronics technology. But, we move ahead by mixing theory with practice—so, put your new knowledge to work in a project or two!

MOVING COIL METER

Learning electronic theory is dull, dull, dull. Right? Not necessarily. In some cases you can learn a lot and still have a lot of fun. How? Leave your theory textbook behind and build a current-measuring gadget that will allow you to see electronic theory in action.

Moving coil meters are used universally in all types of test instruments to measure dc current because they are highly sensitive, rugged and reliable, and relatively inexpensive. They may also be used to measure ac current by first rectifying the ac with a small meter rectifier.

Our project uses the moving coil principle in a simplified form of indicating meter. You can learn more about this form of meter by building our easy-to-construct project.

How It Works

The operation of the moving coil type of meter is based on the attraction between a permanent magnet and the magnetic field of a movable coil of fine wire. The coil is pivoted in the center of the space between the poles of the magnet, and has a return spring (to return the meter pointer to zero). This spring is usually of a spiral form in commercial meters, but out meter unit uses a rubber band coil suspension in place of both the pivot and spiral zero return spring.

When dc current flows through the coil, it produces a magnetic field that is attracted to the permanent magnet's magnetic field. This attraction imposes a turning force on the coil, that rotates the coil and moves the attached pointer over the meter scale. The amount of turning force is dependent on the amount of dc current flowing through the coil. The more dc current, the more the coil rotates. The meter is calibrated in dc current indications.

Construction

As can be observed from our photos and drawing, our model of a moving coil meter has been made in a very simplified form to facilitate construction. It's a taut-band moving coil instrument by virtue of the rubber band suspension of the moving coil assembly. We used wood for the various supporting structures because it's easier to work with and most everyone has the few hand tools required.

Size is relatively unimportant. However, we suggest you follow the dimensions and construction details given in the drawing and parts list. In this way you should have no difficulty in making the meter and and you won't have to fiddle with changing the number of turns of wire for the moving coil to compensate for a change in physical size. Refer to Fig. 1-23 for the following steps.

You should cut out all of the various pieces of wood and sand them smooth before actually starting to assemble the meter. Mount rubber feet on the bottom four corners of the base (A) and then glue the 4 supports (B) to base (A), as shown in the

pictorial drawing. Next cement the scale platform (C) to these supports. We used our electric glue gun, but epoxy cement, Elmer's glue. Pliobond, or similar adhesives can be used with equal success.

Now you're ready to cement the magnet and moving coil assembly supports to base (A). Pieces D, E, G, and I are made from 1/4-inch plywood. First step is to cement D and E in their respective locations and fasten the magnet in place. The magnet used in our unit has a mounting hole. If the magnet you use isn't drilled at the bottom center of the U to allow a bolt to go through it to hold the magnet in place, it too can be cemented to D and E.

At this point the main support block (H) should be readied for cementing. But first you must notch it out so that piece I can be properly fastened to it. Hold H on the base (A) near piece E and mark

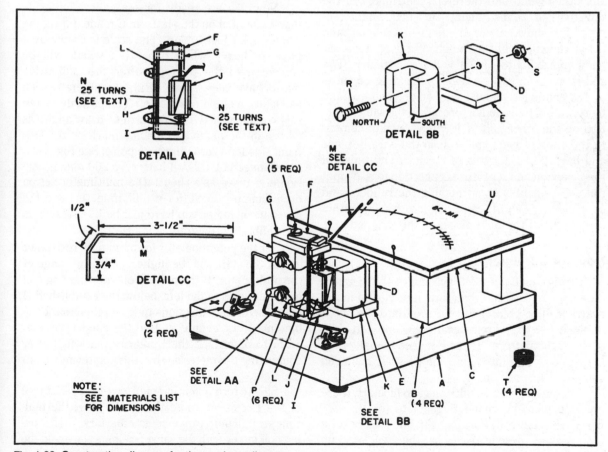

Fig. 1-23. Construction diagram for the moving coil meter.

H so that the top of the notch will be even with the top about 1/4-inch deep. The best way to determine its depth is to hold piece G in position at the top of H and place piece I so that its notched end is even with the notched end of G. Mark the depth of the notch in block H based on the position of the end of piece I that will be inserted in the notch where its end is matched with piece G as mentioned above. Be sure that the notch in block H is cut square so that the surface of piece I will be square with the surface of block H where I is cemented in place. The notches in the free ends of I and G are required only to hold the rubber band in position. Cement block H in position, and also piece G to block H as shown in drawing.

The form block J for the moving coil is made from balsa wood, which is lighter in weight than any other wood and therefore contributes to the sensitivity of the instrument. Cut a notch in the center of J as shown in our drawing. The rubber band (L) is cemented in this notch. We used a rubber band approximately 6 3/4 × 3/8 × 1/16 inch. The coil is made in two sections by winding 25 turns of #38 enameled magnet wire on one half of J and by repeating this winding process in the same direction on the other half of J. Put a touch of cement to the ends of each coil to hold the wire in place and have 6-inch lengths of the start and finish of the 2-section coil for future connection to it. Mount the coil assembly by stretching the rubber band over pieces G and I, centering it vertically within the height of the pole pieces of the magnet.

Now for a Pointer

Straighten out a 4 3/4-inch length of #18 gauge bare copper wire and then form it as shown in the drawing. The pointer is cemented into the notch in block J so that it rests near the O end (left side) of the scale platform. Piece F is used to make final O rest position adjustments after a scale has been cemented in position.

Fasten two double solder lugs to block H; these are intermediary connecting points for the two wires from the coil. Form a helix like a hairspring with each of these leads so that they will wind up

as the coil assembly moves clockwise. Solder the end of the wire from the top helix to the top lugs and the bottom helix to the bottom lugs. Mount two Fahnestock clips or binding posts along the front edge of the meter baseboard and connect them to the solder lugs on H, using #18 solid base wire. Since meter polarity is determined by magnet polarity and the direction of current flow, established by how the coil is wound, the correct polarity markings of the meter should be determined when you calibrate the instrument.

Calibration

In order to calibrate this instrument, you'll need a potentiometer having roughly 20 ohms resistance, a 1 1/2-volt battery and a dc milliammeter, preferably a multi-range one available as part of a VOM.

Now you are ready for the calibration scale that's mounted on the platform C made during the framework construction. The scale is drawn on a piece of heavy white paper (U) which will be cemented to the platform after the calibration marks have been drawn. (Rub-on numerals, such as Datak, make a neat scale.) Temporarily fasten this white paper (U) to platform C, draw an arc as shown in the photo and place a mark on the left-hand side for a zero reference point. See Fig. 1-24.

Connect a 1 1/2-volt battery, a 200-ohm potentiometer (used as a rheostat) a multimeter set on dc milliamp ranges (for a milliammeter) and the moving coil meter you have just built, as shown in the calibration diagram, Fig. 1-25.

Set the potentiometer for maximum resistance and at the start use the highest milliamp range of the multimeter. If the pointer on your moving coil meter deflects to the left, below the established O point, reverse connections to it and then mark the binding posts + and −. Use the connection diagram to determine their polarity markings after connecting the meter so that the pointer moves to the right.

Slowly turn potentiometer to reduce resistance in the circuit and note the readings of the multimeter milliamp range selected. Mark your moving coil meter with the same readings shown on the

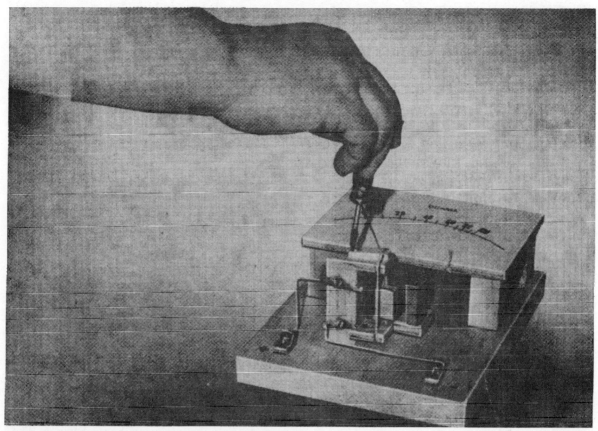

Fig. 1-24. To zero the pointer of your Moving Coil Meter project, all you need to do is loosen the screw as shown, and move the wooden block, thus repositioning the coil assembly.

milliammeter. We divided the 0-100 scale into 10 mA divisions. In the manufacture of dc moving coil meters spring tensions, spacing and coil weight are carefully controlled so that these meters are linear. For this reason commercial milliammeters have uniform spacing between divisions. Our moving coil meter doesn't have such uniformity because of the variations in the rubber band used for suspension and tension, and because it's difficult to maintain accuracy of positioning the various pieces and to be assured of the strength of magnetic field developed by the magnet. Once you have established the calibration points they can be considered accurate.

Now that you have marked the scale in pencil you can remove it from the platform and apply the permanent markings. Permanently fasten the sale

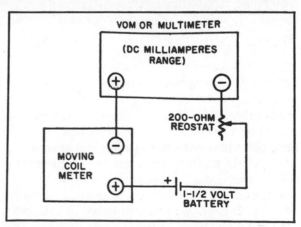

Fig. 1-25. Any 0-100 mA or higher milliameter will test your MCM just as well as a VOM or multimeter, provided its accuracy is fairly good.

in position and stand back to admire your work. If you used reasonable care in following the instructions, you'll have good reason to be proud of your handiwork.

CUSTOM RELAYS . . . AT MASS PRODUCED PRICES

Custom build your experimental relays from magnetic reed switches and save a bundle. The reed switches are very inexpensive and all other components can be found in your junk box. The simplest relay will run you about thirty cents. There are even other advantages. The relays are highly sensitive and can be coupled directly to audio circuits for experimental purposes, their light weight and tiny size make them ideal for model applications, and they are even applicable to high speed switching circuits because of their extremely short response times.

The Basic Relay

Wrap a coil of wire around a reed switch (Radio Shack Cat. 275-034 "Mini" or 275-035 "Micro Mini") and hold it on by end pieces cut from some thin, rigid material such as cardboard. The reed switches—especially the "Micro Mini" size—are quite fragile, so play it safe and wrap the coil around a form of the same diameter as the reed switch (coat hanger wire, for example, for the "Micro Mini") then replace the form with the actual switch when the coil is complete. The length of wire used to wind the coil is not critical; about five feet of #24 gauge enameled magnet wire (Radio Shack Cat. No. 278-004) is sufficient. The coil will hold together better if you coat it with lacquer or model airplane dope.

A relay of this type will respond to as little as 0.5 volt. When connected to an audio signal generator, the relay responds to frequencies approaching 3000Hz and to somewhat higher resonant frequencies.

The basic relay can be modified in a number of ways. Though you will undoubtedly find more, here are a few basic examples.

Multi-Role Relays

Make these by using additional reed switches inside the coil. Four and five pole relays are simple to make, though extra windings may be needed to retain a high degree of sensitivity. If you need a relay with more than five poles, gang several smaller, fully assembled relays together by wiring their coils in parallel.

Latching Relays

Once triggered by a short pulse, this relay will remain on, it can be made by using two reed switches in the coil (see Fig. 1-26). One switches the load, while the other is wired into the coil power circuit. When the momentary-on switch is pressed, the coil is energized, closing the two reed switches. Once the left-hand reed switch is closed, current will continue to flow through the coil even after the momentary-on switch is released. To turn the relay off, a normally-on, momentary-off switch is pressed to break the flow of current to the coil, thereby cutting off both reed switches.

Biased Relays

In the simplest, basic relay the only magnetic field around the switch is that created by the trigger current flowing through the coil and it is this magnetic field that activates the reed switch. The sensitivity of the relay to the trigger current can be increased by biasing the magnetic field with either a permanent magnetic field or an electromagnetic field.

The permanent magnetic bias is made by simply mounting a small magnet at the proper distance from the coil. To find the best positioning, move the magnet close to the relay until you hear the reed switch click on, then back off a tiny distance. The field created by the permanent magnet should be almost strong enough to turn the switch on, but not quite. Now only weak trigger current sent through the coil will be strong enough to kick the magnetic field above the threshold level needed to activate the reed switch.

A more flexible way of creating the magnetic bias is to double wind the coil using two wires instead of one. Connect your trigger input through one, as shown, and connect the other through the

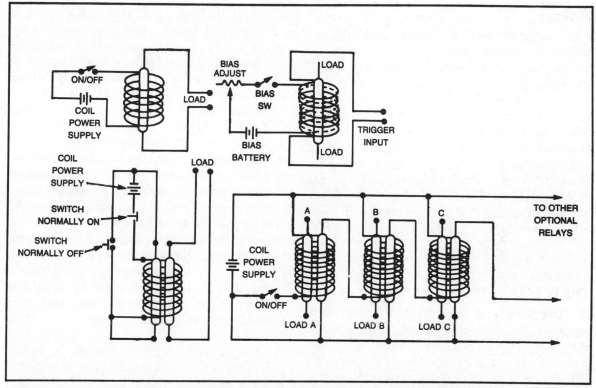

Fig. 1-26. A basic relay (upper left) is simply a coil of wire wrapped around a magnetic relay switch. The coil is connected to a power supply and the switch to the load. A bias relay (upper right) is the next step in complexity and consists of a double-wound coil about a reed switch. The first coil is biased slightly so that a trigger input into a second coil can, with great sensitivity, trip the switch to the load. A latching relay (lower left) is a coil of wire wound about two magnetic reed switches; both of which remain closed once the relay is activated. A normally-on switch unlatches the relay. Finally, there is the relay cascade (lower right) which is simply a series arrangement of double pole relays. It can switch on any number of loads in a rapid, preprogrammed order.

bias battery (see Fig. 1-26). The rheostat lets you set the bias field to the correct level, which, again, should be almost strong enough to make the reed switch click on. The resistance value of the rheostat will depend on what voltage bias battery you use.

One side note to all of this: if you use a transformer instead of a battery to power the relay coils, use a full-wave rectifier between the transformer and the relays. Alternating current or half wave dc will make the relay buzz on and off at 60Hz.

A Relay Cascade

This device lets you turn several items on with one flip of a switch, and have them come on in a specific order, one after another. The coil of relay A (see Fig. 1-26) is wired to the start switch, and the coil of each consecutive relay is wired through the reed switch of the previous relay. Thus, when the On/Off start switch is closed, relay A will come on, then relay B, then relay C, and so on. Theoretically, there is no limit to the number of relays you can cascade this way, although the power source may have to be increased to supply enough current. The current carrying capacities of both types of reed switches is 0.5 amps at 125 Vac.

The relays close and open extremely quickly—a "Micro-Mini" can cycle up to at least three thousand times per second, according to my rough tests, and will respond to resonant frequencies even higher. Thus, the closing time of the relay is, obviously, very short.

In Closing

The applications of these relays are limited only by your imagination and the type of projects you build. Once you design something using one of these miniature marvels you may never again want to use one of the store-bought, bulky variety.

One tip: do not forget coating the coil of each relay with at least one good coat of lacquer or model airplane dope. Nothing is more aggravating than, sometime after the project is already built and functioning, having to rewind a relay coil which has spilled out of the form.

You're sure to find that switching with these relays is nearly as much fun as building them.

CUSTOM SWITCHES . . . THAT YOU COULDN'T AFFORD TO BUY

How often have you searched fruitlessly for a special switch? Probably dozens of times—if you're at all an active builder. The next time this happens, consider custom-building your own complex switches using inexpensive magnetic reed switches and small ceramic magnets. Such do-it-yourself switches offer several advantages. They are relatively inexpensive, silent, and long lasting, as there are no rubbing contacts and the reed contacts are sealed in glass, away from corrosive atmospheric gases.

You can purchase two sizes of magnetic reed switches and the ceramic magnets from Radio Shack. The larger switch (Cat. No. 275-034; 1 3/4" overall length) comes in a 4-for-79¢ blister package. The smaller "Micro Mini" switch (275-035; 1 1/8" long) comes 10 to a package, for $2.99. The magnets cost 10 cents each, regardless of size. The smallest, 1/2" diam. disc ("button") magnet is the most useful, but you may need the larger 1 1/8" disc or 1" × 3/4" rectangular magnets to build really large, complex switches.

The several custom-built switches shown in this article only hint at the virtually limitless design combinations that are possible. Study the drawings to learn how magnet orientation and direction of travel past the reed switches affect switching action.

Carpetak Tape, a cloth tape with adhesive on both sides that is used to hold down carpets, is excellent for mounting the reed switches to panels. The switches adhere firmly, yet can be removed without damage. For greater permanence, you may wish to use epoxy cement for mounting once you know exactly where to locate the reed switches. Generally, it is best to locate the magnet and reed switches on the same side of the panel; however, it is also possible to put the switches on one side of a non-magnetic panel and orient the magnet on the other side. The ceramic magnets are of extremely hard material, and you may have poor success if you try to hacksaw them smaller. Try breaking the magnet by clamping in a vise and striking with a chisel; it may not break cleanly across, but grinding on an emery wheel may be practical. When possible, just use the magnets as they are. Mount them in aluminum holders as shown here, or glue them to support arms with epoxy adhesive.

The following brief descriptions of various switch types should help clarify the principles of building switches:

Single-Throw, Multi-Pole

These can be constructed simply by mounting reed switches in parallel, and passing the edge of a vertically-mounted magnet over them to trip all switches simultaneously (see Fig. 1-27). If you need a sequential switching action, just angle the magnet about 30 degrees so that the parallel reed switches are tripped in 1, 2, 3, 4 order. If the magnet movement continues in the same direction, the switches will go off in the same 1, 2, 3, 4 sequence, on the other hand, if magnet movement is reversed when all switches are on, the switches will go off in the reverse 4, 3, 2, 1 order.

Multi-Position, Single-Pole

Arrange the reed switches one after the other, like cars of a train. You can keep the switch smaller by using two lines of staggered switches, as shown. As the vertically-oriented disc or rectangular magnet passes over the switches, each "on" switch goes

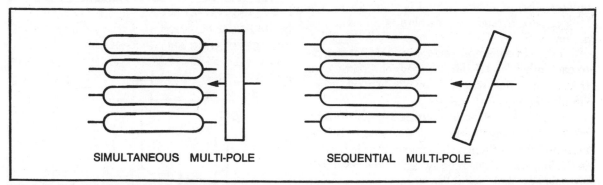

Fig. 1-27. Two different multi-pole switches.

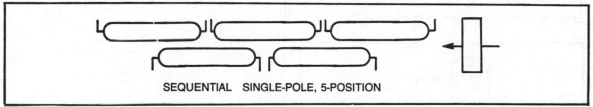

Fig. 1-28. Here are various magnet and reed switch orientations all of which achieve different switching actions. Position the magnets and reed switches exactly as shown, and as further discussed in the text, for best results.

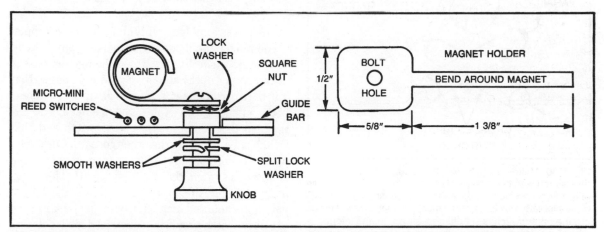

Fig. 1-29. Here is a sliding switch designed to function as a double-pole, single-pole, double-pole sequencer. A locking device of a lock washer under the knob on the other side of the panel permits locking the movement at any desired position. The support arm is positioned to keep the magnet aligned properly.

off before the next switch comes on (see Fig. 1-28).

A simple locking device consisting of a lock washer under the knob on the other side of the panel permits locking the movement at any desired position (see Fig. 1-29). Note the "guide" strip near the slot; a square nut that holds the magnet support arm on the knob shaft bears against this guide to keep the magnet properly aligned over the reed switches.

Rotary Switches

These are easier to build than slide switches, and there are many ways to achieve special switching characteristics. Note that when the edge (diameter axis) of a disc magnet is aligned with the long axis of a reed switch there is no switching action.

Thus if you mount several reed switches next to each other, and rotate the magnet directly over the center of the switches, you obtain more or less simultaneous on-off action.

If two switches are crossed, a vertically-mounted rotating magnet will turn one switch on and the other off when the magnet axis is parallel to the long axis of one reed switch. In the intermediate position, both switches are on; thus you can have on-before-off action with a very simple physical arrangement. To make a double-pole version, cross four reed switches in pairs (see Fig. 1-30).

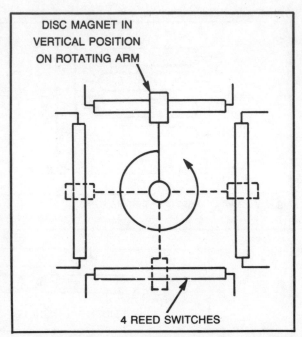

Fig. 1-31. A single-pole, 4-position switch is accomplished by a vertically-oriented disc magnet passing over four reed switches, which are arranged in a square.

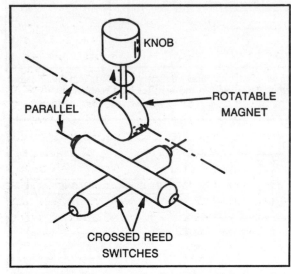

Fig. 1-30. Make a single-pole, 2-position, on-before-off rotary switch with two crossed reed switches and a rotatable disc magnet positioned above them. When the magnet's axis is parallel with a switch's long dimension, that switch remains off; the other switch is simultaneously on. In the intermediate, 45° position, both switches are on. Use this arrangement when the second switch must come on before the first switch turns off.

A 4-pole, 4-position rotary switch can be made by arranging four reed switches in a "square" and adding a vertically-oriented disc magnet so that it can be swung in a circle over the centers of the reed switches. This provides an off-before-on switching action, each "on" switch first going off before the next one comes on (see Fig. 1-31).

Some strangely useful things begin to happen if you mount the disc magnet horizontally instead of vertically (see Fig. 1-32). As the magnet passes over a corner of the square of reed switches so that it is partly over the ends of two adjacent switches, both switches go on. Rotate the magnet a little further, so that it is over just one switch and that switch stays on while the other goes off. Curiously, when the horizontally mounted magnet is over the center of a switch, that switch goes off. This is exactly the opposite of the on-action caused by a vertically-mounted magnet. Consequently, this type of rotary switch provides sequential double-pole and single-pole action, with four fully off positions.

Multi-Pole Rotary

Such switches can be constructed by stacking additional reed switches atop the first four that make up a basic square. Mount the rotatable magnet inside the "box" formed from the stacked reed switches. When the long dimension of the magnet is perpendicular to stacks on opposite sides of the

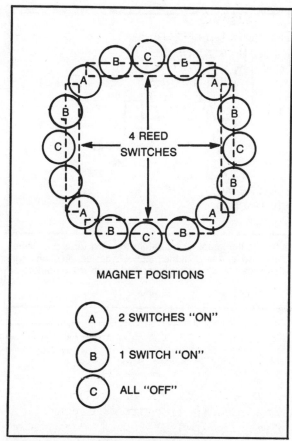

Fig. 1-32. A complex switching method is achieved by passing a horizontally-oriented magnet over a square of four reed switches. When the magnet is in a "corner" two adjacent switches are on; in other positions only one switch is on.

box, all of those switches will go on; other stacks at 90° to these will remain off because the magnet axis is parallel to them. By using one of the larger rectangular magnets, you can easily stack at least a half dozen switches on a side, for a total of 24 switches; 12 would be on at any one time, 12 off. When the magnet is in the intermediate, 45° position, all switches are off (see Fig. 1-33).

Linear Off-Before-On

Mount parallel switches far enough apart so that, as a vertically positioned magnet approaches the switches from one side, the first switch will go on and off before the next switch is affected. Here's a handy trick that enables you to pull the parallel reed switches much closer together to form a more compact switch: Position a small disc magnet over the center of the first switch so that its long axis (diameter) is parallel to the long axis of the switch. If you have been paying attention, you already know that in this position the magnet has no effect on the switch. Now slowly rotate the switch away from this parallel orientation until you hear the switch click on. Mount the magnet in its sliding holder so that it passes over the center of the reed switch in this slightly angled position. This deliberately weakened magnetic action permits location of the next switch much closer to the first—as close as about 3/8″—and still obtain off-before-on switching (see Fig. 1-34).

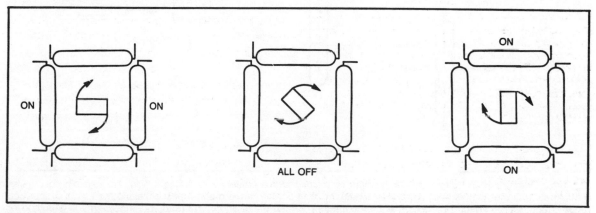

Fig. 1-33. By positioning a rotatable magnet in the center of a square of four reed switches you have a double-pole rotary switch. By stacking magnets on top of the basic four, and using a larger magnet, as many as twelve on-positions are possible at each active orientation.

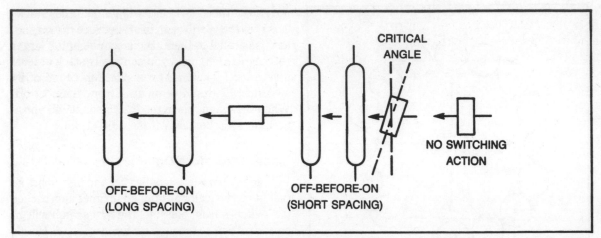

Fig. 1-34. Spacing of adjacent reed switches is important if the first switch must go off before the next turns on. When the magnet is in its strongest orientation (left), the reed switches must be far apart. If the magnet is positioned at an angle slightly removed from where it does not switch, the two reed switches can be closer together and retain the on-before-off action.

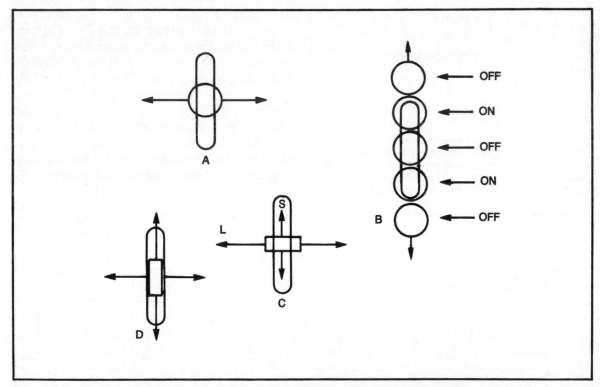

Fig. 1-35. Orientation and direction of movement of a disc magnet influence switching action. No switching occurs as a horizontal magnet moves across the reed switch as at upper left. If the magnet passes along the length of the reed (upper right), switching to "on" occurs when the magnet is near either end of the reed, but not when it is directly over the contact points in the center of the reed. Switching occurs if the magnet is vertically oriented as at lower left, but over a shorter range if the magnet moves along the "S" path than along the "L" path. If the magnet is turned 90° (lower right), no switching occurs when it is moved along either of the indicated paths.

There's no problem, of course, if you want on-before-off action because then you can mount the reed switches as close to each other as you like. A magnet approaching from the side will turn the first on, then the second, before turning the first off. Bear in mind that if the magnet approaches the pair of switches from the end directions, you obtain approximately simultaneous double-pole switching.

If you have but one reed switch, and the vertically-oriented magnet approaches from one side of the reed switch, it has a longer "reach" and switching action occurs while it is relatively far from the center of the switch. This relative sensitivity, relating to direction of magnet travel, could be an important factor in some switch-design problems (see Fig. 1-35).

Special Designs

As you play around with your reed switches and magnets you will undoubtedly discover many variations on the ideas given here. For example, suppose you wanted a sliding multi-pole switch that always switches the reed switches on in the same sequence. As the magnet travels over the parallel reeds, the switches come on in 1, 2, 3, 4 order. But as you slide the magnet back to its original starting position, the reeds would go on in reverse 4, 3, 2, 1 sequence—which is what you do not want. So what's the answer? Simply mount the magnet on a holder that permits it to be turned 90° at the end of each sweep. This way the magnet can be in its "active" orientation going one way, and in its "dead" orientation going the other way. Thus it is possible to return the magnet to the starting position, for subsequent normal switching order, without affecting the switches on the return sweep.

I have not tested these ideas, but it seems likely that you could construct such truly off-beat switches as, for example, a level-indicating switch by suspending the magnet on a short pendulum so that it will swing close to either of two parallel magnets to electrically signal tilting. And it may be feasible to create a vibration-detector in much the same manner, by mounting the magnet on the end of a flat or coil spring so that vibrations will swing it in-and-out of the switching range.

DIAL-AN-OHM

As every electronic experimenter knows, a good resistance substitution box is an invaluable aid—a timesaver in breadboard and troubleshooting work. They range in price from less than $6.00 on upward—depending upon accuracy, number of resistance values available, and their power capabilities.

There are three commonly used varieties, each with different applications. The simplest circuit is a selector switch (Fig. 1-36) which picks one of several different-value resistors, usually ±10 or ±20% tolerance for quick substitution in radio and TV repair work. These are inexpensive but have two drawbacks; First only a limited number of resistance values are possible leaving many wide gaps and unless ±1%, or better tolerance, resistors are used they are not too useful when accurate substitution is required.

The second, and most commonly used type, is the resistance decade box which consists of several selector switches, with each selector switch having 10 positions, with 9 resistors (see Fig. 1-37). For

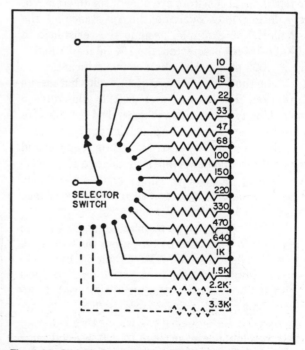

Fig. 1-36. Circuit of resistance substitutor.

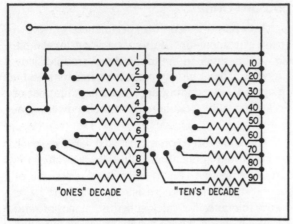

Fig. 1-37. Nine resistors and a single-gang selector switch are needed for a decade.

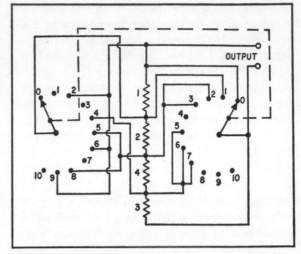

Fig. 1-38. (top, right) Four resistors and a 2-gang switch form one resistance decade.

example, a 6-switch decade would be capable of any resistance value from 1 ohm to 999,999 ohms in increments of 1 ohm. Of course, this unit would be rather expensive. Considering ± 1% resistors at one dollar a piece it will cost (prices vary, of course, with type, manufacturer and power ratings) $54.00 plus selector switch, etc. Another disadvantage is when several resistors are added, the tolerance of the larger may override the resistance of the smaller. For example, assume the resistance of 100,000 ohms is selected, the 1% value of 100,000 is ± 1,000 so the 100 ohms is insignificant.

The third type is more of a novelty but merits attention. The circuit in Fig. 1-38 illustrates a switching type decade in which only 4 resistors are required per switch. The disadvantage of this type are first, a more expensive switch is required and again the tolerances create a cumulative error overshadowing the smaller values and second if one resistor should become damaged several resistance values would be lost.

A New Approach. A simpler, and quite precise method has been used by the author for some time with excellent results. The circuit in Fig. 1-39 shows simply two, ten-turn potentiometers (pot) (with calibrated turn-counting dials) used as independent substitution resistors. Both are ± 3% accurate with .25% linearity. With the turn-counting dials, resolution is accurate to 1/1000 the total value or .1 ohm for the 100-ohm pot and 100 ohms for

the 100K pot. This would be equivalent to having a decade box with 7 selector switches and 63 precision resistors.

Using the Variable Decade. Connect the variable decade in the circuit being worked with and adjust the knob until the circuit is functioning properly. Then read the calibrated dial. With the 100-ohm pot each scale division is .1 ohm—each full turn is 10 ohms. The 100K dial reads 100 ohms for each scale division—10K for each turn.

After reading the resistance indicated on the dials, refer to Table 1-1 and select the standard value of the desired tolerance nearest the indicated resistance reading and readjust the variable decade to the standard value you intend using and make certain the circuit still functions properly, if not perhaps a closer tolerance resistor must be used.

As with any substitution box caution must be

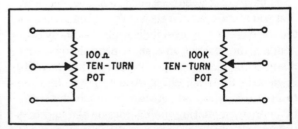

Fig. 1-39. A circuit using 2 10-turn pots for resistance substitution.

Table 1-1. Standard Fixed Resistor Values.

20%	10%	5%	20%	10%	5%
10	10	10	33	33	33
		11			36
	12	12		39	39
		13			43
15	15	15	47	47	47
		16			51
	18	18		56	56
		20			62
22	22	22	68	68	68
		24			75
	27	27		82	82
		30			91

Higher standard values may be formed by adding zeros up to 22 megohm

observed to keep the current to a safe value. Current should not exceed 200 milliamperes in the 100-ohm pot and 200 microamperes in the 100K pot if you use units identical to those used here. Check the specifications of your units carefully. Some 10-turn potentiometers have ratings of 1 1/2 watts—others are rated as 2, 3 and 5 watts.

Sometimes wattage, current and voltage ratings conflict—for example you may not be able to get maximum wattage at maximum resistance without exceeding the voltage rating. Check all potentiometer specifications carefully.

UNDERSTANDING TRANSFORMERS

A transformer is a device for changing the voltage of ac electricity. Transformers work on the principle of induction. Basically, a transformer has two windings—a primary and a secondary—wound on the same core. This core can be laminated iron, ferrite, or air.

Through the principle of *induction*, the alternating current flowing through the primary winding sets up an alternating magnetic field in the core. This magnetic field, in turn, *induces* an alternating voltage in the secondary winding (or windings). In this way, *energy is transferred* from the primary to the secondary.

A transformer that reduces the voltage in a circuit is called a *step-down* transformer. This is true, for example, of a radio-receiver filament trans-

former, which steps the 117-volt main supply down to 6.3 volts.

A transformer that is used to increase the voltage in the circuit is known as a *step-up* transformer. An example is the high-voltage transformer which produces the several thousand volts needed to operate a television picture tube.

The basic transformer has two windings—primary and secondary—wound on a laminated-iron core. The two windings are insulated from each other and from the core (see Fig. 1-40).

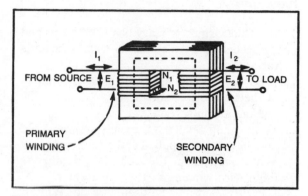

Fig. 1-40. A basic transformer.

The primary winding is connected to the energy source, and the secondary winding is connected to the load. As alternating current flows through the primary, a pulsating magnetic field is set up in the core. As the constantly changing magnetic field cuts the turns of the secondary, a voltage is induced in the secondary winding.

The amount of voltage induced in the secondary winding depends on how many turns of wire the secondary contains compared to the number of turns of wire in the primary winding. So, if the secondary has only half as many turns as the primary winding, the voltage will be stepped down to half its original value. If the secondary has twice as many turns as the primary, the voltage will be stepped up to twice its original value.

The difference in the number of turns is known as the *turns ratio* of the transformer. If the primary winding has N_1 turns and its voltage is E_1, the secondary winding with N_2 turns produces voltage E_2.

27

$$\frac{E_1}{E_2} = \frac{N_1}{N_2}$$

The power consumed in the secondary circuit of a transformer must be supplied by the primary. Since the voltages are constant in each circuit, the current in the primary circuit must vary to supply the amount of power demanded by the secondary. Current in the primary depends on the current drawn in the secondary circuit.

Questions

1. If a transformer primary has 1,000 turns and the secondary has 6,500 turns, what is the turns ratio?
2. If 85 volts is applied to the primary winding of the transformer in Question 1, what is the voltage at the secondary?
3. What would happen if the leads were reversed and 85 volts was applied to the 6,500-turn coil?
4. What happens if 130 volts is fed into the 6,500-turn winding of the transformer?
5. Can a transformer be used with dc? Why?
6. What will be the phase relationship between the voltage across the primary of a transformer and the voltage across the secondary, assuming the coils are wound in the same direction?
7. If there is no load between the terminals of the secondary of a transformer, will current flow in the secondary?
8. Will there be a magnetic field produced by current in the secondary?
9. Will there be a magnetic field produced by current in the primary?
10. What effect will this magnetic field have on the impedance of the primary circuit?
11. If the magnetic field were weaker, would more or less current flow in the primary circuit?

Answers

1.
$$\frac{N_1}{N_2} = \frac{1,000}{6,500} = 1 \text{ to } 6.5$$

2.
$$\frac{E_1}{E_2} = \frac{1}{6.5}$$

$$E_2 = E_1 \times 6.5 = 85 \times 6.5 = 552.5 \text{ volts}$$

3. If you reverse the leads, the turns ratio is:

$$\frac{N_1}{N_2} = \frac{6,500}{1,000} = \frac{E_2}{E_1}$$

The output would be:

$$E_2 = \frac{1,000 \times 85}{6,500} = 85 \times 0.153$$

$$= 13 \text{ volts (approx.)}$$

4. The voltage appearing at the 1,000-turn winding will be

$$\frac{1,000}{6,500} \times 130 = 20 \text{ volts.}$$

5. A transformer cannot be used with direct current. A direct current in the primary does not produce a pulsating magnetic field.
6. The voltage across the secondary will be 180° out of phase with the voltage across the primary.
7. No current will flow.
8. If no current flows, no magnetic field will be produced by the secondary.
9. Yes.
10. The stronger the magnetic field, the greater will be the impedance of the primary circuit.
11. More current would flow in the primary.

Transformer Power

If the transformer was 100% efficient, all the power from the primary winding would be transferred to the secondary and delivered to the load.

Suppose a transformer has 1,000 turns in the primary and 6,500 turns in the secondary. If 100 volts is applied to the primary, 650 volts will appear at the secondary. Now suppose the load connected to the secondary is a 65-ohm resistor. It will draw a current of 650/65, or 10 amperes, and the power consumed will be 650 × 10, or 6,500 watts. This power must be supplied by the primary winding. Assuming no loss in the transformer, the primary winding must supply 6,500 watts. The primary current, therefore, will be 6,500/100 watts = 65 amperes.

Questions

12. What happens to current in the secondary of a transformer when a load is connected across its terminals?
13. Will a magnetic field be produced by the current in the secondary?
14. Will the magnetic field add to or oppose the magnetic field produced by the primary? (Remember the coils are wound in the same direction but the currents are in opposite directions.)
15. How will the magnetic field produced by current flow in the secondary affect the current drawn by the primary?
16. What will happen if the load resistance in the circuit above is increased to 6,500 ohms?

Answers

12. There will be a current in the secondary when a load is connected across its terminals.
13. A magnetic field will be produced by a current in the secondary.
14. The secondary magnetic field will oppose that of the primary.
15. The secondary magnetic field will decrease the total magnetic field acting on the primary and, therefore will decrease the impedance of the primary circuit. The primary will draw more current.
16. Current in the secondary will be

$$\frac{650 \text{ volts}}{6,500 \text{ ohms}} = 0.1 \text{ ampere.}$$

Power dissipated in the secondary will be 0.1 ampere × 650 volts = 65 watts. Therefore, power drawn in the primary must be 65 watts. The current in the primary will then be

$$\frac{65 \text{ watts}}{100 \text{ volts}} = 0.5 \text{ ampere.}$$

Transformer Efficiency

So far we have assumed that no power is lost in the transfer from the primary winding to the secondary winding. However, no transformer has absolutely 100% efficiency. Some power is lost in heating the core, and some is lost in the resistance of the windings. But, transformers are very efficient; their efficiency often reaches very nearly 100%. Therefore, for rough calculations, it is permissible to assume 100% efficiency.

As with any other device, the efficiency of a transformer is equal to:

$$\frac{\text{output power}}{\text{input power}}$$

Most transformers have an efficiency in the range of 97 to 99%. So, even if you neglect the losses, your calculations using 100% as the transformer efficiency will still be accurate within 1 to 3%.

Transformer Losses

The power loss in transformers is due to three factors. The first is simply *resistance* in the windings; no winding is a perfect conductor.

The second factor that causes power loss in transformers is *eddy currents*. The iron in the core of a transformer is a conductor. When the changing magnetic field produced by the primary coil cuts through the iron of the core, small currents are generated in the core material. These currents dissipate power as they pass through the resistance of the iron. These currents are called eddy currents. This type of loss is held to a minimum by using thin sheets of iron, called *laminations,* in the core. These thin sheets are insulated from each other (often by oxidizing the surface of the sheets) and thus shorten the conducting path for the eddy currents.

The third factor that causes power loss in transformers is *hysteresis*. It takes a certain small amount of power to magnetize a piece of iron. This power must be expended again when the magnetic field is reversed. Since the magnetic field in a transformer is reversed many times each second, these tiny expenditures of power add up to a noticeable loss. Hysteresis loss can be reduced by constructing the core with a type of iron that is very easily magnetized and demagnetized.

Questions

17. If a transformer supplies 1.9 amperes at 100 volts to a resistive load in the secondary circuit, and if it dissipates 200 watts of power in the primary circuit, what is the efficiency of the transformer?
18. This transformer has a relatively (high, low) efficiency.
19. If the secondary of a transformer supplies 0.99 watt at 1,000 volts and the transformer has an efficiency of 99%, what power will the primary draw at 120 volts?
20. How could you find the amount of power lost due to resistance in a transformer?
21. Does an air-core transformer have hysteresis or eddy currents?

Answers

17. The power dissipated in the secondary will be 1.9 × = 190 watts. The efficiency of the transformer will be 190/200 = 95%.
18. It has a relatively low efficiency. (An efficiency below approximately 97% is considered to be low)
19. The voltages have no effect on the problem. The efficiency of the transformer is equal to output power divided by input power.

$$\frac{0.99}{?} = 99\%$$

The input power must be 1 watt.

20. You would have to measure the resistance of both windings and then calculate the power dissipated due to the current in the windings.
21. An air-core transformer has neither eddy-current nor hysteresis losses.

Types of Transformers

There are many varieties of transformers, ranging from huge power-station units to tiny subminiature radio-frequency types.

Most transformers are designed to transfer power. Others, however, are built to transfer only signal voltages.

Power distribution transformers (see Fig. 1-41) are rated in KVA (kilovolt-amperes) rather than in kilowatts or other power units. The KVA rating refers to the apparent power carried by the transformer—the real power is smaller by the load power factor.

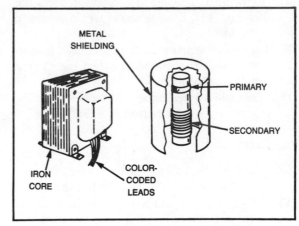

Fig. 1-41. Power-supply transformers and radio-frequency transformer.

Special transformers, wound to precision specifications, are used in metering applications to measure the current and voltage passing through large power-transmission lines.

A step-up transformer increases voltage (which increases impedance) and decreases current (resulting from an increased impedance) at the same time. A step-down transformer decreases voltage (which decreases impedance) and increases current (which results from a decreased impedance) at the same time. Therefore, a transformer changes impedance, but the impedance change is more pronounced than the voltage change. In fact, a transformer changes impedance by the square of the turns ratio:

$$\frac{Z_1}{Z_2} = \frac{N_1^2}{N_2^2}$$

Figure 1-42 shows an impedance matching transformer.

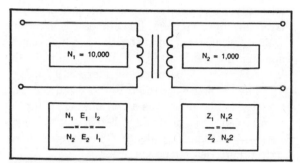

Fig. 1-42. An impedance matching transformer.

Questions

22. If the primary of a transformer has 10,000 turns and the secondary has 1,000 turns, what is the turns ratio?
23. If 100 volts is applied to the primary, what voltage will appear at the secondary?
24. If the load impedance of the secondary circuit is 1 ohm, how much current will flow in the primary?
25. What is the impedance of the primary?

Answers

22.

$$\frac{10,000}{1,000} = 10 \text{ to } 1 \text{ turns ratio}$$

23.

$$\frac{N_1}{N_2} = \frac{10}{1} = \frac{100}{E_2} \; ; \; E_2 = 10 \text{ volts}$$

24. Current in the secondary is 10 amperes, so,

$$\frac{N_1}{N_2} = \frac{I_2}{I_1} \; ; \; \frac{10}{1} = \frac{10}{I_1}$$

$$I_1 = 1 \text{ ampere}$$

25. The impedance of the primary circuit is:

$$\frac{E_1}{I_1} = \frac{100}{1} = 100 \text{ ohms}$$

Magnetic Amplifiers

Magnetic amplifiers are special transformer-like devices that use a small amount of power to control larger amounts of power, thus acting as amplifiers. They are simple, rugged, and efficient as compared to other forms of amplification.

Magnetic amplifiers take advantage of a special property of iron or steel in a strong magnetic field. To explain how a simple magnetic amplifier works, let's first review the basic principles of a coil.

When a current flows in a coil, a magnetic field (flux) is set up inside and around the coil. If the current is ac, the field also alternates. But, in any case, the strength of the magnetic field (the number of lines of flux produced) depends on the material inside the coil as well as how much current is flowing through the coil.

A very simple type of magnetic amplifier (see Fig. 1-43) is based on the fact that an iron core normally allows greater changes in the magnetic field and, therefore, increases the inductive reactance of a coil at a given frequency.

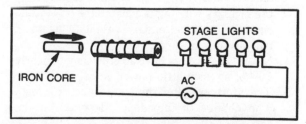

Fig. 1-43. A magnetic amplifier used to control stage lights.

Questions

26. A coil with an air core has a (greater, smaller) inductance than a similar coil with an iron core.
27. Inductive reactance is the result of a (constant, changing) magnetic field.
28. How would you increase the inductive reactance of the device illustrated in Fig. 1-43.
29. What effect would increasing XL have on the brightness of the lights?
30. How should the core be set to obtain maximum brightness of the lights?
31. Would this device work with a dc power supply?

Answers

26. A coil with an air core has a smaller inductance than an iron-core coil.
27. Inductive reactance is the result of a changing magnetic field.
28. Push the iron core into the coil.
29. Increasing XL would dim the lights.
30. The iron core should be totally removed.
31. The device would not work with dc.

What You Have Learned

1. The changing magnetic field produced by the primary winding in a transformer induces a changing voltage in the secondary winding.
2. The ratio of the primary voltage to the secondary voltage is the same as the ratio of the number of turns in the primary winding to the number of turns in the secondary winding.
3. If a transformer steps up voltage, it steps down current, and vice versa. The power drawn by the primary winding is equal to the power dissipated in the secondary circuit of an ideal transformer.
4. Most transformers have an efficiency of nearly 100%, so very little power is lost in them.
5. Transformers alter the impedance of a load. The change in impedance depends on the square of the turns ratio.
6. Magnetic amplifiers control the inductive reactance of a coil by altering the magnetic property of its core.
7. A very simple magnetic amplifier is basically a coil with a removable iron core. When the core is inserted, XL increases, and the power supplied to the load decreases.

INSIDE YOUR POWER SUPPLY

The catalog of a leading electronics supplier contained this glowing description: A superhet shortwave receiver covering the standard broadcast band through 20 meters. Its cabinet was luxurious walnut, its audio output push-pull into a high-quality speaker. The set boasted low current drain and the latest circuitry. The price?—a mere $49.75.

The catalog was Allied Radio's and the date was 1932. The radio was a console meant for the living room, and it no doubt pulled in the A&P Gypsies with reasonable fidelity. The thing is, it required batteries for power.

Here's the battery complement for the handsome, but hungry, Knight 8 vintage receiver: three 45-volt "B" batteries for tube plates; one 2-volt "A" cell for lighting filaments; one 22.5-volt "C" battery for biasing tube grids. This mountain of Evereadys cost $9.00, a rather steep tab even in the good old days. And they could have pooped out right in the middle of a Herbert Hoover speech.

Super Supplies

That danger is gone, thanks to power supplies. Now a receiver takes raw electricity from the utility company and converts it to filament, plate, or bias voltages. It does the same for transistorized circuits. Or it perhaps participates in the growing trend to 3-way operation, where you use the same device at home, in a car, or carry it as a portable. The supply not only powers the equipment in the home, it also recharges the portable batteries. Cost is low because ac power is priced about 3¢ per kilowatt hour—which means you can operate a plugged-in table radio for about 100 hours on a penny.

Though power supplies operate circuits of vastly different voltage and current requirements, the basic principles are the same. In most instances a supply accepts house current—usually 117 volts ac alternating at 60 Hz (cycles)—and performs the following steps.

Transforming Voltage. The power company provides 117 volts for home outlets, but it's hardly the value that many electronic devices demand. The plates of receiving tubes require about 100 to 250 volts for operation, while transmitting tubes may need a "B+" several hundred volts higher. Transistors, on the other hand, usually function at less than 30 volts. So the first task of the supply is to transform voltage to the desired value. In many CB sets, for example, there's plate-voltage requirement of 250 and filament-voltage requirement of 12.6 Vac. The power transformer delivers these levels.

Changing ac to dc. Furnishing correct voltage is not enough. Those voltages must often be dc—and the power company provides alternating current. So, the second function of a supply is to *rectify*, or convert ac to dc. If a rectifier malfunctions in your radio you'll soon learn its function. The symptom is annoying hum in the speaker (caused by 60-Hz alternations in the audio). In a TV set, suffering rectifiers can put a thick, dark, "hum" bar across the screen.

Filtering. Though rectifiers change ac to dc the product is far from suitable because it contains objectionable ripple. This will be attacked by the filter, which smooths the pulsations to pure dc.

The final step of the supply depends on the designer. He can add a bleeder, choose a regulator, or insert a divider at the output. We'll look at these extras, but first consider how the supply's basic parts operate.

The Transformer

In Fig. 1-44 is a typical power transformer that's been produced by the millions with only slight variations. As we'll see, the transformer acts to create a voltage change between its primary and various secondary windings. The trick's based on the turns-ratio between the various windings. If turns in the secondary number twice those of the primary, then output voltage doubles; if turns in the sec-

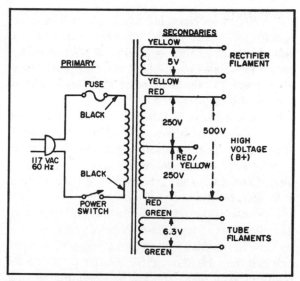

Fig. 1-44. Schematic of typical power transformer, showing voltages and EIA color-coding of windings.

ondary are a fraction of those in the primary, then a stepdown in voltage occurs.

Thus, in Fig. 1-44, the rectifier filament, which operates at 5 volts, has few turns compared to the primary; the high-voltage winding at 500 volts, however, has about five times as many turns as the primary. The colors shown for the windings, incidentally, are standard and observed by many transformer manufacturers.

The centertap connection of a winding splits the voltage in half. In our example, the high-voltage secondary is capable of 500 volts across the full winding (red to red), but only 250 volts between the centertap (red/yellow) and either end. The most important job for a centertap occurs in a full-wave supply, as we'll see in a moment. Note that a protective fuse and a power switch are located in one primary lead of the transformer.

Rectification

The two filament voltages from our transformer (5.0 for the rectifier and 6.3 for other tubes) will need no further processing. Ac can be applied directly for filament heating (or for lighting pilot lamps on the front panel). High voltage, however, must be converted to dc before powering tube plates or transistor collectors and drains.

A circuit for changing ac and dc is a half-wave rectifier, shown in Fig. 1-45. It's based on a diode's ability to conduct current in only one direction. The rectifier cathode boils off electrons (negative) which are attracted to the plate when the plate is driven positive by incoming ac.

When the next half-cycle of the ac appears, the plate is driven negative, so electrons are repelled at this time. The net result is shown in the output: a series of positive voltage pulses appearing at the load. (The dotted line shows where the negative side occurred.)

In practical circuits the half-wave rectifier is usually reserved for light-duty power supplies. It's inefficient because it fails to make use of ac voltage half the time (during the negative pulses). Secondly, those wide spaces between pulses are difficult to filter because of low ripple frequency. In a half-wave rectifier, the pulsations occur at 60 Hz, the same frequency as the applied line voltage. But don't underrate the half-wave supply because it's been used in just about every 4- or 5-tube table radio now playing. After all, its power requirements are low and the circuit is inexpensive to manufacture.

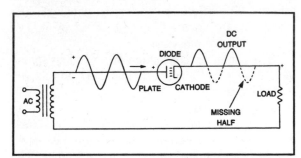

Fig. 1-45. Half-wave rectifier, showing how diode produces pulsating dc output by repelling electrons when plate is driven negative.

Full-Wave Supplies

Transmitters and higher-power equipment overcome the half-wave's shortcomings with the full-wave system. It's nothing more than a pair of diodes that are driven alternately so they consume every bit of ac input voltage. The key to full-wave operation is the centertap on the transformer's secondary winding. As applied ac appears across the complete winding, it makes the top end negative (as shown in Fig. 1-46) and the bottom end positive.

The centertap at this time establishes the zero voltage point because it's at the common, or grounded, side of the circuit. During the time the lower diode (No. 2) has a positive plate, it does the conducting. Next, the applied ac voltage reverses and makes the top diode plate (No. 1) positive so this tube now conducts.

This load-sharing combination of two diodes and a centertapped power transformer not only improves efficiency, but doubles the ripple frequency. An input of 60 Hz emerges as 120 Hz in a full-wave arrangement because every half-cycle appears in the output. This reduces the pulsating effect (cycles are closer together) and the dc becomes easier to filter.

If you purchase a transformer, watch out for one pitfall. It may be rated, say, "250 volts CT" and appear to be suitable for a rig with a 250-volt plate supply. In a full-wave supply, however, the transformer voltage output would be only 125, since a centertap reduces the voltage of a winding by one half. This can be avoided by specifying a transformer that has 250 volts each side of centertap or, stated another way, "500 volts CT."

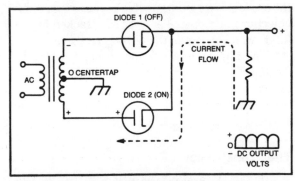

Fig. 1-46. Full-wave rectifier is a pair of diodes driven alternatively to take advantage of both halves of ac input voltage.

Solid-State Rectifiers

Tube rectifiers are still widely found in electronic equipment, but they're destined for the Smithsonian Institution. Solid-state equivalents are superior because they don't need filaments or heaters to accomplish the same rectifying action. They're several hundred times smaller and much cooler in operation. Instead of a huge 5U4 vacuum-tube rectifier in your TV set you're now more apt to find a pair of tiny silicon diodes.

Circuits using these semiconductors, though, are similar to those of vacuum tubes. As shown in Fig. 1-47, diodes can be used in equivalent half- and full-wave arrangements.

Unlike tubes, though, solid-state diodes rectify ac and dc by a semiconductor effect at the diode junction (a region between the anode and cathode). The action, in simplified fashion, occurs when "current carriers" in the material flow toward and away from the junction under the influence of applied ac. When few carriers appear at the junction, little current gets through the diode; conversely, when many carriers are in the area, they reduce the junction's opposition to current flow. Depending on the way the diode is connected in the circuit, it can recover either the positive or negative half of the ac.

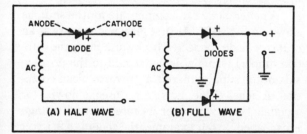

Fig. 1-47. Solid-state selenium or germanium diodes in similar half- and full-wave rectifier circuits are better than tubes since they don't need filaments or heaters for rectifying action.

Bridge Rectifiers

Another common arrangement is the full-wave bridge (Fig. 1-48). Though it uses four diodes, it offsets this disadvantage by an ability to produce the same output as a regular full wave supply without a centertapped transformer. It accomplishes the feat by operating one pair of diodes during each half cycle. And as one diode pulls current out of the load, its partner pushes current into it.

The net effect is a total voltage across the load which is about equal to the applied ac. We've shown how it occurs for diodes 1 and 2 in the diagram (Fig.

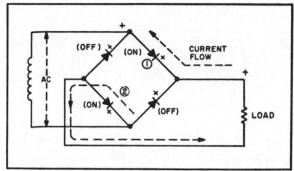

Fig. 1-48. Solid-state bridge rectifier provides full-wave rectification with center-tapped transformer by using four diodes.

1-48) but a comparable action occurs in the other diodes when the ac switches polarity.

Filtering

The next major section of the supply is the filter, which smooths out the ripple. Its two major components are often a capacitor and a choke which eliminate pulsations by dumping a small amount of current from the peak of each ripple into the "valleys" between them. The result, as shown in Fig. 1-49, is pure dc fit for a tube or transistor.

In operation, pulsating dc arrives at the filter choke, a coil of wire wound on a soft iron core. As the name implies, the choke attempts to oppose any change in current flow. The rippling part of the wave, therefore, encounters high reactance in the choke and fails to get through. This is aided by the filter capacitor which is charged by ripple voltage.

As the ripple falls (between pulses), the capac-

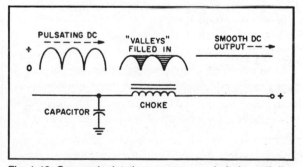

Fig. 1-49. Curves depicts how reactance of choke and discharge of capacitor eliminates ripple and fills in valleys for smooth dc.

itor discharges part of its stored current into the "valley." Thus the combined effect of choke and capacitor results in smooth dc which can have ripple as low as a few percent of the total voltage.

You won't find the choke in some power supplies because it's an expensive item. Many designers eliminate it (especially in mass-produced equipment) by using a resistor instead, as shown in Fig. 1-50. The resistor does the job of filtering, but with one penalty: it reduces the amount of available voltage at the output. Yet, the loss can be tolerated in many circuits and filter resistors are common.

Another use for resistors in a supply is to serve as a bleeder, also shown in Fig. 1-50. In this function, it protects parts in the supply from possible damage due to sudden voltage surges when the supply is first turned on. Also, a bleeder helps stabilize voltage output when the load changes (as in a keyed ham transmitter) by always drawing some small degree of load current. Bleeders, too, are found in dangerous high-voltage circuits where they bleed-off the stored charge of filter capacitors that could deliver a lethal shock to a repairman (even after the equipment has been turned off.)

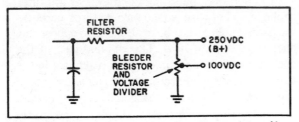

Fig. 1-50. Choke can be replaced by filter resistor. Also shown is bleeder resistor that serves both as output regulator as well as voltage divider.

Note that a tap can be added to the bleeder to provide a second output voltage from the supply. Now the bleeder becomes a voltage divider. As such, it can supply the designer with multiple output voltages for operating various devices in a circuit.

Voltage Regulation

A ham who's received a "pink ticket" from the FCC for chirpy signals, a color TV that's gone fuzzy, a shortwave receiver that won't stay on frequency—all may suffer from a problem in voltage regulation. Line-voltage fluctuations or other electrical swings can cause poor, unstable operation. So the engineers have come up with methods for "stiffening" a power supply.

If, say, line voltage changes from 105 to 130, they design the circuit to operate at 100 volts. Whatever voltage arrives over the line is reduced to 100, and the surplus is dumped (usually in the form of heat). To perform this task, the regulator establishes a reference point, then regulates around it.

A common example is the zener diode found in the power supply of many CB transceivers. Since these rigs can operate from a car's battery or generator, supply voltage can swing from 11 to 15 volts. This could happen if you're standing for a traffic light, then pull away, causing a shift between car battery and generator. If the CB set is on at this time, receiver tuning could be thrown off because of large changes in local oscillator voltage.

A zener diode can compensate for the shift, as shown in Fig. 1-51. At first glance it appears as an ordinary diode connected backward. Since the cathode (upper) terminal is connected to the positive side of the supply, there's a "reverse bias" condition. A zener diode, however, "breaks down" (or "avalanches") whenever its rated (zener) voltage is exceeded. In our example, the zener is a 9.1-volt unit, so the diode conducts current as the supply voltage shifts from 11 to 15 Vdc.

Yet we see 9.1 volts indicated at the output. Secret of the zener's ability to hold at 9.1 is that it

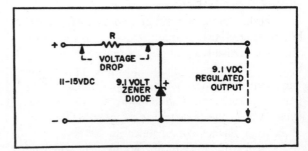

Fig. 1-51. For more efficient regulation than produced by bleeder resistor, zener diode shunted across dc output will hold voltage to specified limit.

detours part of the supply current as the voltage increases. Since a resistor is in series with that current flow, a voltage drop (as shown) appears across the resistor. Thus, any increase in supply voltage is dissipated across the resistor and effectively subtracted from the output. This automatic and continuous action occurs for any voltage above 9.1—the zener's nominal rating—so the output is said to be regulated.

More and Merrier

This barely brushes the subject of power supplies, since the variations are nearly endless. More than 20,000 volts for the picture tube of a color TV are derived from a special "flyback" transformer. It captures voltage from rapidly moving magnetic fields in the set's horizontal scanning section. An oscilloscope power supply contains strings of adjustable voltage dividers to move the pattern of light on the screen in any direction.

There are also high-current supplies with massive rectifiers for battery charging and super-smooth lab supplies for circuit design. But behind most of them are the simple principles which transform, rectify, filter, and regulate a voltage so it can do the job at hand.

DESIGNING REGULATED POWER SUPPLIES

Up until a few years ago, the task of designing a regulated power supply was both complicated and time-consuming. As a result, the average experimenter either made do without regulation or copied someone else's circuit. Things have changed a lot since then. Now, even a beginner can design his own regulated supply using one of the integrated-circuit voltage regulators. No fancy oscilloscope is necessary; in fact, you don't even need a calculator. Simply by consulting the tables and graphs in this article, you can custom-design your own regulated supply in a matter of minutes.

The supplies to be covered here range in output from 5 to 18-volts at currents up to one-ampere. Both positive and negative outputs are possible. Let's start by examining the basic positive-regulator circuit shown in Fig. 1-52. Voltage from transformer T1 is full-wave rectified by diodes D1 and D2, and smoothed by filter capacitor C1. Voltage regulator VR + converts the unregulated dc across C1 into a regulated potential of the desired size at its output, pin 2. Capacitor C2 bypasses this output and thereby stabilizes the circuit and improves transient response. On the primary side of T1, fuse F1 protects the circuit should a malfunction cause excessive current to be drawn from the ac line.

Similar, But Not Equal

The similarity between the positive-supply circuit and the negative-supply circuit (Fig. 1-53) is apparent. Note, however, that D1, D2, C1 and C2 are reversed in the negative circuit. Furthermore, the pin designations of negative regulator VR − are different from those of positive regulator VR +. For the positive regulator, pin 1 is the input, while pin 2 is the output, and pin 3 is ground. On the negative regulator, however, pin 1 is the ground connection. Pin 3 is now the input, and pin 2 remains as the output of the voltage regulator.

Both the positive and negative regulators are available in two case styles, a "T" package and a "K" package; see the base pin diagram.

Regardless whether a regulator is positive or

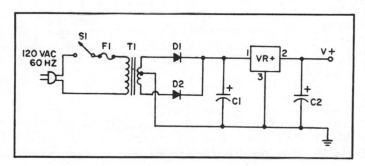

Fig. 1-52. Here is the schematic for the typical positive-regulated supply. Note the pin connections on the voltage regulator chip.

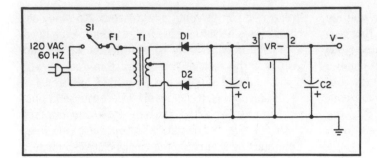

Fig. 1-53. The negative supply is almost identical to positive, with the exception of the reversals of the diodes and the pinouts of the regulator.

negative, the same pin-numbering scheme applies. Remember, however, that the numbers have different meanings for positive and negative regulators. For example, on the "T" package, pin 3 is always the middle pin. If the regulator is positive, the middle pin is ground. But if the regulator is negative, then the middle pin is its input.

In the design procedure to follow, the same tables and rules will be used to specify F1, T1, D1, D2, C1 and C2, whether a positive or negative supply is being built. This is certainly reasonable since the two circuits are so similar. However, the positive and negative supplies must use different types of regulator ICs, and these may not be interchanged. With all the preliminaries out of the way, let's get down to the basics of this easy seven-step method for designing the supplies.

Determine the Required Voltage

You have your choice of seven positive voltages and seven negative voltages, as shown in the middle column of Fig. 1-54. Note that +10V has no negative counterpart. Be sure that you know the maximum current that your load can draw; it must

be no more than one ampere. If you are powering a construction project or a kit, you should find a supply-current specification somewhere in the literature. If you have no idea as to how much current your intended load will draw, you can measure it directly. Connect the device you intend to power to a variable bench supply set to the desired voltage. Measure the current drain with an ammeter in series with one of the power leads.

Select a Transformer

Refer to Fig. 1-54, and locate the desired output voltage in the middle column. For a positive supply, you will find the necessary transformer listed in the right-hand column, and in the same row as your selected voltage. The proper transformer for a negative supply will be found in this same row, but in the column furthest to the left. The transformers are specified according to the RMS voltage from one end of the secondary to the other. Note that all secondaries must be center-tapped (CT). The transformers listed are standard, although they may not seem so if you are accustomed to the usual 6, 12, and 24-volt transformers that

Fig. 1-54. Here's a listing of the more commonly used transformer and regulator combinations for both positive and negative.

NEGATIVE SUPPLIES			POSITIVE SUPPLIES	
TRANSFORMER (RMS VOLTS)	REGULATOR	OUTPUT VOLTAGE	REGULATOR	TRANSFORMER (RMS VOLTS)
16 ct	7905/320-5	5	7805/340-5	20ct
20 ct	7906/320-6	6	7806/340-6	20 ct
24 ct	7908/320-8	8	7808/340-8	24 ct
24 ct	7909/320-9	9	NOT AVAILABLE	
NOT AVAILABLE		10	7810/340-10	28 ct
34 ct	7912/320-12	12	7812/340-12	34 ct
40 ct	7915/320-15	15	7815/340-15	40ct
44ct	7918/320-18	18	7818/340-18	48 ct

flood the hobby market. Finding a source is not hard; check the catalogs of any of the large electronics retailers. At least one transformer company, Signal, will sell you these transformers by direct mail-order. Before ordering, request a catalog and price list (Signal Transformer Co., 500 Bayview Ave., Inwood, N.Y. 11696).

You do have a little bit of leeway in the selection of a transformer, particularly at the higher voltages. If a 34-VCT transformer is called for, and you have on hand one that measures 32-VCT, go ahead and use it. Also, you could hook up the secondaries of two 12-volt transformers in series (and in the proper phase) to obtain the equivalent of a 24-VCT transformer.

In addition to the voltage, you must also specify your transformer's current rating. A convenient rule-of-thumb is to pick a transformer whose secondary-current rating is about 1.2 times the maximum current that is to be drawn from the supply. If you use a transformer whose current rating is too small, it will overheat. On the other hand, if you choose a transformer that can supply much more current than is necessary, it will be bulkier and more expensive than a transformer of the proper size.

Pick a Regulator

Here again, you should use Fig. 1-54. Positive regulators can be found in the column just to the right of the "Output Voltage" column, and negative regulators are just to the left. As you can see, a positive regulator may be chosen from either of two IC families: The 7800 series, or the 340 series. Furthermore, each family comes in either the "T" package or the "K" package (see Fig. 1-55). Thus, when selecting a 6-volt positive regulator, you can pick from any of the following: 7806K, 7806T, 340K-6 or 340T-6. If you were looking for a negative 6-volt regulator, the 7900 and 320 families would offer the following candidates: 7906K, 7906T, 320K-6 or 320T-6. Actually, there is no significant distinction between the 7800 and 340 families, nor between the 7900 and 320 families. The "K" package, however, can facilitate high power more readily, so it might be preferred at the higher

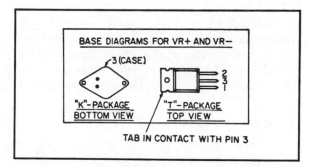

Fig. 1-55. Above are the pin diagrams for both the "T" and "K" package regulators. Note difference between pos. and neg.

supply-current levels. On the other hand, the "T" package is probably preferable if you intend to build your supply on a PC board.

At all but the smallest load currents, these voltage regulators will have to be heat-sinked. This will be covered in more detail later. When you buy a regulator, try to get a specification sheet, too. It will provide you with more complete information on your particular IC.

Choose Your Rectifier Diodes

The factors to be considered here are the diodes' voltage rating, average-current rating, and surge-current rating. Since the supply's load current is restricted to a maximum of one ampere, each diode must see an average current of less than half an ampere. Therefore, a rectifier diode with an average-current rating of one-ampere should suffice. A voltage rating of 100-PIV would be adequate, but it is even safer to use diodes with a 200-PIV rating. These will survive most power-line transients. The surge-current rating becomes an important consideration at the instant when the supply is turned on. At that moment, filter capacitor C1 is uncharged. Transformer T1 charges the capacitor with a current through one of the rectifier diodes. Since this current is limited primarily by the small resistance of the transformer's secondary, it is very large. When all of the above factors are taken into account, the 1N4003 emerges as a good rectifier with transformers of 28-VCT or less. Its higher-voltage cousins, the 1N4004 and 1N4005, also will work well. For transformers of 34-VCT to 48-VCT, use a 1N5402 rectifier or a higher-voltage relative (1N5403, etc.) The 1N5402 is a 3-ampere diode that will handle higher surges than the 1N4003. Both rectifier types are readily available from many suppliers, including Radio Shack.

Specifying Capacitor C2

This is easy, since anything greater than 25-μF will be fine. The capacitor's voltage rating should be from 1.5 to 2-times the output voltage of the supply you are building. If a capacitor with too small a working voltage is used, it will not last long. Conversely, using a capacitor with a working voltage greater than twice the supply voltage is wasteful of space and money.

Selecting Filter Capacitor C1

First, determine this component's working-voltage rating from the chart. A range of satisfactory working voltages will be found opposite the transformer voltage that you selected in step 2. Use a filter capacitor with a voltage rating as high as possible within the recommended range of working voltages.

The minimum capacitance of C1, in microfarads, can be found from the graph. Locate your supply's maximum current drain (see step 1) on the x-axis of the graph. Project a line upward to strike the one line (out of the three in the graph) that is appropriate to the transformer voltage being used. The y-value at the point of intersection is the minimum capacitance necessary. Use a standard electrolytic capacitor that is greater than or equal to the value determined from the graph.

In most cases, you can afford to be generous with capacitance. A larger capacitor will have less ripple voltage across it. As a result, it will heat less and last longer. So, when a low-current supply demands only 200-μF, you can use 500-μF if you like. But when the capacitor must have a high working voltage (50 to 75-volts), extra microfarads come in a bigger package and at a higher price. Therefore, you may not wish to be so generous.

In order to locate a suitable electrolytic capacitor, consult the catalog of a large mail-order supplier, such as Allied or Burstein-Applebee. You will find some electrolytics listed as "computer-grade." These cost a little more, but they last longer in heavy-duty service. Whether or not the extra cost is warranted is a decision that is up to you.

Finding the Right Fuse

The fuse rating table will be of assistance here. Locate the row corresponding to the transformer being used, and the column appropriate to the maximum expected load current. Check the zone in which the row/column intersection lies for the proper fuse rating. Be certain to buy a slow-blow (3AG) fuse, since this type is less prone to blow on the current surge at turn-on.

Now, let's consider a practical design example. Suppose that a 15-volt, 350-milliamp, positive supply is required. The table indicates that a 40-VCT transformer will be needed. Estimate the transformer's current rating: $350 \times 1.2 = 420$. A look through a transformer catalog reveals the nearest commercially available unit to be 40-VCT @ 500 milliamps.

Referring once more to the table, let's choose a 7815K regulator IC. Since a 40-VCT transformer is being used, 1N5402 rectifier-diodes are a good choice.

For capacitor C2, let's use a 100-μF unit with a standard working voltage of 35-volts. Because the voltage rating is about twice the supply's output voltage, this is a safe selection.

Figure 1-56 reveals that filter capacitor C1's working voltage should lie between 40 and 60-volts. Turning to Fig. 1-57, and using line "B," we find the minimum capacitance to be about 750-μF. The nearest commercial unit turns out to be 1000-μF @ 50 volts. You can use more capacitance if desired.

Finally, Fig. 1-58 indicates that a 1/4-amp, slow-blow fuse is appropriate for this particular combination of transformer voltage and maximum load current.

Now that you know how to design your supply, let's talk about how to build it. Most manufacturers recommend that a voltage regulator be mounted fairly close to C1. This means 3-inches or less of interconnecting wire. Likewise, C2 should be

TRANSFORMER RATING (RMS VOLTS)	WORKING VOLTAGE OF CI (VOLTS DC)
16	16 – 25
20	25 – 35
24	25 – 35
28	30 – 40
34	35 – 50
40	40 – 60
44	50 – 75
48	50 – 75

Fig. 1-56. Simply look across from left to right in order to determine what the working voltage of C1 will need to be.

mounted close by—right on the pins of the regulator, if possible.

Rectifiers D1 and D2 are cooled by heat conduction through the two mounting leads. To assist conduction, mount these rectifiers with short leads. If the rectifier is mounted on a terminal strip, then the lugs of the strip will act to sink some heat. Printed-circuit mounting requires the use of large

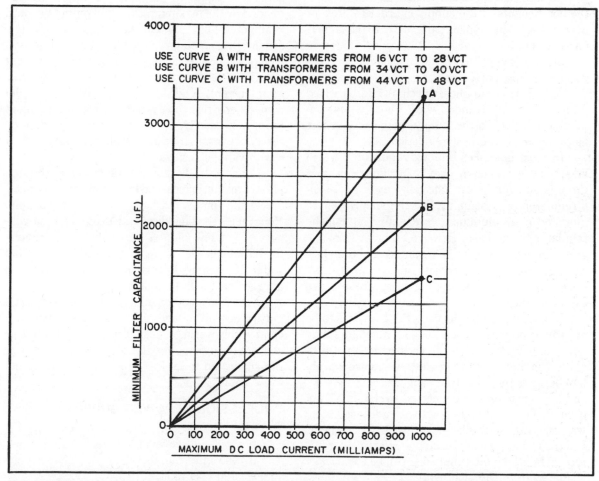

Fig. 1-57. After consulting Fig. 1-56 for the voltage rating, use this graph to determine the correct capacitance for capacitor C1.

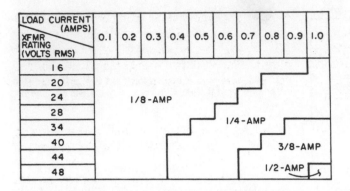

LOAD CURRENT (AMPS) XFMR RATING (VOLTS RMS)	0.1	0.2	0.3	0.4	0.5	0.6	0.7	0.8	0.9	1.0
16										
20										
24		1/8-AMP								
28										
34					1/4-AMP					
40							3/8-AMP			
44										
48							1/2-AMP			

Fig. 1-58. To calculate what size fuse is needed for your supply, find your transformer's output rating in the vertical column, and your regulator's rating at top. Draw a line out to the center of the chart from each box. Where they meet is the fuse rating in amps.

pads and thick connecting traces to draw heat away from the rectifier's leads.

Be sure that there is adequate air flow around the components of the supply in order to prevent overheating. This applies particularly to the higher-current supplies.

Short, heavy wires should be used for interconnecting components. Again, this is most important for high-current supplies, which should be wired with #16 or #18 stranded wire. Those wires connecting the load to the supply should be as short as possible for the best regulation.

In most instances, voltage-regulator ICs will need to be heat-sinked. They're just fine. However, there is an even better, cheaper way to heat-sink a regulator IC: Assuming that the supply will be mounted in an aluminum case, simply attach the regulator to the case. Remove all paint from the area where the IC is to be mounted, and then bolt the regulator to the chassis. Silicone grease between the chassis and the regulator will improve the heat transfer.

If, as is generally the case, the chassis is to be at ground potential, then positive regulators may be mounted directly to the chassis with no difficulty. Negative regulators, however, pose a problem because the mounting flange on both the "T" and "K" packages is connected to the input, not ground. The solution here is to use mica insulating wafers, coated with silicone grease, between the IC and the chassis. Heat will still be effectively transferred, but the mounting flange will be electrically insulated from the chassis.

Once your supply is finished, check it out be-fore permanently wiring it to a load. You will need a dummy resistor to test the supply. Its resistance should be equal to the supply's output voltage divided by the maximum expected output current, in amperes. For the supply that was designed in this article, that amounts to 15/35, or about 43-ohms. The resistance should have a power rating of about two-times the product of output voltage and maximum current. Again, for the supply that was designed here, this comes to $2 \times 15 \times .35$, or about ten-watts. Usually, you can build up such a dummy resistance from series and parallel combinations of lower-wattage resistors.

Connect the dummy resistance across the supply's output terminals, and then connect a voltmeter across the dummy resistance. Turn on the supply. Your meter should indicate the desired output voltage. After a few minutes, carefully feel the regulator IC's flange. It should be no hotter than hot tap water. If touching the regulator case is painful, use a larger heat-sink to cool it down.

If, at the end of ten minutes, your supply is still putting out full voltage, and the regulator is not uncomfortably warm, you can turn the supply off. Disconnect the dummy resistance and voltmeter, wire the supply up to its load, and start pumping out those happy amps.

PROFESSIONAL POWER SUPPLY

Sure, I'm a dyed-in-the-wool experimenter/hobbyist, and I've had the fever for some time. And if you're like me, there's a good chance your budget is just as tight.

That fiscal fact plus an appreciation for a good,

efficient design is the "need" that helped provide the "shove" that got the ball rolling to crank out this handy power supply for my own use. Looking over the line-up of commercial units and talking to people in the field gives a pretty good picture of just what features are important and which are popular. You'll find them all here with an experimenter/hobbyist's parts budget to boot! Not a bad deal, actually.

You get the benefits of a commercial lab supply for as little as twenty-five dollars—all new parts, complete with case—by building it yourself. A full-blown version complete with switchable front-panel voltmeter/ammeter will peak out at about thirty-five dollars; but if you can scrounge up a 25-volt, 2 or 3-amp power transformer, don't need the meter, and you have a case, all new parts go for about $17. Any way you build it, performance is never sacrificed.

Background: Having the right level of dc power available to test a transistor circuit, a motor, or the like is all too often a problem. It is the old story of not having the right tool at the right time. Batteries don't offer variable voltage or much power. Purchasing an inexpensive, unregulated supply may be satisfactory in some cases, but when transistors in the test circuit begin switching on and off, you may find the supply voltage going up and down. Ideally, one would like to have a selectable voltage level that will not change as the load changes, a fair amount of available power, and an adjustable current limit in order to protect both the supply and the item being tested.

Although ICs are available that deliver regulated voltage selectable over a range of around 0 to 20 volts, the power delivered by these ICs is only a few watts. Finally, to purchase a supply that has the desired features would cost a fair amount mainly because one would have to buy a professional-type supply. The answer to all this, however, is really very simple. The power supply described here can be built in only a few hours at low cost, and the features are outstanding.

While the basic principle of operation of this regulated supply is well known—mainly an operational amplifier controlling a power transistor—we have designed this particular unit using components that offer the most for the money and simple circuit "tricks" that provide the best return for your efforts. The result is a supply that uses a handful of electronic parts costing about $20 with the following features:

- Twenty watts of available output power (above 20 watts, for safety, the voltage begins to decrease automatically).
- Adjustable current limiting (maximum current fed to the load can be pre-set to any value between 0.1 amp and 1.0 amp).
- One-half percent regulation (at 10 volts output, for example, the voltage will drop only 0.05 volt between no load and full load).
- Adjustable output voltage of 0.6 volt to 30 volts.
- Short circuit protection (the output of the supply can be accidentally short circuited without harming the supply or even blowing a fuse; try it!).

How It Works

This regulated power supply has a "heart" and a "brain." The brain is a 741 operational amplifier IC which detects error signals. The heart is a power transistor which regulates power to the load. Figure 1-59 is a simplified schematic showing how it works. The unregulated voltage comes from a transformer and full wave rectifier. Placing a load across this voltage directly would cause it to drop sharply—which is what we want to avoid.

Resistors R1 and R2 determine a voltage gain for the 741 op amp by (1 + R1/R2). The output of the op amp, and therefore the regulated output V_{OUT} is given by $V_{OUT} = 0.6 \times (1 + R1/R2)$, where 0.6 is the reference voltage built into the circuit. This equation holds only when the voltage drop across R2 equals the 0.6 reference voltage, so it is the job of the op amp to force this to happen. The process is basically simple, V_{out} is selected by adjusting R1 with, for example, no load on the output. As a load is applied, it momentarily causes V_{OUT} to drop since point A in Fig. 1-59 is "pulled" closer to ground than before. The voltage across R2 is then less than the reference voltage, so the

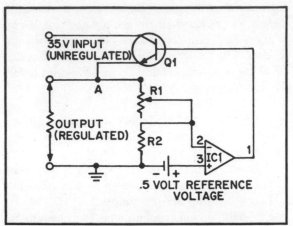

35 V INPUT (UNREGULATED)

Q1

A

R1

OUTPUT (REGULATED)

R2

2

3 IC1

1

− +

.5 VOLT REFERENCE VOLTAGE

Fig. 1-59. Author's simplified schematic to show the principle of operation. Reference voltage is not necessarily a battery. It could be, but it's not very practical. In this supply, it consists of pre-regulator zener D2 and the one-amp silicon power diode called D1.

op amp sees an imbalance, or error voltage, at its input which is amplified and sent to Q1 to turn it on (make it conduct) more. Q1 then "pumps" more current into the load, thereby maintaining the output voltage at its desired level.

In addition to regulating voltage, this unit limits current. In the complete schematic we see that the desired current limit is selected by adjusting R6. When current through R7 causes the voltage at the base of Q2 to be about 0.7 volt, Q2 begins conducting from collector to emitter thereby grounding the output of the op amp and lowering the output voltage, which in turn has the desired effect of limiting the current to the pre-selected level.

The 741 op amp is an ideal device to use here because it is inexpensive and has built-in short circuit protection for its output which allows Q2 to ground the output to limit current. When selecting among the various 741 op amps on the market, choose one that, according to its specification sheet, has an offset voltage of less than 10 millivolts; otherwise the lowest output voltage from the power supply will be proportionately greater than the 0.6 volt specified here.

Power transistor Q1 is a darlington type, which means it has a current gain of about 1000. Inside, it is basically one transistor driving another. This results in the high current gain. This high gain is needed to prevent the op amp output from being overloaded, which would reduce regulation quality.

Our Overdesign

Transistor Q1 is rated at 90 watts, but remember that such ratings are at room temperature (25 °C). If you set the output voltage to 0.6 volt and draw 1 amp through a load, Q1 will "drop" about 35 volts across it; at 1 amp, that's 35 watts. Without an ice cube on it, Q1 on the heat-sink we have suggested will heat to about 80 °C. At this temperature it is capable of dissipating 50 watts, which is well enough above the actual 35 watt requirement for safe operation.

To obtain the low reference voltage for pin 3 of the 741, a regular diode (D1) is used since voltage in the forward direction causes a sharp knee (the voltage at which conduction begins) at about 0.6 volt. It is serving, therefore, as a low voltage zener diode at a fraction of the cost. To greatly improve regulation, D1 is fed by a 12-volt zener, D2, so we have a reference within a reference and a very inexpensive way to obtain a stable low voltage.

Nuts, Bolts 'n Solder

Construction is straightforward. See the full schematic and parts list in Fig. 1-60. All components will fit on a 4 × 5-in. perf board and within a 3 × 5 × 6-in. cabinet. The transformer may have a center tap (yellow on the Radio Shack version) which can be cut and taped since it is not needed. All 120 Vac leads that go to S1, the fuse holder, and T1, must be covered with insulating tape to avoid the shock hazard associated with these points. In addition, a 3-prong plug should be used with the ground prong going to the cabinet—as with any properly protected electrical tool. Capacitor C1 may be increased to 2000 μF if better regulation is desired. It is best to use a 4-pin socket for D3 and a mini-DIP socket for the IC to avoid heating the devices themselves when soldering.

The heat-sink for Q1 can be mounted directly on the perf board. Mounting hardware and a socket (see parts list) should be used to hold the device firmly to the heat-sink. The mica insulator in the

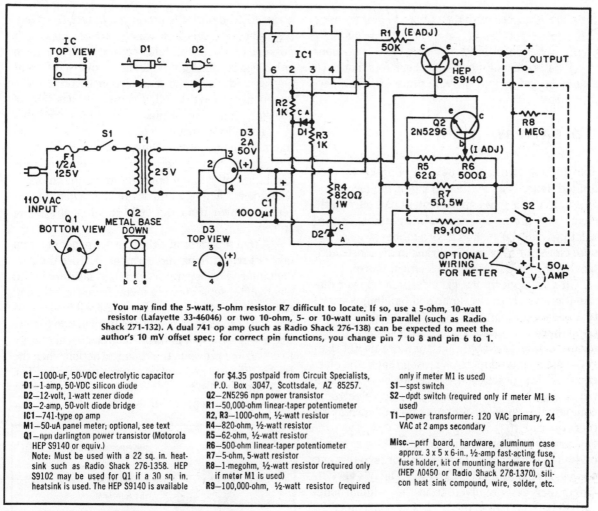

You may find the 5-watt, 5-ohm resistor R7 difficult to locate. If so, use a 5-ohm, 10-watt resistor (Lafayette 33-46046) or two 10-ohm, 5- or 10-watt units in parallel (such as Radio Shack 271-132). A dual 741 op amp (such as Radio Shack 276-138) can be expected to meet the author's 10 mV offset spec; for correct pin functions, you change pin 7 to 8 and pin 6 to 1.

C1—1000-uF, 50-VDC electrolytic capacitor
D1—1-amp, 50-VDC silicon diode
D2—12-volt, 1-watt zener diode
D3—2-amp, 50-volt diode bridge
IC1—741-type op amp
M1—50-uA panel meter; optional, see text
Q1—npn darlington power transistor (Motorola HEP S9140 or equiv.)
 Note: Must be used with a 22 sq. in. heat-sink such as Radio Shack 276-1358. HEP S9102 may be used for Q1 if a 30 sq. in. heatsink is used. The HEP S9140 is available

for $4.35 postpaid from Circuit Specialists, P.O. Box 3047, Scottsdale, AZ 85257.
Q2—2N5296 npn power transistor
R1—50,000-ohm linear-taper potentiometer
R2, R3—1000-ohm, ½-watt resistor
R4—820-ohm, ½-watt resistor
R5—62-ohm, ½-watt resistor
R6—500-ohm linear-taper potentiometer
R7—5-ohm, 5-watt resistor
R8—1-megohm, ½-watt resistor (required only if meter M1 is used)
R9—100,000-ohm, ½-watt resistor (required

only if meter M1 is used)
S1—spst switch
S2—dpdt switch (required only if meter M1 is used)
T1—power transformer: 120 VAC primary, 24 VAC at 2 amps secondary

Misc.—perf board, hardware, aluminum case approx. 3 x 5 x 6-in., ½-amp fast-acting fuse, fuse holder, kit of mounting hardware for Q1 (HEP A0450 or Radio Shack 276-1370), silicon heat sink compound, wire, solder, etc.

Fig. 1-60. Schematic and parts list for the professional power supply.

mounting kit can be coated with silicon heat-sink compound to aid in cooling Q1. To further aid in cooling Q1, holes should be drilled in the bottom of the cabinet, and holes should be present along the top or sides of the box. Q2 can be nearly any transistor with a gain of at least 50 and a rating of 40 volts and 25 mA. The Q2 suggested here does not require a heat-sink.

Finally, a voltmeter is not needed in the cabinet since once the voltage is set with an external meter it will not change unless the pre-set current limit or power limit (20 watts) is exceeded. If a meter is desired, however, the schematic shows how

one can be connected to serve as both an ammeter and a voltmeter.

Calibration

To calibrate the voltage control, R1, connect an external meter, turn R1 to different voltage levels, and mark these voltages on the panel next to R1. To calibrate the current limit control, R6, set R1 to 10 volts, apply a 10-watt, 10-ohm load and turn R6 down until the voltage just begins to drop. This is the 1-ampere point; it can be marked on the panel next to R6. To get the 0.1-ampere mark, change the load to 100 ohms at 10 volts (1-watt resistor). Turn R6 until the voltage begins to drop, and you've got the 0.1 amp limit. Current limit points in between are obtained in similar fashion.

This power supply takes about four hours to assemble and should provide years of stable performance.

C-Zn BATTERY THEORY

There are several sources of electricity available for experimenters now as opposed to very limited sources at the beginning of the electronic age. Initially, early experimenters had only static electricity, produced essentially by rubbing an insulating material such as a hard rubber or glass rod with cloth or fur, or as Ben Franklin demonstrated, by flying a kite during an electrical storm.

In this modern age of widespread power distribution nearly every home and building is wired to a power company's generating station. In addition, there are various kinds and shapes of batteries readily available that are more useful than static electricity. The main reason that static electricity is of no practical use is because modern electrical machinery, appliances, and electronic equipment require a continuous flow of current for their operation.

Since the subject of this discussion is the zinc-carbon battery, we'll confine our words to this one source of reliable electrical power. Today's very efficient dry cells evolved from the original zinc-carbon battery, called the Leclanché cell, named after its inventor, Georges Leclanché. Before the advent of electronics they were used extensively for door bells, alarms, telephones, and other applications where current is needed only intermittently.

How Batteries Are Made

There's a great deal of similarity between the original Leclanché cell and modern zinc-carbon batteries. Everyone's familiar with the conventional round single cells, such as AA, C, D, and #6 sizes, which are packaged and wired together to make up higher voltage batteries. In addition, there are flat rectangular cells, that stack one on top the other, which have been developed for higher voltage bat-

teries. These flat cells produce a longer-lived battery since there is less wasted space, making it possible to produce a higher capacity cell in a given cubic space. Though available in many different shapes and sizes, the zinc-carbon battery, more commonly called dry-cell, is comprised basically of the same materials originally used by Leclanché.

His cell was made up of a positive carbon element, a zinc negative element formed to serve as a container, and an electrolyte. The electrolyte is a solution of sal ammoniac (ammonium chloride) that doesn't actively attack the zinc when no current is drawn from the cell, or when it's being stored.

A thin separator of either porous paper or a thin layer of wheat flour and cornstarch, lines the zinc container. The separator, which is saturated with electrolyte, separates the metal from the mix and prevents the cell from discharging itself in short order. The separator permits chemical action to take place when the cell is furnishing electrical energy to a load and prevents the chemical action when the load is disconnected and no current flows. See Figs. 1-61 through 1-63.

When current is drawn from the cell for

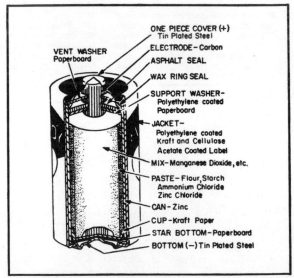

Fig. 1-61. Cutaway view of a flashlight cell, either AA, C, or D size. This view shows various components making up cell. Study of this and reference to text helps to understand general makeup of carbon-zinc battery.

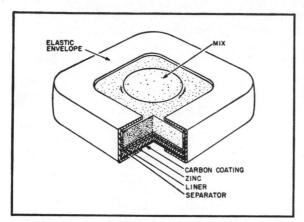

Fig. 1-62. Cutaway view of square "minimax" zinc-carbon cell. It develops 1.5V—the same as round cells; chief advantage is that for the same volume of space it has a greater capacity.

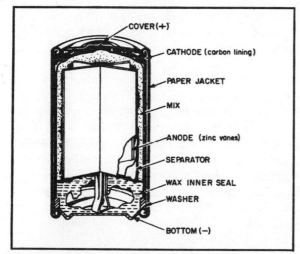

Fig. 1-63. Cutaway view of external cathode or "inside out" type of battery. Molded carbon wall is both container and current collector. Zinc vanes are inside cell, ensuring efficient zinc consumption.

reasonably long periods, hydrogen gas accumulates on the carbon element. This accumulation of hydrogen gas bubbles polarizes the cell, which, in turn, appreciably reduces the current it will deliver. The cell, however, doesn't revive after a rest period.

Depolarizing Agent

Continuous heavy current drain initiates the generation of hydrogen within the cell that causes it to become polarized, which soon results in low cell output. Leclanché added a chemical depolarizing agent, manganese dioxide, which is really an oxidizing agent. By definition, an oxidizing agent is a chemical that releases its oxygen readily. Since oxygen and hydrogen have a strong affinity for one another, the hydrogen that accumulates on the carbon element unites chemically with the oxygen from the manganese dioxide and forms water. In essence, the depolarizer (MnO_2) reacts with and removes the hydrogen to avoid polarization.

The term "dry cell" is a misnomer, since the electrolyte, though not a liquid, is a wet paste that also contains the depolarizing agent and fine particles of carbon to reduce internal cell resistance. Cell design, customized for specific applications, is based primarily on the percentage of carbon particles in the mixture. The cell won't spill, evaporate, or run over because, on commercially manufactured cells, the top is sealed. When the battery no longer produces electrical energy it isn't because the wet paste has dried up or because any one particular chemical has been used up. Instead, it's because all of the active ingredients are chemically united to form new compounds that are not active, thus for all intents and purposes creating a worn-out cell.

A dry cell remains inactive until a load is connected, at which time electricity is produced by chemical reaction. Each zinc atom gives up two electrons to the load circuit and forms a positive zinc ion (Zn^{++}) that goes into the electrolyte. The chemical equation is:

$$Zn \text{ (metal)} \rightarrow Zn^{++} \text{ (ion)} + 2 \text{ electrons}$$

The electrons return to the cell through the positive electrode and enter into another reaction with ammonium ions (NH_4^+) and the manganese oxide (MnO_2). These electrons are absorbed in the reaction and produce manganic oxide (Mn_2O_3), ammonia (NH_3), and water (H_2O). The equation for this reaction is:

$$2MnO_2 + 2NH_4 + 2 \text{ electrons}$$
$$\downarrow$$
$$Mn_2O_3 + 2NH_3 + H_2O$$

In addition, the ammonia (NH_3) combines with the zinc ion to form a complex zinc ion.

Some cells may contain zinc chloride ($ZnCL_2$) which create other reactions. Regardless of the chemicals used, the electrons that make up the current flow come from the zinc metal, which is consumed in the process.

Shelf Life

Open circuit voltage of a dry cell, regardless of its size, is 1.5 volts. As the active ingredients become depleted, the internal impedance or cell resistance increases until the cell becomes useless. The resistance of new AA, C, D, and #6 cells normally is less than 1/2 ohm. Shelf deterioration results from two major factors: (a) loss of moisture through evaporation because of poor seals, or (b) low-level chemical reactions that occur within the cell independent of those created by current drain. Internal current leakage causes the cell to discharge itself at a slow rate. This accounts for the gradual depletion of battery output even though the cells are not connected in a circuit to supply power. This gradual depletion of battery life is commonly referred to as shelf life.

Since raising the temperature of chemical mixtures speeds up most chemical reactions, the storage of dry cells in abnormally high ambient temperature environments will hasten wasteful zinc corrosion and other side chemical reactions within the cell to reduce its shelf life. Storage in lower than normal, but not freezing temperatures, will appreciably reduce shelf life deterioration. Temperatures above 125° will effect rapid deterioration and possible leakage. Ideal storage temperature is from 40° to 50°F. The average shelf life for dry cells not in use under ideal temperature conditions is two to three years.

Capacity

Ordinarily, dry-cell batteries are tested on circuits of constant resistance and the capacity is expressed as the time of discharge rather than in ampere hours. It's relatively easy to calculate ampere hours by determining the average value of current drain. To calculate the average drain you must first determine the average voltage by plotting voltage readings taken at regular intervals from full voltage to cutoff voltage. From this and the known fixed resistance used as a fixed load, the average current is computed, which, in turn, is multiplied by the total time of actual discharge to arrive at ampere hour capacity. Since voltage characteristics of different brands of batteries differ, the average current delivered by a particular size cell will be only an approximation of the capacity of other cells and batteries under comparable conditions.

Other factors affecting battery capacity are: (a) temperature—discussed previously, (b) cutoff voltage—capacity is greater as cutoff voltage is lowered, (c) relative time of discharge and recuperation—performance normally is better when discharge is intermittent, and (d) rate of discharge—capacity is greater as discharge current is less, down to a certain level, at which point efficiency decreases because of spontaneous reactions within the cells.

No definite statement can be made, but, as an example, maximum service efficiency for continuous discharge of a #6 cell is obtained on a 60- to 100-ohm circuit, or at a current of 10 to 20 mA. For smaller cells this current will be proportionately smaller. From this it can be seen that other factors such as size, weight, convenience, and initial cost must be taken into account to determine the ultimate service efficiency that can be obtained (see Fig. 1-64).

Selecting Batteries

From the variety of different sizes and types of batteries available one might get the impression that battery selection is a difficult task. You can reduce the problem considerably by first outlining basic operational requirements and then matching up a battery that most nearly fulfills them.

To obtain factual information on the many types of batteries available, we suggest you get a copy of a publication titled *Battery Applications Engineering Data*, published by Union Carbide, the makers of Eveready brand batteries (Burgess also publishes a similar handbook). In addition to being

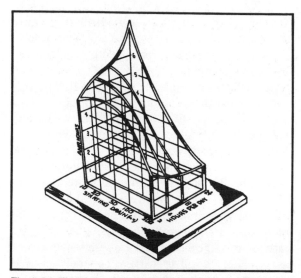

Fig. 1-64. This three-dimensional graph plots service life as a function of initial current drain and duty cycle of a typical D-size carbon-zinc cell.

loaded with battery characteristics, standard test procedures, etc., it contains a most comprehensive listing of a wide variety of Eveready batteries being manufactured as well as cross-referencing to batteries of other manufacturers.

There is a certain minimum amount of information that must be tabulated before a suitable battery can be selected. You must know such things as nominal operating requirements of the circuit, its current drain, its operating cycle, its desired service life, temperatures in which equipment will be used, size and weight limitations, type of terminals, cost, etc.

If there is a limit in voltage below which the equipment will no longer function properly (called cutoff voltage) this must also be taken into account when selecting a battery. Some circuits have a high initial current drain and then operate at a more nominal drain once started—a consideration when arriving at the circuit's current drain. In arriving at the ampere-hour capacity necessary, current drain along with discharge schedule and required service life are determining factors.

Battery Charging

Dry cells generate electricity by chemical ac-

tion which eats away the negative electrode. Once this has been completely destroyed, and since the structure of the cell is such that they are sealed, it's impossible to replace the negative electrode. To truly restore the charge in a dry battery you must replace this electrode. However, the operating life of the dry cell can be extended in some cases. This would be more like a rejuvenation process rather than a recharging one. As pointed out previously, the chemicals added to the electrolyte deter the formation of gas around the positive electrode, which reduces the polarization and increases the life. The longer a battery is used the more these chemicals are used up and polarization sets in, weakening the battery.

By applying a reverse polarity with current flowing in an opposite direction, electrolysis takes place in the electrolyte. This ionizes the gas atoms around the positive electrode, clearing it for more efficient chemical action, which will determine how well the life of the cell can be extended. Recharging is economically feasible only when the cells are used under controlled conditions using a system of exchange of used cells for new ones.

Though dry cells are nominally considered to be primary cells, they may be restored for a limited number of times if the following conditions are used: (1) the operating voltage or discharge of the cell is not below 1 volt per cell when the battery is removed from service and charged, (2) battery is placed on charge immediately after it's removed from service, (3) ampere-hours of charging should be 120% to 180% of the discharge, (4) the charging rate must be low enough so that the recharge takes 12-16 hours, (5) the battery must be put into service soon after charging.

SUPERCHARGER BATTERY CHARGER

Proliferation of portable electronic gadgets such as calculators, tape recorders, walkie-talkies, radios, etc., gave a big boost to sales of rechargeable batteries. This article should bring your knowledge on the rechargeable battery up-to-date and tell you about a truly universal charging circuit with an electronic timer which you can build.

Rechargeable sealed batteries, besides many

other advantages, make the operation of portable equipment quite inexpensive. Do you still remember the high cost of B and filament batteries for portable tube radios? But even with transistorized equipment, the cost of "cheap" throw-away batteries may be quite high. For example, a portable calculator or a radio using four AA throw-away cells needs battery replacement about once a week if it is used for 2 to 3 hours each day. This comes to about $50 per year. A set of four rechargeable AA-size Nickel-Cadmium (NiCad) batteries costs around $8 and with proper care should last 3 to 5 years or more. The cost of electricity used for recharging comes to only about 10 cents per year. Quite a difference in cost!

What Proper Care?

We mentioned that a rechargeable NiCad battery will last for many years if proper care is exercised. Our charger described in this article will give your rechargeable batteries such proper care. There are three rules to observe when handling rechargeable batteries. They are all expressed in terms of battery capacity in milliampere hours (mAh). This value is usually given by the manufacturer on the battery label. If no battery capacity is given, some common values are shown in this table. However, watch for the figures given by the manufacturer. For example, you may find a sub C cell in a D cell package.

Battery Size	Capacity (mAh)	10-Hour Rate (mA)	5-Hour Rate (mA)
AA	450	45	90
sub C	1000	100	200
C	1500	150	300
D	3500	350	700

Rule 1. Do not discharge continuously at more than the hourly rate (450 mA for AA cells). Whether this rule is satisfied depends on the kind of equipment you are using. This rule will seldom be violated. Just don't try to run your electric power mower on a bunch of AA cells!

Rule 2. Do not continue discharging when the battery voltage is 0 volt (cell reversal). If you have several batteries in series, one will always have slightly smaller capacity than the others. When that battery is completely discharged, the other batteries will still pump current through it. The only way to avoid this condition is to turn off your appliance immediately when the total series battery voltage drops significantly (by more than 1 volt). You will notice it when, for example, your radio starts distorting. Turn it off immediately.

Rule 3. Do not charge at more than the 10-hour rate (45 mA for AA cells) and do not continue charging at that rate beyond full capacity for more than a few hours. Slightly higher charging rates of up to the 5-hour rate are permissible as long as the battery is still discharged. To satisfy this rule, you need to control the charging current and the charging time as is provided by this charger. Some so-called universal battery chargers put either a too-high or a too-low current into your batteries. As a result either the battery will be damaged and its life shortened or it will not get fully charged in a reasonable amount of time.

These are general and safe rules. Specially-constructed batteries (for example, the so-called quick-charge batteries) may let you break one or more of these without causing permanent damage. However, unless the battery manufacturer assures you to the contrary you better stick with our three rules; otherwise permanent damage may result. Either the battery will fail (go dead) immediately or its life-span and capacity will be shortened.

Battery Charger

This charger is capable of charging one to six cells from AA to D size. It lets you control the charging current and the charging time. You turn the charger on, set the current to the 10-hour rate for a full charge or 5-hour rate for a quick boost, and forget it. After 14 hours (or 1 3/4 hours for a quick boost) the charger will turn itself off. In other words, we pump in 140 percent of battery capacity to charge it fully (40 percent is the typical loss in the charging process). For a quick boost of 1 3/4 hours when the battery is completely or partially discharged, we can go up to the 5-hour rate to obtain about one-quarter full battery capacity. For special quick-charge batteries follow manufacturer's recommendations. The schematic and parts list are shown in Fig. 1-65.

The charger makes use of a newly-developed integrated circuit which combines a built-in oscillator (similar to the 555-type) and a frequency divider of up to 65,536 (2^{16}). This way we can choose a basic oscillator frequency of 0.77 Hz which can be obtained with reasonable resistance and capacitance values and divide it by 2^{16} to obtain timing values of up to 14 hours. The basic frequency, f, is determined by C2, R3, and R4. The frequency

$$f = \frac{1}{2 \times R3 \times C2}$$

where R4 = 2 × R3. The IC is connected in such

a way that the timer resets itself when the circuit is first turned on. When its timing interval is up, it will turn the SCR off permanently until the circuit is first removed from, then connected to the power line again. The rest of the circuit is straightforward. The output of the IC (pin 8) controls the gate of the SCR and lights up the LED. The charging current is controlled by the variable resistor R9. The current range with the values shown is between approximately 40 and 500 mA for up to 6 cells. Switch S1 selects the IC divider output of either 2^{16} or 2^{13}.

The lowest divider ratio the IC is capable of, 256, is particularly useful during the charger calibration. To select this counting/dividing mode, disconnect pins 12 and 13 from S1 and temporarily connect pin 12 to pin 14 and pin 13 to pin 5. When you have finished the test, reconnect pins 12 and

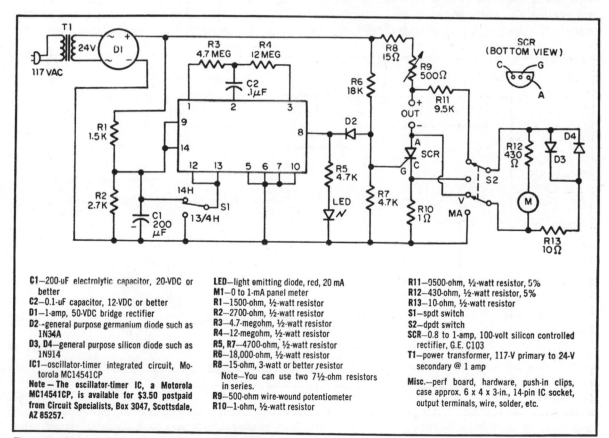

C1—200-uF electrolytic capacitor, 20-VDC or better
C2—0.1-uF capacitor, 12-VDC or better
D1—1-amp, 50-VDC bridge rectifier
D2—general purpose germanium diode such as 1N34A
D3, D4—general purpose silicon diode such as 1N914
IC1—oscillator-timer integrated circuit, Motorola MC14541CP
Note — The oscillator-timer IC, a Motorola MC14541CP, is available for $3.50 postpaid from Circuit Specialists, Box 3047, Scottsdale, AZ 85257.

LED—light emitting diode, red, 20 mA
M1—0 to 1-mA panel meter
R1—1500-ohm, ½-watt resistor
R2—2700-ohm, ½-watt resistor
R3—4.7-megohm, ½-watt resistor
R4—12-megohm, ½-watt resistor
R5, R7—4700-ohm, ½-watt resistor
R6—18,000-ohm, ½-watt resistor
R8—15-ohm, 3-watt or better resistor
Note—You can use two 7½-ohm resistors in series.
R9—500-ohm wire-wound potentiometer
R10—1-ohm, ½-watt resistor

R11—9500-ohm, ½-watt resistor, 5%
R12—430-ohm, ½-watt resistor, 5%
R13—10-ohm, ½-watt resistor
S1—spdt switch
S2—dpdt switch
SCR—0.8 to 1-amp, 100-volt silicon controlled rectifier, G.E. C103
T1—power transformer, 117-V primary to 24-V secondary @ 1 amp

Misc.—perf board, hardware, push-in clips, case approx. 6 x 4 x 3-in., 14-pin IC socket, output terminals, wire, solder, etc.

Fig. 1-65. Schematic and parts list for supercharger.

13 to S1 after removing your temporary connection. In this mode the timer should turn itself off after 3 minutes 17 seconds plus or minus 10 seconds. The meter M1 is used as a volt meter (0 to 10 volts) across the batteries or as a charging current milliamp meter of 0 to 500 mA. Its function is selectable with S2. The diodes D1 and D2 protect the meter from overload.

Put It Together

You can mount all components on a perfboard as shown in Fig. 1-66. The wiring is not critical. The MOS integrated circuit is internally protected against static charges, however we still recommend using a 14 pin socket. Do not insert the IC until you are (1) finished with the wiring, (2) have checked all connections, (3) and made sure the power is off.

If you plan to charge the batteries outside your equipment, then you must provide battery holders for various size batteries which you want to connect to the charger. Under certain conditions, you

may be able to connect the charger directly to your appliance without removing the batteries, usually via the "adapter" jack. You may have to look at the schematic of your radio or walkie-talkie to find out if the "adapter" jack is connected to batteries when a plug is inserted. If so, you can charge the NiCads in the unit.

Once construction is complete, apply power and check to see whether or not the LED pilot lamp is on. If so, it should remain on for either one and three quarters of an hour or fourteen hours, whichever time you have selected with the time select switch. To check the correct operation of the timing circuit in less time, you can make the following temporary connections to enable the divide by 256 function. Connect pin 12 and 13 of the IC temporarily to pins 14 and 5 respectively to select the 256 divider ratio. Try different values of capacitor C2 till you get a timing interval of approximately 3 minutes and 17 seconds. Of course, this is not a critical parameter, but it should be accurate to at

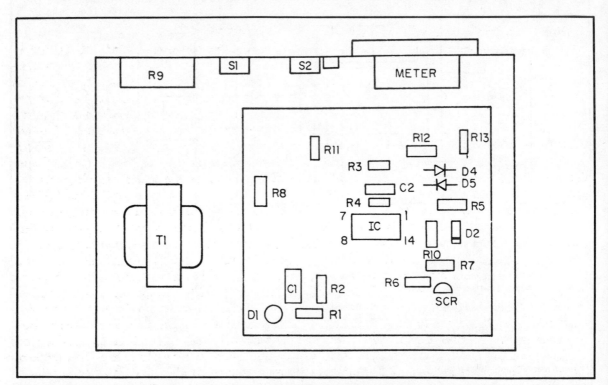

Fig. 1-66. With out artist on the job, you should have little difficulty locating parts on your supercharger perf board. While it is possible to build this unit in a much smaller area if you wish, beginners will find the extra room a benefit.

least 3 minutes and 17 seconds plus and minus 30 seconds.

More Savings

Besides rechargeable batteries, regular, throw-away zinc-carbon batteries can also be recharged under certain conditions. Those conditions follow.

- Battery should not be completely discharged (battery voltage should stay above 1 volt).
- Battery should not be leaking.
- Battery should be used soon after being recharged.

Other popular "throw-away" batteries are alkaline and mercury batteries. Mercury batteries are used where high energy concentration in low volume is required. A camera or a hearing aid is a prime example of such an application. The mercury cell has three to five times the capacity of a carbon-zinc cell of the same size but it costs five to ten times as much.

Non-rechargeable alkaline batteries have about twice the capacity of a comparable carbon-zinc cell at approximately three times the price. Mercury and alkaline cells have similar nearly constant discharge voltage and low internal resistance characteristics as the NiCad cells. However, they are not leakproof and should be removed from equipment if not in use. We strongly discourage you from trying to recharge mercury or non-rechargeable alkaline batteries. Gases generated by the recharging process in the sealed cell may cause an explosion and spread the caustic electrolyte.

You may also run across rechargeable alkaline batteries. They are not as popular as NiCad batteries, but are slightly cheaper and have similar characteristics to NiCad batteries. They are not, however, as long-lived. Many other excellent types of batteries are used in military and commercial applications. They did not yet find their way to the consumer market because of high cost.

From this short description, you may deduce that the NiCad battery is the most cost-effective battery in many applications where the appliance is in frequent use.

On the Inside

A NiCad battery consists of layers of sintered cadmium and sintered nickel separated by fiber soaked in potassium hydroxide electrolyte.

Sintering consists of baking a powdered metal to the consistency of a solid. A sintered material is highly porous. Its active area is several hundred times larger than that of a solid plate of the same dimension.

During the latter part of the charging cycle, during overcharging and during high discharge, hydrogen, oxygen and electrolyte fumes are being generated. These gases will normally reach an equilibrium condition reacting with each other and with the porous electrodes. Sealed cells also have a safety venting mechanism (activated above 100 PSI) assuring that the cell will not rupture under extreme conditions. Repeated venting however, causes loss of the electrolyte and subsequent battery deterioration. For this reason controlled charging is beneficial to NiCad batteries.

Other Advantages

A major advantage of NiCad cells, in particular when used for portable radios and walkie-talkies, is a nearly constant voltage during the discharging cycle. Regular zinc-carbon batteries lose their voltage at a fairly constant rate and thus affect the performance of the equipment they are powering; however, rechargeable batteries keep their voltage nearly constant until they nearly completely discharge. For example, the voltage of a carbon zinc battery drops by approximately 0.3 volts per cell when it is 50 percent discharged. The voltage of a NiCad battery drops by only 0.1 volt during the same period. Another important feature of NiCad batteries is the low internal resistance on the order of about 30 milliohm (AA cells)—about ten times less than for a comparable zinc carbon battery. This feature is particularly important for class B type audio circuits which require more power during peaks of speech or music. Batteries with a low internal resistance can supply the sudden surges of power required for good, low distortion sound. Another important feature of NiCad batteries, as compared to zinc carbon, is that they can be stored in a charged or discharged state and are virtually leakproof.

For additional information about batteries in general and/or NiCad batteries in particular, refer to the following material. "More Staying Power for Small Batteries," *Machine Design* magazine, December 13, 1973; *Nickel-Cadmium Battery Application Engineering Handbook,* General Electric publication number GET-3148; *Nickel-Cadmium Battery Application Engineering Handbook Supplement,* General Electric publication number GET-3148-S1; *RCA Battery Manual,* RCA publication BDG-111B; *Eveready Application and Engineering Data Book.*

From flashlight to photoflood, from toys to 2-way, NiCads are in widespread use. Everyone is ready to save a buck these days; from a money-saving standpoint, NiCad batteries have some definite advantages. Maybe, if you are a heavy battery user, NiCad rechargeable batteries can help you. Why not check it out?

BATTERY MONITOR AND CELL CONDITION TESTER

Are you one of the many who are servicing his own car? It pays to make sure that the battery is in good shape to prevent that slow, grinding start when you are in a big hurry. Just adding water at intervals isn't always enough to ensure that the battery will be in top condition when you need it.

With our expanded-scale battery tester you can make periodic tests of your battery to insure that the battery is in good shape. The tester is built in a compact plastic cabinet and includes easy-to-make special probes for the cell electrolytic tests as well as overall battery voltage tests. The construction of the tester is simplified for ease in building.

Tester Circuit

Refer to Fig. 1-67 for the schematic and parts list. When S1 is set to the "single wet cell" position and voltage is at J1 and J2 (from the test leads), M1 will indicate only when the test voltage at J1 and J2 is higher in value than 1.4-volt battery B1. For example, if the test voltage is 1 volt (positive

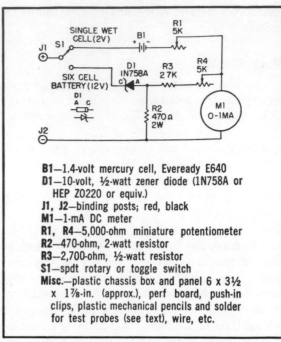

B1—1.4-volt mercury cell, Eveready E640
D1—10-volt, ½-watt zener diode (1N758A or HEP Z0220 or equiv.)
J1, J2—binding posts; red, black
M1—1-mA DC meter
R1, R4—5,000-ohm miniature potentiometer
R2—470-ohm, 2-watt resistor
R3—2,700-ohm, ½-watt resistor
S1—spdt rotary or toggle switch
Misc.—plastic chassis box and panel 6 x 3½ x 1⅞-in. (approx.), perf board, push-in clips, plastic mechanical pencils and solder for test probes (see text), wire, etc.

Fig. 1-67. Parts list and schematic for battery monitor.

polarity at J1 and negative polarity connected to J2), the meter will not indicate since the B1 voltage is 1.4 volts. When the test voltage is 1.5 volts, there is a 0.1 volt difference over that of B1, and M1 will indicate a current flow (voltage) in the circuit. The 1.4-volt meter scale marking is equivalent to meter zero.

When S1 is set to the "six cell battery" position, zener diode D1 operates similarly to battery B1 in the other position. Since D1 is a 10-volt zener diode, a test voltage higher than 10 volts is required to allow M1 to indicate voltage.

Potentiometer R1 is the calibration pot for the single wet cell meter circuit, and R4 is the calibration adjustment for the six cell battery circuit. Series resistor R2 provides a minimum current flow through the zener so that it will operate properly.

Construction

The Tester is built in a 6 x 3 1/2 x 7/8-in. plastic box with a plastic panel. The box dimensions are not critical, and any convenient size can be used. To minimize possible electrical short circuit hazards, do not use a metal box. Most of the components are installed with push-in clips on a 3 × 2 1/2-in. perfboard with remaining parts mounted on the box panel.

The best way to start construction is to cut out the M1 mounting hole in the panel and install the meter in approximately the same position shown in the panel photo. Then locate and mount S1, J1 and J2. Cut a section of perfboard to size, and drill two holes to fit the M1 terminal screws to mount the board. Install the perfboard to the meter terminals with two solder lugs supplied with the meter.

Mount the board components with push-in clips at the approximate locations shown in Fig. 1-68. Use short leads for best mechanical rigidity, and wire as shown in the schematic. Make sure that D1 and B1 are connected with the proper polarities as shown in the schematic. Carefully solder B1 to the push-in clips with a minimum of heat, or the mercury cell may be destroyed. If desired, you can use commercial mounting clips for the battery that do not require soldering.

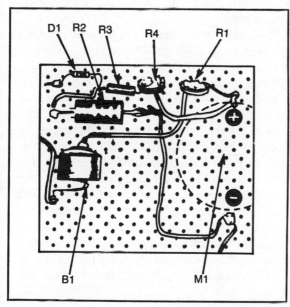

Fig. 1-68. Perfboard showing components including location of meter as dashed line. Mercury cell battery will last its shelf life, which is generally two years for a fresh battery. Eliminate D1, R2, R3, R4, and S1 for a dunk-test only meter. 2-V is center scale.

Wire the remainder of the tester circuits and the panel components. Carefully check the wiring and make sure that M1 is connected with the proper polarity.

Test Probe

The tester requires special probes for the electrolyte test. As shown in Fig. 1-69, the probes are made from solder wrapped around the end of a plastic tube (we used a plastic body of a mechanical pencil and #18 60/40 rosin core solder).

Begin construction by selecting a pair of mechanical pencils with black and red plastic bodies for your test leads. Carefully cut off the metal pointed end of each pencil and remove the entire mechanical assembly from inside the pencil. Clean out the inside of the pencils so they are completely hollow and have no inside obstructions.

Drill two holes spaced 3/4-in. apart approximately 1/4-in. from the end of each pencil body, and wrap wire solder between the holes as shown. Insert the ends of the wire solder into the holes to hold the turns in place. The end of the wire solder in the hole toward the other end of the pencil body (the former eraser end) should be long enough to reach through the body end to be carefully soldered onto the test lead. Then carefully push the solder back into the plastic body with a portion of the test lead. Do not try to stretch the wire solder or use

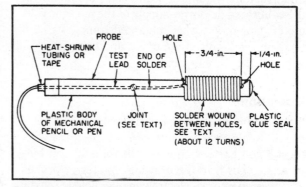

Fig. 1-69. Use the plastic body of a mechanical pencil or modify a set of old VOM leads. Either way, wrap 10 to 18 turns of "wire" solder around the end to serve as the electrolyte contact surface. Shrink tubing makes a neat job. Connect the wire lead and the solder together before trying to put the lead into the hole.

too much tension or the solder will break. Carefully inert short plastic sections into the body end to wedge the test lead in place and prevent it from being pulled out, then tape or use heat shrink plastic tubing on the lead end of both test probes. We used hot plastic from an electric glue gun to seal up the open end of the test prod and at the places where the solder is fed into the holes. Do not put any hot plastic over the solder turns.

Calibration

Set S1 to the single wet cell (2 volt) range and connect the tester to an exact source of 2 volts dc. Adjust R1 for an M1 indication of 2 volts (at center scale). Then set S1 to the six cell battery (12 volt) range. Adjust R4 for a 12-volt center scale indication with exactly 12-volts input to the tester. Make sure that you have connected the right polarity input for these calibration adjustments (J1 connected to positive (+) voltage and J2 connected to negative (−) voltage terminals).

For a more accurate meter calibration (and if you are using a different size 1 mA meter or a different type of 10-volt zener diode) you will need a calibrated variable voltage dc power supply or a dc supply with a potentiometer and a monitor voltmeter. Calibrate both ranges of the tester by adjusting R1 and R4 for midscale indications as in the previous (cemented meter scale) procedure, and then marking the meter scales in accordance with the calibrated dc power supply or the monitor voltmeter. Our model was calibrated from 1.4 to 2.6 volts on the 2-volt range of S1, and from 10 to 14 volts on the 12-volt range.

Operation

Automobile storage batteries consist of a number of 2-volt cells connected in series—three cells for a 6-volt battery and six cells for a 12-volt battery. As shown in the drawing, the tester probes are inserted into the electrolytic filler holes of a pair of adjacent (series-connected) cells so that the tester will indicate the voltage between the electrolytes in each cell. This voltage is approximately 2 volts, depending on the condition of the battery cells. The test will show the condition of the positive plate in one cell and the negative plate in the paired cell. By making tests of each pair of cells along the battery, the overall condition of the battery can be determined. Make sure that you observe proper test probe polarities.

If you are not sure which cell is the correct mate of another cell (since the arrangement of cells under the plastic top of the battery cannot be seen), momentarily place the probe into the electrolyte of a cell and quickly withdraw the probe if the meter (M1) swings sharply upscale, indicating overvoltage. The 1/4-in. plastic section at the end of the probes should minimize the possibility of shorting out the cell between the plates, but use care in placing the probes into the battery holes; hold them in your hands—do not just drop them into the electrolyte while taking readings. Place the probes just far enough into the electrolyte to obtain an M1 indication. The probe electrodes may have slight tendency to polarize (act like little miniature storage batteries due to electrochemical action on the solder) and affect the meter indication. To prevent this, slightly agitate the probes in the electrolyte while testing.

Test your storage battery at periodic intervals and note the cell readings. This will give you a performance record to check when you suspect that the battery may be defective. When a battery starts to go bad, it will show up as widely different voltages between cells (usually one cell will start to go bad before the others—not all the cells at once). For best results, make your periodic tests when the battery is in approximately the same electrical state of charge; the battery should be fully charged and have stabilized for some time before making tests. The probes should be washed and dried after each use to prevent corrosion from affecting the readings. The 12-volt scale of the tester can be used with a normal set of test probes to periodically check full battery voltage across the battery terminals.

INTRODUCTION TO THE TRANSISTOR

Using transistors in your projects is easy once you understand how they work. This section will give you the basics of modern transistor theory enabling you to use these tiny dynamos in your construction projects.

The Transistor as a Switch

The transistor is undoubtedly the most important modern electronic component. It has made great and profound changes in electronics and in our daily lives since its discovery in 1948.

In this chapter the transistor will be introduced as an electronic component which acts similarly to a simple mechanical switch, since it is actually used as a switch in much modern electronic equipment. The transistor can be made to conduct or not conduct an electric current—which is exactly what a mechanical switch does.

An experiment in this chapter will help you to build a simple one-transistor switching circuit. This circuit can be easily set up on a home workbench, and it will enhance your learning if you obtain the few components required and actually perform the experiment of building and operating the circuit.

From this basic idea we will progress to simple circuits which use several transistors to accomplish the same end. This affords an easy introduction to why the transistor is used, and to how it is used in computers and other modern circuits.

When you complete this chapter you will be able to:

- describe the basic construction of a transistor;
- specify what transistor switching action is;
- differentiate between the two most common types of transistors;
- tell which currents flow through a transistor;
- specify the relationship between base and collector current in a transistor;
- calculate the current gain for a transistor;
- explain how a transistor can be ON or OFF;
- compare the transistor to a simple mechanical switch;
- do simple transistor current calculation.

The Basic Transistor

Figure 1-70 shows several common transistors

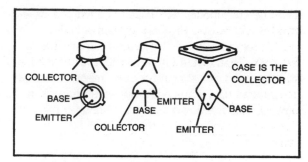

Fig. 1-70. The three types of transistor body.

in use today. For each transistor, the lower diagram shows how the leads are designated and how to identify them in most cases. In its simplest form a transistor can be considered as two diodes, connected back to back, as in Fig. 1-71. However, in the construction process one very important modification is made. Instead of two separate P regions only one very thin region is used.

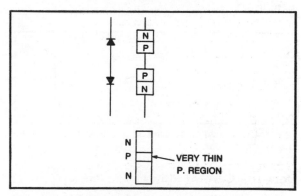

Fig. 1-71. A transistor may be seen as two diodes back to back, with a very thin p region.

The three terminals of a transistor—the base, the emitter, and the collector—are connected as in Fig. 1-72.

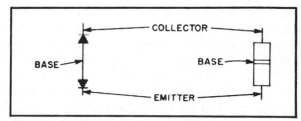

Fig. 1-72. The three parts of a transistor.

The two diodes are usually called the base-emitter diode, and the base-collector diode.

The symbol used in circuit diagrams for the transistor is shown in Fig. 1-73 with the two diodes and the junctions shown for comparison. Because of the way the semiconductor materials are arranged, this is known as an npn transistor.

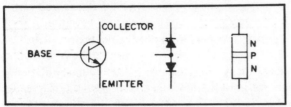

Fig. 1-73. The schematic symbol, and its analogous parts in an npn transistor.

It is also possible to make transistors with a pnp configuration, as shown in Fig. 1-74. Both types, npn and pnp, are made from either silicon or germanium.

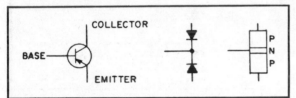

Fig. 1-74. The schematic symbol, and its analogous parts in a pnp transistor.

How the Current Flows

If a battery is connected to an npn transistor, then a current will flow as shown in Fig. 1-75.

This current, flowing through the base-emitter diode, is called base current and is given the symbol Ib.

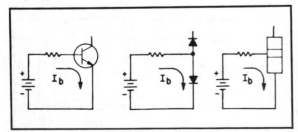

Fig. 1-75. The base current.

Would base current flow if the battery were reversed? Base current would not flow as the diode would be back biased.

In the circuit in Fig. 1-76, the base current can be calculated using Ohm's law, where

$$I = \frac{E}{R}, \ E = IR, \text{ and } R = \frac{E}{I}$$

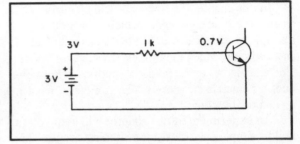

Fig. 1-76. Circuit for calculating base current by Ohm's law.

Find the base current in this circuit. (Hint: Do not ignore the 0.7 V drop across the base-emitter diode.) Your calculations should look something like this.

$$Ib = \frac{(Vs - 0.7V)}{R} = \frac{(3 - 0.7)}{1 \ k\Omega} = \frac{2.2 \ V}{1 \ k\Omega}$$
$$= 2.3 \ mA$$

In the circuit in Fig. 1-77, as the 10 V battery is much higher than the 0.7 V diode drop, we can consider the base-emitter diode to be a perfect diode, and thus assume the voltage drop is 0 V. The base current is calculated like this:

$$Ib = \frac{(10 - 0)}{1 \ k\Omega} = \frac{10}{1 \ k\Omega} = 10 \ mA$$

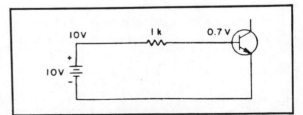

Fig. 1-77. Circuit for calculating base current by Ohm's law.

Will current flow in this circuit in Fig. 1-78? Why or why not? It will not flow as the base-collector diode is reversed biased.

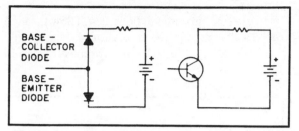

Fig. 1-78. Circuit with the base-collector diode reverse biased.

When both the base and the collector circuits, as in Fig. 1-79, are connected, it demonstrates the outstanding characteristic of the transistor, which is sometimes called transistor action: If base current flows in a transistor, collector current will also flow.

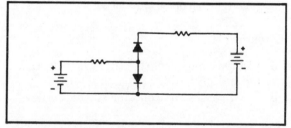

Fig. 1-79. A circuit showing that the base current controls the collector current.

Examine the current paths in Fig. 1-80.

Base current (Ib) flows through the base-emitter diode and causes the collector current (Ic) to flow through the base-collector diode.

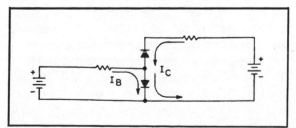

Fig. 1-80. Transistor circuit showing base and collector current.

No current flows from the collector to the base, as shown by the dotted line in Fig. 1-81.

The reason why the collector current takes the path shown in Fig. 1-80, rather than the dotted line path, is beyond the scope of this book. This is the domain of semiconductor physics and is not needed in electronic circuit design and analysis at this time.

Up to now we have been using the npn transistor, solely for the purposes of illustration. A pnp transistor could have been used. There is no difference in how the two types work or behave. What is said about one is equally true for the other.

There is, however, one important circuit difference which is illustrated below. This is caused by the fact that the pnp is made with the diodes in the reverse direction from the npn.

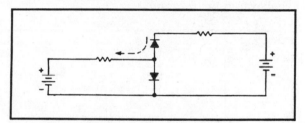

Fig. 1-81. No current flows from collector to base.

Note how the battery polarity is reversed and the current flows in the opposite directions through the diodes. Figures 1-82 and 1-83 show the battery connections to produce currents for both circuits. In both diagrams the current flow is counterclockwise.

As stated earlier, there is absolutely no difference between npn and pnp transistors. Both are used equally in electronic circuits; one is not favored over the other. Base current causes collector current to flow in both. To avoid confusion, the rest

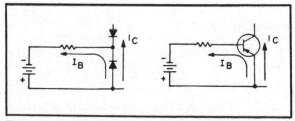

Fig. 1-82. Circuit for a pnp transistor.

59

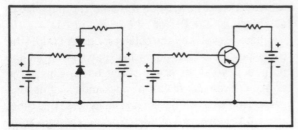

Fig. 1-83. Circuit for a pnp transistor.

of this discussion will be conducted using npns only as examples. And from now on, we will use the circuit symbols only.

Consider the action of the circuit in Fig. 1-84. It uses only one battery to provide the base and the collector current. The path of the base current only is shown in the diagram.

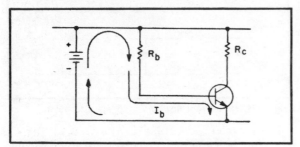

Fig. 1-84. Transistor circuit with one battery.

Questions

1. Name the components through which the base current flows.
2. Into which terminal of the transistor does the base current flow?
3. Out of which transistor terminal does the base current flow?
4. Through which terminals of the transistor does no base current flow?

Answers

1. the battery, the resistor Rb, and the transistor
2. base
3. emitter
4. collector

Can you remember the outstanding physical characteristic of the transistor? When base current flows in the preceding circuit, what other current will flow, and which components will it flow through?

Collector current will flow. It will flow through the resistor Rc and the transistor.

The path of the collector current is shown in Fig. 1-85.

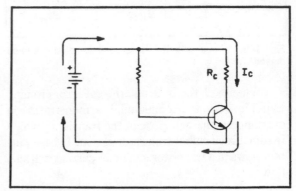

Fig. 1-85. The path of the collector current.

Questions

5. List the components through which the collector current flows.
6. What causes the collector current to flow?

Answers

5. the resistor Rc, the transistor, and the battery
6. base current (Collector current cannot ever flow if base current is not flowing first.)

It is a peculiar property of the transistor that the ratio of collector current to base current is constant. The collector current is always much larger than the base current. The constant ratio of the two currents is called the current gain of the transistor and it is a number much larger than 1.

Current gain is given the symbol β, called beta. Typical value's β range from 10 to 300. 100 is a good typical value from many transistors, and we will use this number for convenience in our calculations.

The mathematical formula for current gain is as follows.

$$\beta = \frac{Ic}{Ib}$$

where:

Ib = base current   Ic = collector current

From this you can see that if no base current flows, no collector current will flow. And if more base current flows more collector current will flow. This is what is meant when we say the "base current controls the collector current."

Current gain is a physical property of the transistor. Its value can be taken from the manufacturer's published data sheets or it can be determined experimentally by the user.

In general, β is a different number from one transistor type to the next, but it remains constant for a given transistor. Transistors of the same type have β values within a narrow range of each other.

One of the most often performed calculations in transistor work is determining the values of either collector or base current, when β and the other current are known.

For example, suppose a transistor has 500 mA of collector current flowing and it is known to have a β value of 100. Find the base current. To do this, use the formula as shown below.

$$\beta = \frac{Ic}{Ib}$$

$$\beta = \frac{Ic}{Ib} = \frac{500}{100} = 5 \text{ mA}$$

The Transistor Experiment

The object of the following experiment is to find β of a particular transistor by measuring several values of base current with their corresponding values of collector current. These values of collector current will be divided by the values of the base current to obtain β. The value of β will be almost the same for all the measured values of current. This will show that β is a constant for a transistor.

As long as the circuit is set up, measure the collector voltage for each current value. This will demonstrate experimentally some points to be made in future frames. Observe how the collector

voltage Vc drops toward 0 V as the currents are increased.

If you do not have the facilities for setting up the circuit and measuring the values, just read through the experiment to find out how it would be done. If you do have the facilities, you will need the following equipment and supplies.

1 9-V transistor radio battery (or a lab power supply)
1 current meter, maximum reading 100 μA
1 current meter (maximum reading 10 mA)
1 voltmeter, maximum reading 10 V
1 resistor substitution box, or a 1 MΩ potentiometer, or assorted resistors with values in the table
1 1-kΩ resistor
1 transistor, preferably npn

Almost any small commercially available transistor will do for this experiment. The measurements given in this book were obtained using a 2N3643. If only a pnp is available, then simply reverse the battery voltage and proceed as described.

Finally you will need several clip leads to join the components together. If you have adequate facilities, soldered joints can be used.

Set up the circuit shown in Fig. 1-86. Follow this procedure.

(1) Set Rb to its highest value.
(2) Measure and record Ib.
(3) Measure and record Ic.
(4) Measure and record Vc.
(5) Lower the value of Rb enough to produce a different reading of Ib.
(6) Measure and record Ib, Ic, and Vc.
(7) Lower Rb again and get a new Ib.

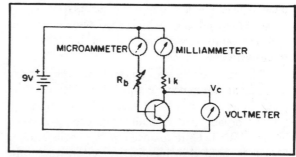

Fig. 1-86. Circuit for the transistor experiment.

Rb	Ib	Ic	Vc
1 MΩ	9 uA	0.9 mA	8.1 volts
680 kΩ	13	1.3	7.7
470	19	1.9	7.1
330	27.3	2.8	6.2
270	33.3	3.3	5.7
220	40	4.1	5.0
200	45	4.5	4.5
180	50	5	4.0
160	56	5.6	3.4
150	60	6	3
120	75	7.5	1.5
110	82	8.0	1.0
100	90	9	0.3

Table 1-2. Results of the Transistor Experiment.

(8) Measure and record all the values again.

(9) Continue this until Vc = 0 V.

(10) Further reductions in the value of R2 will increase Ib, but will not increase Ic or Vc.

Check the figures in your table to make sure you got a consistent pattern. Then compare your measurements with the ones given in Table 1-2.

The figures in Table 1-2 were obtained in an experiment conducted with considerable care. Precision resistors were used, and a commercial 2N3643 transistor was used. With ordinary 10% or 20% tolerance resistors and a transistor chosen at random, different figures will obviously be obtained. So if your figures are not as precise as those here, do not worry.

RIG-QWIK BREADBOARD SYSTEM

Rig-Kwik, is a modern version of the experimenter's "breadboard" which can be used for a wide variety of projects, ranging from the simplest which use only one power supply voltage to those advanced ones which need plus and minus voltages up to 15 volts as well as a third supply of plus five volts.

Though we still use the term "breadboard" to describe anything used to wire experimental or prototype circuits, it's been a long, long time since kitchen breadboards actually were used to develop circuits. While Grandpa used to drive nails into the board to hold down coils, capacitors and tube

sockets, today a complete circuit often takes up less space than the nail itself.

Over the years specialized electronic breadboard systems were developed to keep pace with new technologies. As the transistor replaced the tube the breadboard hardware was changed, eliminating the special clamps needed for heavy wire and substituting miniature multi-wire locking terminals that could handle the extra fine wire of solid state devices. Finally, we now have the integrated circuit (IC), and even solid-state electronic breadboards are too large—the hardware just doesn't make for easy breadboarding with subminiature components.

Now that solid-state component terminals are mostly standardized on 0.1-in. spacing, it has been possible to come up with a "breadboard" that accommodates virtually all the small signal solid state devices of the types used by hobbyists. A typical example is the QT socket strip from Continental Specialty Corp. These American-made QT sockets are available in many different configurations, but basically they all allow any component or wire lead to be plugged into a "board" and instantly get four multiple terminals for additional connections. Use a small U-shaped jumper and you have eight connections—and you can add jumpers until you get as many terminals as needed. The QT sockets snap together so you can easily construct a breadboard of any size of configuration needed, and if you look carefully at those professional-type developmental kits costing many hundreds of dollars you'll find many of them use the very same QT breadboard socket strips.

Along with the standardization of solid-state component lead spacing there are "standard" hobbyist voltages in the sense that many, though not all, projects use 5, 15, ±15 (bipolar) or 24-30 volts as the required dc power. By combining such a power supply with a matrix of Continental Specialty QT sockets we have come up with a prototype breadboard unit for well under $50 that compares favorably with larger laboratory breadboard kits that are priced well into the hundreds of dollars.

Just such a unit is shown here. Costing less than $40 (the final price depends mostly on how many and which QT sockets are used), Rig-Kwik provides regulated power supplies of 5.0 volts at 1.5 amperes, and ±15 volts at 150 mA. QT sockets have been used in Rig-Kwik to provide two component boards for transistors, diodes and ICs, two power distribution rails (one on each side) and three power distribution pads for the power supplies.

QT Test Socket Strips

These sockets let you breadboard any circuit, as fast as you can stick short pieces of #22 solid wire into the holes in the sockets. Each temporary terminal consists of five connected solderless tie points. The individual points are spaced so that standard DIP-packaged ICs, transistors, Op Amps,

all resistors (under 1-watt size), capacitors, and other small components can be directly plugged in and then interconnected. When the circuit has been tested, improved and finalized, the components are simply pulled out and the breadboard is ready to go again with another experimental circuit.

Figure 1-87 shows how the QT socket strips are hooked up internally. There are ten different kinds of QT sockets (strips), ranging from $3.50 to $12.50 each, and carrying from 14 to 108 5-point terminals (holes) each.

Our Rig-Kwik uses two each of the following QT strips: QT-35S (70 terminals × 5); GT-35B (two bus strips each, for GND or power voltages); and QT-7S (voltage bus pads). This configuration would cost you $27.00 for the breadboard strips, and it can accommodate about six or seven IC packages plus lots of associated circuitry. You could save $8.50 by getting just one QT-35 now, and leave room to add more later when your breadboard work gets more complicated. The choice of sockets is an entirely individual matter. Just be sure you use a chassis box large enough to accommodate at least one more QT socket (or more) than you think you might need at first.

The chassis shown is a small deluxe Rig-Kwik so most of its available top surface space is taken up by the two QT sockets. But you can use only one, or as many more, QT sockets as you think you may need.

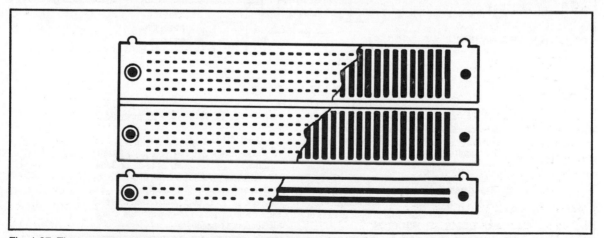

Fig. 1-87. These cutaway views of Continental Specialties QT sockets show (at right) how metal strips under the connecting holes hook rows together.

Fuse blocks are provided so both of the power supplies, which are not themselves internally short-circuit protected (to keep the price down), as well as the experimental circuit of the moment can be protected. More on the fuse setup later.

Construction

Our Rig-Kwik was assembled inside and on top of the two parts of an aluminum box whose dimensions are 7-in. W × 5-in. D × 3-in. H. The power supply is inside, and the QT sockets and fuse holders mount on top of the cabinet. See Fig. 1-88.

While the QT sockets aren't inexpensive, they are a permanent investment because they will be used many times. Figure out what you think you'll need, and add, say, one extra QT socket for more complicated projects later. Before you start construction you should get the catalog of these sockets from Continental Specialties by circling number 75 on the Reader Service Coupon. If you prefer getting the catalog even faster you can write direct to Continental Specialties Corp., 44 Kendall St., New Haven, CT 06509. They sell direct so you can select those sockets you want and order from Continental if they aren't stocked locally.

D.C. Power

The power supply is available in kit form from Bullet Electronics for $12.95. The kit includes the power transformer and the printed circuit board which mounts the entire power supply (except the transformer). This is a good deal because it saves you money (the transformer alone would cost five or so dollars) as well as the time and trouble of getting the parts together and etching the circuit board. Those who have a good junk box of spare parts can of course put it together for even less than the cost from Bullet Electronics. The Bullet kit has all the parts needed to build the regulated power supply which makes available (with one per cent load regulation) (a) a +5-Vdc supply at up to 1.5 amps, (b) a +15-Vdc supply at up to 150 mA, and (c) a negative −15 Vdc supply, also up to 150 mA. The two 15-volt supplies can be hooked together

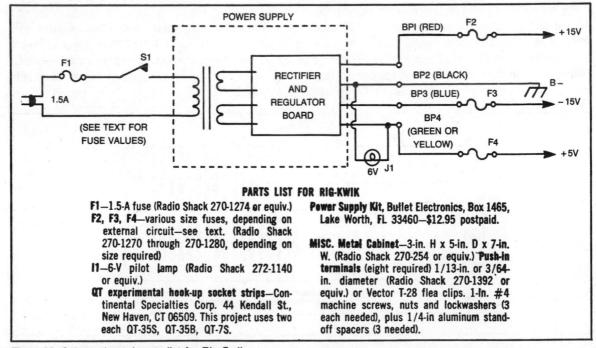

POWER SUPPLY

PARTS LIST FOR RIG-KWIK

F1—1.5-A fuse (Radio Shack 270-1274 or equiv.)
F2, F3, F4—various size fuses, depending on external circuit—see text. (Radio Shack 270-1270 through 270-1280, depending on size required)
I1—6-V pilot lamp (Radio Shack 272-1140 or equiv.)
QT experimental hook-up socket strips—Continental Specialties Corp. 44 Kendall St., New Haven, CT 06509. This project uses two each QT-35S, QT-35B, QT-7S.

Power Supply Kit, Bullet Electronics, Box 1465, Lake Worth, FL 33460—$12.95 postpaid.

MISC. Metal Cabinet—3-in. H x 5-in. D x 7-in. W. (Radio Shack 270-254 or equiv.) **Push-in terminals** (eight required) 1/13-in. or 3/64-in. diameter (Radio Shack 270-1392 or equiv.) or Vector T-28 flea clips. 1-in. #4 machine screws, nuts and lockwashers (3 each needed), plus 1/4-in aluminum stand-off spacers (3 needed).

Fig. 1-88. Schematic and parts list for Rig-Qwik.

to provide one 30-volt supply if desired. Finally, the two 15-volt supplies are so designed that they track each other. That is, if anything should happen to cause one or the other 15-Vdc source to go slightly high or low, the other supply will follow it, in the opposite direction to minimize the effect on the circuit they are powering.

To keep the cost down, these regulated supplies are not internally protected against short circuits. That's why the fuse sockets shown are provided. This is a better way of protecting the supplies, because the fuse sizes can be chosen for each particular project to protect the parts in the project, and they will also at the same time protect the supplies.

The printed circuit board that comes with the power supply kit has a few component lead holes which need slight enlarging. Don't try to force a lead into a hole as you might wind up breaking the printed circuit board. Instead, use a #56 drill bit to enlarge the hole.

It will be easier to install and connect the power supply printed circuit board if you hold off soldering the power transformer and output connection wires until later. The best bet is to provide tie points for the input and output connections. Use Radio Shack #270-1392 terminals and enlarge the connecting holes with a 3/64-inch drill bit. Don't try to jam the terminals into the holes—they just won't go without damage. Solder the terminals to the foil and then cut off any remaining terminal material on the foil side of the board. The printed circuit board has no mounting holes—Bullet Electronics lets you do it your way. Use a three point mounting. Drill holds for #6 screws (but use #4 screws to mount the board) at two corners away from the ground foil running around the perimeter of the board. Drill the third mounting hole on the opposite edge approximately midway between the two sides—anyplace you can get clear of the foil.

To avoid shorting the foil to the cabinet the board must be mounted on standoffs at each mounting hole. A 1/4-in. standoff spacer is sufficient. (Do not use a stack of metal washers unless you are certain no washer comes in contact with the foil on the board.)

Protection

In the unit shown we have provided three fuseblocks on top of the cabinet. See Fig. 1-89. These fuseblocks are made for the 1/4 × 1 1/4-inch fuse (3AG) type, and will accommodate both the 8AG and 3AG sizes. In this way you can use either size fuse without using two sets of fuseblocks. Note, however, that two different types of fuseholders have been used. When working with experimental circuits requiring two or more power supply voltages it is possible to get the wiring crossed when the power wires come from the same general location—and a crossed power wire can wipe out a handful of components. So a different fuseholder was used for the 5-volt power supply. If you can only get hold of one kind of fuseholder paint the 5-volt one a distinctive color that cannot be confused with the fuseblocks used for the two 15-volt supplies. The fuses must be fast-acting (8AG) because solid-state components will blow out long before a standard fuse (such as the 3AG) blows.

Though the power supply kit is not supplied with a fuse for the power transformer's primary (ac power-line side), the instructions included with the kit suggest the use of a fuse, and a fuseholder should be installed in the base of the cabinet, as shown.

To avoid confusing the power output connections the use of different-colored 5-way binding posts is suggested. The standard colors for a bipolar power supply are Black for negative (ground) and red for positive and blue or green for negative voltage. The 5-volt power output should be any other color (don't use red again). If you cannot locate binding posts in assorted colors paint them with Testor's model paints, which come in very small bottles for about 25 cents each. Model paints are available in hobby stores which stock model trains, planes, rockets, etc.

Using Rig-Kwik

The QT socket terminals can handle wire sizes #22 (solid) and #24. You can insert a #20 wire but it takes a strong push with long-nose pliers. The QT sockets provide a firm grip on the wire and can

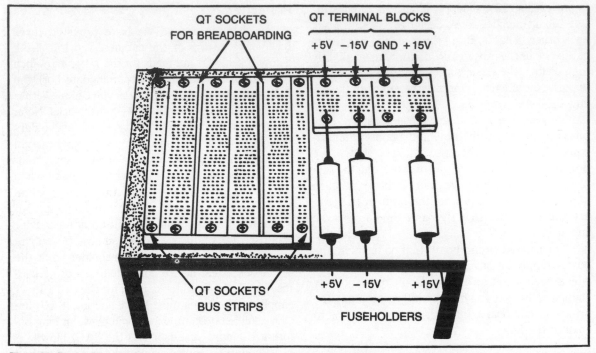

Fig. 1-89. Each of the three power supplies has its own fuseholder, permitting use of fuses of correct size to protect components for whatever project is being built on Rig-Kwik. The four small QT sockets at upper right let you run up to 27 leads from each to QT sockets at left, where breadboarding takes place.

be re-used indefinitely after the breadboard is cleared—this is not a one-shot project board. Most transistor, resistor, capacitor and connecting wires will fit the QT terminals. The wires on high power SCRs and transistors, 1 watt resistors, and high-voltage (250 V and higher) capacitors are just a shade too large for the QT terminals, and if you try to force them in you'll either break the component or damage the socket. If, for some reason, you must use oversize components solder a short piece of #22 wire to their leads so they can be easily connected to the sockets.

Choosing Fuses

Fuses should never be rated higher than the maximum rated current of the associated power supply. For example, if you are using an external 5-ampere/5-volt supply the fuse should be no larger than 5-amperes. If you are using the internal 1.5-ampere 5-volt supply the fuse should be no larger than 1.5 amperes. But fusing for the supply's maximum rating protects only the power supply, not the circuit you're building. Such fusing in the presence of a wiring error could lead to an undamaged power supply—with crispy-fried experimental components! It is better to fuse so that the experimental circuit gets full protection, or as much protection as you can give it. For example, assume you are building a TTL project whose maximum current including the readout display is 150 mA. Using the next higher fuse value, in this instance 3/16 or 2/10 ampere, will protect both the project and the power supply. Thus, whenever you use the Rig-Kwik for breadboarding a project you can protect the project, as well as the power supply, by choosing a fuse just large enough for the project itself (each time). You now have a fast, convenient, and inexpensive laboratory breadboard. Enjoy!

CATHODE-RAY TUBES

The cathode-ray tube (which we'll refer to as

66

CRT from here on) is a large vacuum tube which has three main parts. They are, first *electron gun*, which produces a steady stream of electrons and aims them at the large, flat end of the tube, second, *deflecting* devices, which move the electron beam in accordance with the signal to be observed, and third, the chemical coating on the large flat end of the CRT, commonly called the *screen*.

The oscilloscope displays electrical signals on the screen to show what's going on in electrical or electronic circuits. The TV set shows pictures transmitted from the TV station. In both cases the CRT used in the 'scope or the TV set are almost exactly the same.

The main difference in the picture tube in TV sets and the CRT in scopes today is that the electron beam is moved back and forth in the TV set electromagnetically, by coils of copper wire placed around the neck of the tube, while the electron beam in a scope is moved about by the changing electrostatic voltages between small deflection plates inside the neck of the tube. In fact, the earliest TV picture tubes were electrostatic-deflection CRTs, and during the Korean War, when copper for the magnetic deflection coils was scarce, TV set makers stopped making electromagnetic-deflection picture tubes and went back to the earlier, electrostatically-deflected tubes!

The CRT in Oscilloscopes

The oscilloscope is really a not-very-exact measuring instrument for voltages and waveforms which also shows what the voltages or signals look like. Although it can be pretty exact in its measurement of signals, only the most expensive 'scopes are nearly as precise as even cheap meters, so their main purpose is usually to show what the signals look like.

The oscilloscope contains, in addition to the CRT, a power supply which generally provides 2,000-volts or more, and some control circuits which take the signal voltage(s) to be displayed, amplify and otherwise process them and feed them to the CRT for display. See Fig. 1-90.

'Scope CRTs have a screen usually made of phosphorescent (give off light when struck by elec-

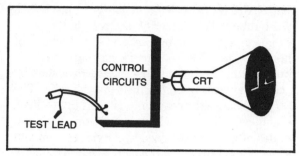

Fig. 1-90. Simplified oscilloscope.

trons) chemicals which create a green display. Some very expensive 'scopes use CRTs with blue, or even purple-emitting phosphor-coated screens. TV sets of course have screens with white light-emitting screens (in black and white sets).

The CRT in oscilloscopes uses electrostatic deflection, with the deflecting voltages applied to the vertical-deflecting plates and to the horizontal deflecting plates, as shown in Fig. 1-91.

The signal voltage size is indicated by the amplitude (height, up-and-down dimension) of the beam movement on the screen. The time period (duration) is shown by the distance the beam travels across the screen horizontally, from left to right.

By relating the time a signal takes to its amplitude (size) and its shape, we can get a very accurate idea of what's going on in most circuits at any desired point.

The CRT in TV Sets

The cathode-ray tube is the display device in the television set. The CRT operates by moving a

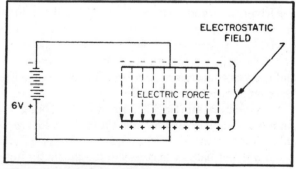

Fig. 1-91. Electrostatic fields.

controllable beam of electrons across the inside face of the tube. The number of electrons in the beam is determined by the blacks, grays, and whites of the scene the TV camera is viewing. White is produced by a large number of electrons striking a chemical coating on the inside of the tube. The electrons cause the coating to give off light. Black is achieved by stopping the electron flow, and shades of gray are obtained by varying the amount of electrons between the amounts required for black and white.

The picture is "painted" on the screen by the narrow electron beam moving back and forth across the tube many times a second. This movement is due to varying magnetic fields produced by a set of horizontal and vertical deflection coils around the CRT's neck.

The principle of putting a picture of a waveform on the screen of an oscilloscope is similar. The movement of the electron beam in the 'scope is controlled electrostatically so that the beam traces out the pattern of the waveform being measured. As in the TV tube, the electron beam illuminates a coating on the inside of the tube.

Electrostatic Fields

To understand how the CRT operates, you must know that an electrostatic field is a space in which electric forces act.

An electrostatic field can be developed between two charged plates. If one plate is negative with respect to the other, the direction of the electric force can be determined.

In Fig. 1-91, lines of electric force take a direction from negative to positive. This means a negatively-charged body entering the field would be moved downward (from negative to positive). A positively-charged body, however, would be moved upward (positive to negative). (Like charges repel, and unlikes charges attract). How do you think an electrostatic field is formed?

An electrostatic field is formed with a voltage source and a pair of metallic plates to hold the charges.

If a 6-volt battery is connected to the plates in the manner shown, the battery will draw electrons from the bottom plate and deposit them on the top plate until the difference in potential between the plates equals the battery voltage. The potential of the plate having an excess of electrons will be negative. The other plate, being deficient in electrons, will be positive.

Electrostatic Forces
Between Circular and Tubular Plates

In Fig. 1-92, an electrostatic field between two plates having center holes is shown. Observe the curvature of the force lines under the holes. Since its path is parallel to the force lines, electron B will pass straight through the axis (center line) of the holes. Electron A starts in the same direction as electron B. When electron A enters the field, it turns in the direction of the force lines. Just before it leaves the field, it is turned even further in the direction of the curvature of the force lines.

Suppose a small and a large cylinder, both charged with a positive potential, are placed so the electrons must pass through them. Also suppose the larger cylinder has a more positive charge. The distribution of the lines of force would look like Fig. 1-93.

An electron in the space at the left of the small cylinder would be attracted toward the cylinder by the positive charge. If the electron was traveling along the axis of the cylinder, it would pass through without crossing a line of force. As it approached the larger, more positively charged cylinder, the ve-

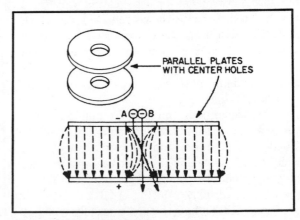

Fig. 1-92. Electrostatic lens I.

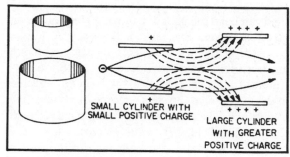

Fig. 1-93. Electrostatic lens II.

locity of the electron would increase.

An electron entering the small cylinder at an angle will cut the lines of force and be turned in their direction as shown by the top and bottom electron paths.

Electrostatic Focus

As it approaches the larger cylinder, the electron will be accelerated by the higher positive potential. Because of the higher electron velocity, the force lines in the larger cylinder will have a smaller turning effect on the electron. If the difference of potential between the cylinders is adjusted properly, the electrons will unite at a given distance after passing through the second cylinder. The action of the electrons as they pass through the influence of the two cylinders provides a convenient method of focusing the beam.

Electron Gun

Cathode-ray tubes used in oscilloscopes consist of an electron gun, a deflection system, and a fluorescent screen. See Fig. 1-94. All elements are

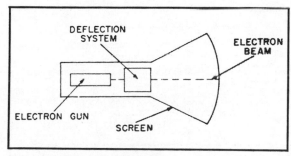

Fig. 1-94. Basic cathode-ray tube.

enclosed in an evacuated container, usually glass. The electron gun generates electrons and focuses them into a narrow beam. The deflection system moves the beam across the screen in the manner desired. The screen is coated with a material that glows when struck by the electrons.

An electron gun has a cathode to generate electrons, a grid to control electron flow, and a positive element to accelerate electron movement. The control grid is cylindrical in shape and has a small opening in a baffle at one end. The positive element consists of two cylinders, called anodes. They also contain baffles (or plates) having small holes in their centers. The main purpose of the first anode is to focus the electrons into a narrow beam on the screen. The second anode speeds up the electrons as they pass. See Fig. 1-95.

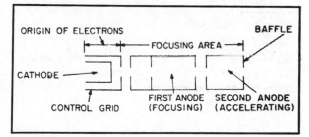

Fig. 1-95. Electron gun.

Cathode and Grid

The cathode is indirectly heated and emits a cloud of electrons. The control grid is a hollow metal tube placed over the cathode. A small opening is located in the center of a baffle at the end opposite the cathode. The grid is maintained at a negative potential with respect to the cathode.

A high positive potential on the anodes pulls electrons through the hole in the grid. Since the grid is near the cathode, it can control the number of electrons that are emitted. As in an ordinary vacuum tube, the negative voltage of the grid can be changed to vary electron flow or stop it completely. The brightness of the image on the fluorescent screen is determined by the number of electrons striking the screen. Intensity (brightness) can, therefore, be controlled by the voltage on the control grid.

Focus Control

Focusing is accomplished by controlling the electrostatic fields that exist between the grid and first anode and between the first and second anodes. Study the diagram. See if you can determine the paths of electrons through the gun.

Electrostatic Lenses

Figure 1-96 shows electrons moving through the gun. The electrostatic field areas are often referred to as lenses. The first electrostatic lens causes the electrons to cross at a focal point within the field. The second lens bends the spreading streams and returns them to a new focal point.

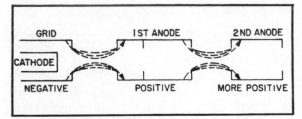

Fig. 1-96. Electron gun "lenses."

The cathode is at a fixed positive voltage with respect to ground. The grid is at a variable negative voltage with respect to the cathode. A fixed positive voltage of several thousand volts is connected to the second (accelerating) anode. The potential of the first (focusing) anode is less positive than the potential of the second anode. It can be varied to place the focal point of the electron beam on the screen of the tube. Control-grid potential is established at the proper level to allow the correct number of electrons through the gun for the desired intensity.

Electron-Beam Deflection System

The electron beam is developed, focused, and pulled toward the screen by the electron gun. It appears on the screen of the CRT as a small, bright dot. If the beam were left in one position, the electrons would soon burn away the illuminating coating in that one area. To be of any use, the beam must move. As you have learned, an electrostatic field can bend the path of a moving electron, or an electron stream. See Figs. 1-97 through 1-99.

Assume the beam of electrons passes through an electrostatic field between two plates. Since electrons are negatively charged, they will be deflected in the direction of the electric force (from negative to positive). The electrons will follow a curved path through the field. When the electrons leave the field, they will take a straight path to the screen at the angle at which they left the field. Although the beam is still wide (the focal point is at the screen), all the electrons will be traveling toward the same spot. This is assuming, of course, that the proper voltages are existing on the anodes which produce the electrostatic field. Changing the voltages changes the focal point of the beam.

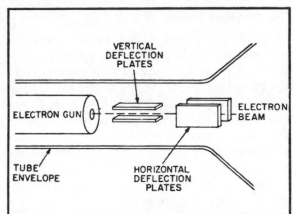

Fig. 1-97. Electron gun and beam formation.

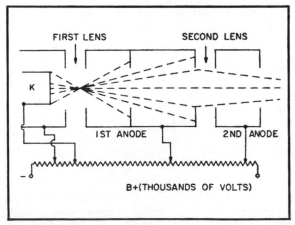

Fig. 1-98. Electron gun fields.

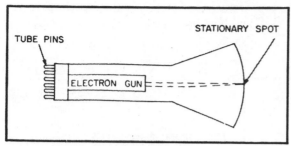

Fig. 1-99. CRT without deflection.

Vertical and Horizontal Plates

If two sets of deflection plates are placed at right angles to each other inside a CRT, the electron beam can be controlled in any direction. By varying the voltage between the two vertical-deflection plates, the spot on the face of the tube can be made to move up and down. The distance will be proportional to the change in voltage between the plates. Changing the voltage difference between the horizontal-deflection plates will cause the beam to move a given distance from one side to the other. There are directions other than up-down and left-right. The beam must be deflected in all directions.

See Fig. 1-100. You can see that the beam may be moved to any position on the screen simply by moving it both vertically and horizontally.

In the left diagram, position A of the beam is in the center. It can be moved to position B by going up two units and then right two units. Movement of the beam is the result of the simultaneous action of both sets of deflection plates. The electrostatic field between the vertical plates moves the electrons up an amount proportional to two units at the screen. As the beam passes between the horizontal plates, it is moved to the right an amount proportional to two units.

Voltage Control of Horizontal Plates

Assume that the resistance of the potentiometer in Fig. 1-101 is spread evenly along its length. When the arm of the potentiometer is at the middle position, there is the same potential on each plate. Since there is zero potential between the plates, an electrostatic field is not produced. The

beam will be at zero on the screen. If the arm is moved downward at a uniform rate, the right plate will become more positive than the left. The electron beam will move from 0 through 1, 2, 3, and 4 in equal time intervals. If the potentiometer arm moves at the same rate in the other direction, the right plate will decrease in positive potential. The beam returns to the zero position when the potential difference between the plates again becomes zero. Moving the arm toward the other end of the resistance will cause the left plate to become more positive than the right. The direction of the electric force reverses, and the beam moves from 0 through 4. If the movement of the potentiometer arm is at a linear (uniform) rate, the beam will move at a steady rate.

Amplitude Versus Time

Do you recall the statement made earlier that waveforms could be described in terms of amplitude and time? You have just seen how the movement of the beam depends on both potential (amplitude) and time.

From zero time to 1-second, the waveform in the diagram is at zero volts. In the CRT the vertical plates remain at the same potential difference while the potential difference between the horizontal plates increases 1 unit in the direction necessary to move the beam toward the right. When time is equal to 1-second, the waveform rises to +2-volts. The potential difference between the vertical plates increases enough to move the electron beam 2 units in the positive direction. From 1 to 4-seconds, the waveform remains at +2-volts and then decreases to −2-volts. As the horizontal-plate potential difference increases by 3 units, the vertical potential remains the same (+2 units) and then drops sharply 4 units. For the next 3-seconds, the waveform remains at −2-volts. In the CRT, the potential difference between the vertical plates remains unchanged as the horizontal potential increases uniformly.

What You Have Learned

An electron gun contains a cathode (to emit

electrons), a control grid (to control the intensity of the trace on the screen), a first anode (to develop the electric lenses that focus the beam on the screen), and a second anode (to accelerate the elec-trons toward the screen). Deflection plates in vertical and horizontal pairs are used to position the beam on the screen.

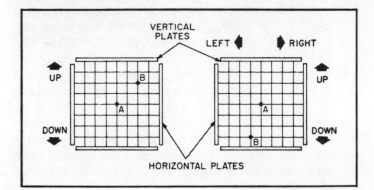

Fig. 1-100. Deflection of CRT beam.

Fig. 1-101. Horizontal plates—top view.

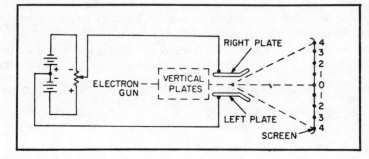

Chapter 2

Audio Electronics

INDUCTANCE AND CAPACITANCE

The lowly resistor is the solid citizen of electronics. It can be relied upon to behave with the same, predictable performance, whether confronted with ac or dc. Unruffled by excursions into the higher frequencies, it continues to live by the guiding rule—Ohm's law—and declares that, no matter what, the current (I) it permits to flow shall depend solely on the applied voltage (E) divided by its own resistance (R).

However, the resistor's component cousins—the inductor and the capacitor—are by no means so stolid in the face of changing frequencies. The inductor, for example, grouchily shuts off more and more of the current flow as the applied frequency gets higher and higher, while the capacitor reacts to higher frequencies in just the opposite manner—it happily allows more and more current to flow as the frequency rises.

Fortunately, the reactionary behavior of these components is just as predictable as is the single-mindedness of their resistive cousin. If we study the strange conduct of these apparently erratic citizens, we not only discover the rules which govern their odd behavior, but also perceive that ultimately, they too, are faithful to Ohm's law—in their fashion—just as are all electronic components and circuits.

Reactionaries in the Lab

To begin our study, let's set up the lab experiment shown in Fig. 2-1.

Here, we have an audio oscillator set to produce an output of 60 Hz, and a power amplifier to amplify that signal to the 100-volt level. The power amplifier drives a load consisting of a large (25-watt) 390-ohm resistor connected in series with an ordinary 1 1/2-volt (0.25-amp) flashlight bulb. An ac meter reads the output voltage from the power amplifier.

Turning on the equipment, we set the audio oscillator to 60 Hz, and gradually turn up the amplifier gain till 100 volts appears at the output. (Note: The ordinary hi-fi-amplifier won't do this—you will

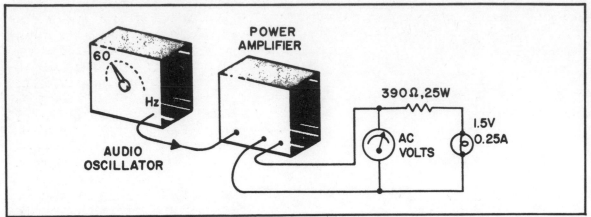

Fig. 2-1. Practical laboratory setup to demonstrate Ohm's law. Power amplifier must have a 70-volt output or a 500-ohm output transformer tap.

need a public address amplifier with a high-voltage (70-volt, or 500-ohm) auxiliary output if you actually want to carry out this experiment.) At this point, the bulb will light to its normal brightness, indicating that the 100 volts is pushing about 0.25 ampere through the combined resistor/light-bulb circuit. Using Ohm's law, we can easily check this:

$$I = E/R$$
$$= 100 \text{ volts}/(390 \text{ ohms} + 6 \text{ ohms})$$
$$= 0.252 \text{ amperes}$$

Note that the light bulb's resistance, R, is

$$R = E/I$$
$$= 1 \ 1/2 \text{ volts}/1/4 \text{ ampere}$$
$$= 6 \text{ ohms}$$

Please also note that it's the 390-ohm resistor, not the bulb, which is the chief authority in establishing the current. The lamp current will change very little, whether the bulb is 6 ohms, 12 ohms, or zero ohms.

Next, let us vary the frequency of the audio oscillator; first, down to 30 Hz, and then, up to 120 Hz. We notice that the bulb stays at the same brightness, indicating that the 390-ohm resistor is behaving in its normal, stolid fashion—that is, it is steadfastly ignoring frequency changes, and permitting its current flow to be determined solely by Ohm's law. Even if the frequency were zero (which

is another way of saying dc), the bulb's brightness would remain the same, if we applied 100 volts to it.

Enter the First Reactionary

Now, let's go to our parts supply bin, pick up a 1-henry inductor, and make a few preliminary measurements on it. Using an inductance bridge, we discover that its real value is 1.05 henry. We next connect it to an ordinary ohmmeter as shown in Fig. 2-2, which informs us that the inductor has a resistance of 45 ohms.

Now, let us replace the 390-ohm resistor of Fig.

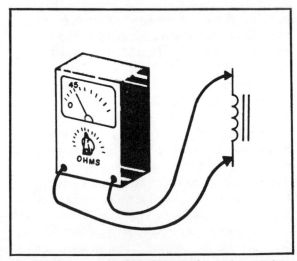

Fig. 2-2. Measuring the dc resistance of a one-henry inductor (choke oil) shows it has 45 ohms of resistance.

74

1 with this 1-henry inductor as shown in Fig. 2-3, and predict what will happen when we turn on the equipment. Since the ohmmeter said "45 ohms" we can predict that the current will be

$$I = E/R$$
$$= 100 \text{ volts}/45 \text{ ohms} + 6 \text{ ohms}$$
$$= 1.96 \text{ amperes!}$$

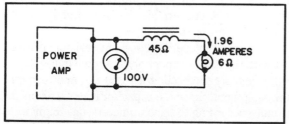

Fig. 2-3. Substituting the one-henry inductor in place of the 390-ohm resistor of Fig. 2-1 lowers the opposition of the circuit to ac, hence more current flows.

With this large current—nearly 8 times normal—the light bulb should burn out almost instantly! However, when we apply 100 volts of 60 Hz to the inductor-plus-bulb, we are surprised to see that the bulb lights to normal brightness! This means that the inductor is behaving like a 390-ohm resistor, and is establishing a 1/4-ampere flow of current—not the nearly-2 amperes calculated from the above ohmmeter measurement.

To compound the mystery, let us now vary the frequency of the oscillator: first, up to 120 Hz—and the bulb gets dimmer!—and then gingerly, down, just a little, to 50 Hz—and the bulb gets uncomfortably brighter. Here, in the lab, is the actual behavior forecast by theory—the inductor grouchily shuts down the current flow for high frequencies, causing the bulb to go dim at 120 Hz, but it is willing to let low frequencies through, thus allowing the bulb to get brighter for 50-Hz input.

A Little Compassion for the Reactionary

To understand this "reactionary" behavior, we must understand how an inductor "feels" about an alternating current. An inductor is, after all, an electromagnet. If a steady direct current flows through it, it fills the space in its vicinity with a magnetic field. If we attempt to cut down the inductor's current, it reacts, quite understandably, by collapsing its magnetic field. But this collapsing field moves across the inductor winding in just the same way that a dynamo or generator field moves through the generator windings to make an output voltage. The inductor, then, reacts to any attempt to change its current by acting as its own generator, generating a new voltage of the correct polarity to try to keep its own current from changing. So, in its own way, the inductor is a solid, but conservative citizen—a citizen who tries to maintain the status quo.

Furthermore, the faster we try to change its current, the harder the inductor works to keep the current from changing. Therefore, the inductor sees a high frequency as an attempt at rapid changes— a threat to the status quo—so it works very hard to generate an opposing voltage (a 'counter-EMF' or 'counter-electro-motive-force') to keep its current from changing. This internally-generated voltage opposes the applied voltage more and more as the frequency rises; hence the actual current which flows drops lower and lower as the frequency rises. This means that the apparent resistance of the inductor rises with frequency. But this apparent resistance is not called resistance—since it is the inductor's reaction to the frequency applied to it, it is called inductive reactance.

A Resistance by Any Other Name

But whether you call it "apparent resistance" or "inductive reactance", it is still measured in ohms, and can be used as a part of the familiar Ohm's law formula. Where a simple resistive circuit answers to the expression

$$I = E/R$$

A similar circuit with resistor replaced by an inductor (coil) is described by the formula:

$$I = E/X,$$

where X is the symbol for reactance. But, since the amount of reactance (X) changes according to frequency, we must have a way to calculate its value at the frequency we are using. The following simple formula does that for us:

Inductive Reactance = $2 \times \pi \times$ frequency $\times$ inductance or, in the familiar algebraic shorthand,

$$X_L = 2\pi fL$$

where L is the inductance in henrys, and the subscript L following the X indicates we are talking about inductive reactance. Therefore, the current in an inductive circuit is:

$$I = E/X_L,$$
$$= E/2\pi fL$$

For Example. Let's take the 1.05-henry inductor and calculate its reactance at 60 Hz:

$$X = 2\pi fL,$$
$$= 2 \times \pi \times 60 \times 1.05$$
$$= 395.8 \text{ ohms.}$$

which, as you can see, is very close to the 390 ohms of the resistive circuit of Fig. 2-1. This explains why the bulb lit to about the same brightness for the inductor as for the resistor.

When we cranked the audio oscillator up to 120 Hz, the inductive reactance became

$$X_L = 2\pi fL,$$
$$= 2 \times \pi \times 120 \times 1.05$$
$$= 791.7 \text{ ohms.}$$

The new current becomes, ignoring, for the moment, the 6-ohm bulb:

$$I = E/X$$
$$= 100 \text{ volts}/791.7 \text{ ohms,}$$
$$= 0.125 \text{ ampere.}$$

which is about half the rated current of the bulb. Hence, it would be dim at this frequency. You can easily calculate that at 50 Hz, the X becomes 329.9 ohms and the current rises to the excessive value of .303 amperes; any further lowering of frequency could burn out the bulb!

Reactionary No. 2: The Capacitor

Returning to the parts-supply bin, we now take a large, oil-filled (—Don't try this with an electrolytic!) capacitor, and, measuring it on a capacitance bridge, find that its true value is 6.8 mfd. An ohmmeter placed across the capacitor's terminals registers an upward 'kick' of the needle as the ohmmeter's internal battery charges the capacitor, but the ohmmeter then settles down to indicate that, as far as it is concerned, the capacitor is—as it should be—an open circuit.

We now replace the 390-ohm resistor of Fig. 2-1 with the 6.8 μF capacitor, as shown in Fig. 2-4.

Again set the oscillator to 60 Hz, and turn on the equipment. Since the capacitor is really an open circuit—according to the ohmmeter—one might expect no current flow at all. We are surprised, then, when the light bulb blithely ignores our oil-filled open circuit, and proceeds to glow as serenely and confidently as it did for the inductor and resistor! When we drop the frequency to 30 Hz, the bulb goes dim—when we gingerly raise the frequency to 70 Hz, the bulb gets brighter. This is just the opposite of the inductive effect, where the bulb got dimmer for higher frequencies.

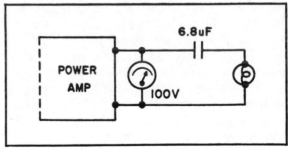

Fig. 2-4. A 6.8 uF capacitor substituted in the test circuit for the inductor. If the capacitor acted as an open (as it would for dc) no current would flow.

Capacitive Reactance

We are obviously dealing with another type of reactance, this time arising from the presence of the capacitor in the circuit, and known as capacitive reactance. Its behavior in the face of changing frequency is exactly the opposite of that shown by inductive reactance. A capacitor's apparent resistance goes down as frequency goes up, and goes up as frequency goes down. This inverse relationship is seen in the expression for capacitive reactance, which is

$$X_C = \frac{1}{2\pi fC}$$

where X is capacitive reactance, and C is the capacity in farads, (not microfarads.)

Mathematically speaking, by placing f (frequency) in the denominator (bottom) of the fraction, we are saying that as f gets larger, the answer (X) gets smaller, which is exactly what we observed in the lab experiment above.

Just as in the inductive case, we can plug X right into the Ohm's law formula and have a way to calculate current or voltage for a capacitive circuit:

$$I = \frac{E}{X}$$

More Examples. As examples of how the above formulas can be used, let's calculate reactances and currents of our 6.8-μF capacitor at various frequencies at 60 Hz,

$$X_C = \frac{1}{2\pi fC}$$

$$= \frac{1}{2 \times \pi \times 60 \text{ Hz} \times 6.8\mu F}$$

$$= 390.1 \text{ ohms.}$$

(Note that 6.8 microfarads must be expressed as 6.8×10^{-6} farads, since the formula is always written for C in farads. Alternately, you could write 6.8 microfarads as 0.000 006 8 farads, but that's a little more awkward to handle.)

At 30 Hz, a lower frequency, the capacitive reactance increases:

$$X_C = \frac{1}{2 \times \pi \times 30 \text{ Hz} (6.8 \times 10^{-6}) \text{ farads,}}$$

$$= 780.2 \text{ ohms,}$$

and at a higher frequency, say 70 Hz, the capacitive reactance becomes less:

$$X_C = \frac{1}{2 \times \pi \times 70 \text{ Hz} (6.8 \times 10^{-6}) \text{ farads,}}$$

$$= 334.4 \text{ ohms.}$$

The current, in any case, can be found by Ohm's law. At 70 Hz, the current is

$$\begin{aligned} I &= E/X, \\ &= 100 \text{ volts}/334.4 \text{ ohms,} \\ &= 0.299 \text{ ampere,} \end{aligned}$$

while at 30 Hz the current is:

$$\begin{aligned} E/X &= 100 \text{ volts}/780.2 \text{ ohms,} \\ &= 0.128 \text{ ampere.} \end{aligned}$$

So, in their way, both inductors and capacitors are obedient to Ohm's law. Their reactances—X_L and X_C, respectively—can replace the R in the familiar Ohm's law expression, $I = E/R$, enabling us to calculate current flow for ac circuits which include inductors or capacitors.

Adding Apples and Oranges

But, what of circuits which combine an inductor and a resistor? Or an inductor and a capacitor? Can we simply add the two 'ohms' together? Do resistance and reactance add like apples and apples?

Unfortunately, this is not the case. Consider, for example, the circuit of Fig. 2-5. Here, our 1.05-Henry inductor and a 150-ohm resistor are connected in series across the 100-volt, 60-Hz source. What is the current flow?

Obviously, we need an Ohm's-law-like expression—something like I = E divided by the apparent "resistance" of R and L, combined.

We know from our previous work that a 1.05-henry inductor has an X inductive reactance of about 396 ohms. We wish that we could simply add the 396 ohms of reactance to the 150 ohms of resistance to get 546 ohms—but reactance and resistance simply don't add that way. Instead, they

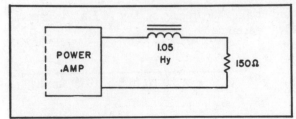

Fig. 2-5. Test circuit load is now combination of inductor (1.05 henry) and resistor (150 ohms). As the text explains, their combined reactance is computed by adding them at right angles!

add at right angles! And how, you ask, does one add at right angles?

A Journey at Right Angles. To understand how resistance and reactance can add at right angles, consider another type of problem: If I travel 150 miles due east, and then 396 miles north, how far am I from my starting point? See Fig. 2-6.

You obviously cannot get the answer to this problem by adding 396 to 150, because you're certainly not 546 miles from home. But notice that the figure is a right triangle—a shape which that old Greek, Pythagoras, solved long ago. He said that if you square 150, and square 396, add the squares, and then take the square root, you will get the length of the longest side:

$$\sqrt{(150 \times 150) + (396 \times 396)},$$
$$\sqrt{179,316, 432.3 \text{ miles}.}$$

This, then, is a way of adding two quantities that act at right angles to each other. Since inductive reactance is a kind of "north-bound resistance", operating at right angles to the "east-bound resistance" of an ordinary resistor, we combine the two by adding at right angles, just as the two right-angle distances were added in the above mileage problem. The effective resistance of the 396-ohm reactance and the 150-ohm resistor is therefore:

$$\sqrt{(150 \times 150) + (396 \times 396),}$$
$$= 432.4 \text{ ohms}.$$

What do we call this combination? It is obviously neither resistance nor reactance, but a combination

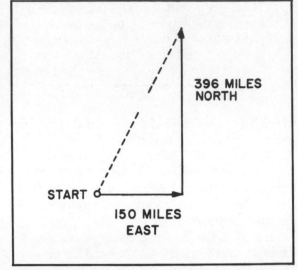

Fig. 2-6. Adding traveling distances in different directions yields resultant which is the diagonal (the shortest distance between the two points), also a right triangle. Back to the Pythagorean theorem!

of both. Since it represents a general way that a circuit can impede the flow of electrons, it is called impedance, and is represented by the symbol Z. The general formula for impedance is, therefore:

$$Z = \sqrt{R^2 + X^2}$$

Another Candidate for Ohm's Law

Impedance is measured in ohms; just as are reactance and resistance. If we know the impedance and voltage in a circuit, we can find the current by plugging Z into the familiar Ohm's Law expression:

$$I = E/Z,$$
$$= E/ \sqrt{R^2 + X^2}.$$

Using this expression we can calculate the current in the example of Fig. 2-5:

$$I = E/Z,$$
$$= 10 \text{ volts}/423.4 \text{ ohms},$$
$$= 0.326 \text{ ampere}.$$

78

Southbound Capacitors

The knowledge that inductive reactance adds at right angles to resistance leads immediately to the question, "What about capacitive reactance? Does it also act as a 'northbound' resistance?"

As you might expect, two circuit elements as different as inductance and capacitance could never agree on the 'direction' of their reactances. If inductive reactance is 'northbound', the capacitor obstinately declares that its reactance is 'southbound,' acting in direct opposition to the inductive direction, as shown in Figs. 2-7 and 2-8.

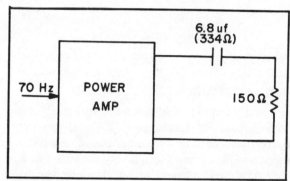

Fig. 2-7. The reactance of the capacitor at this frequency (70 Hz) is 334 ohms. This may be combined with the pure resistance, 150 ohms, by using the formula discussed in the text.

However, this makes no difference in the equation for impedance, which is still given by

$$Z = \sqrt{R^2 + X^2},$$

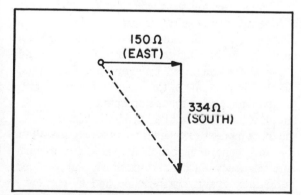

Fig. 2-8. This drawing shows how the two reactances are added, as also shown in Fig. 6 and described in the text.

where X is, in this case, X_C, capacitive reactance.

As an example, let's calculate the impedance of the circuit of Fig. 2-9.

$$Z = \sqrt{R^2 + X^2}$$
$$= \sqrt{(150)^2 + (200)^2}$$
$$= \sqrt{62,500} = 250 \text{ ohms}$$

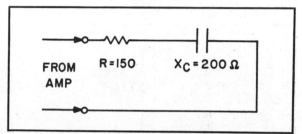

Fig. 2-9. Schematic showing reactance of capacitor. The two reactances add according to the formula, to yield a combined reactance (at the particular frequency used) of 250 ohms.

As a further calculation, let us determine the current which will flow if 50 volts is applied to the terminals at the left of Fig. 2-10:

$$I = E/Z,$$
$$= 50/250$$
$$= 0.2 \text{ ampere.}$$

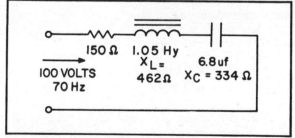

Fig. 2-10. Combining capacitive reactance and inductive reactance is also handled. Reactance of each at 70 Hz is computed, they are added together, and the difference is put into the formula with the pure resistance.

All Together, Now

The final question is this: If a circuit includes resistance, inductance and capacitance, all at once, what is its total impedance?

An example of such a series circuit is shown in Fig. 2-10.

Here, 100 volts at 70 Hz is applied across a series circuit of 150 ohms resistance, 1.05 henry inductance (X_L = 462 ohms), and 6.8 μF capacitance (X_C = 334 ohms).

As a first step in determining the total impedance, we can draw the 'directions' of the resistance and the two reactances, as shown in Fig. 2-11.

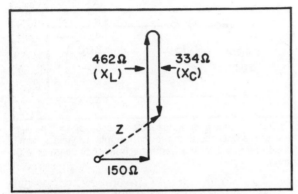

Fig. 2-11. The relative "directions" of capacitive and inductive reactances along with that of the pure resistance. Z (the diagonal) is the resultant of the 150-ohms resistance plus the difference between the two reactances.

The first thing that strikes us about this figure is that the effect of the 'northbound' (inductive) 462 ohms is partially cancelled by the 'southbound' (capacitive) 334 ohms. The net reactance of this circuit is therefore:

$$X = X_L - X_C,$$
$$= 462 \text{ ohms} - 334 \text{ ohms,}$$
$$= 128 \text{ ohms.}$$

This combining of X_L and X_C by simple subtraction reduces the problem to a simpler one, resembling a problem we've already solved. This is graphically shown in Fig. 2-12.

Applying the formula for impedance

$$Z = \sqrt{X^2 + R^2}$$
$$= \sqrt{(128)^2 + (150)^2},$$
$$= 197.2 \text{ ohms.}$$

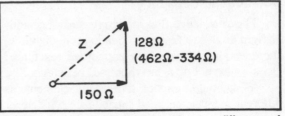

Fig. 2-12. Combining the reactances leaves a difference of 128 ohms and provides a directional diagram similar to that of Fig. 2-6. Such directional drawings are called "vector" diagrams.

The current flow is:

$$I = E/Z,$$
$$= 100 \text{ volts}/197.2 \text{ ohms,}$$
$$= 0.51 \text{ ampere.}$$

North vs. South

In the above problem, we saw that the 'northbound' inductive reactance (462 ohms) was very nearly cancelled by the 'southbound' capacitive reactance (334 ohms). It's pretty obvious that by changing some values, or by changing the frequency, we could make X_L exactly equal to X_C, and they would cancel each other completely, leaving the circuit with no net reactance whatsoever—just 150 ohms of simple resistance. This condition, where $X_L = X_C$ exactly, is called resonance, and that's an interesting story, too.

FREQUENCY

The increasing sophistication of the home experimenter has resulted in his being required to make ever more demanding measurements. High on the list is the need to measure frequencies and phase shifts generated by experimental circuits. Short of buying one of the many frequency counters available, such measurements can be a problem. But they need not be a problem, because even the most modest experimenter probably has all of the equipment on his bench that is required to measure frequency quickly and accurately. All you need is an inexpensive oscilloscope and a frequency source such as an audio oscillator or a signal generator.

The simple equipment interconnections required are shown in Fig. 2-13. Notice that all you have to do is connect the output of your frequency source to the vertical input of your oscilloscope, and the frequency that you wish to measure to the horizontal input. Then by making a few quick control adjustments you can determine the unknown frequency.

Frequency measurement with an oscilloscope is accomplished using Lissajous figures or patterns. Lissajous patterns are the displays that appear on an oscilloscope when voltages of different frequency, amplitude, and phase relationships are applied to its deflection plates. You have probably seen them in older science fiction movies when "weird" patterns are used to indicate abnormal conditions aboard a spaceship.

Getting back to the test set-up, it is obvious that the signal applied to the vertical input will cause the CRT beam to move up and down at a rate determined by the frequency of the signal. The same action can be obtained in the horizontal direction by switching your oscilloscope sweep controls to the positions that bypass the normal sweep circuits and applying signals connected to the horizontal input directly to the horizontal channel amplifier. The result is that the CRT beam will be pulled up, down, right, and left all at the same time. The resulting display will literally resemble a tangled up ball of string unless the two signals are harmonically related to one another. When this condition exists, the display will become steady as a rock, and the unknown frequency can be determined by making a quick mental calculation.

The basis of using your oscilloscope to measure frequency is that you adjust the frequency controls of your frequency source to induce the steady display. Then by reading the frequency dial of your source one of the two frequencies is known and the other can quickly be determined. Simple?

Here's How

Returning to Fig. 2-13. You should now have your equipment connected as shown. Next, adjust the oscilloscope vertical and horizontal sensitivity controls to obtain a suitable deflection both vertically and horizontally. About 1-in. wide and 2-in. high is more than adequate. As mentioned before, at this point the display probably looks like a real mess. But that is normal.

Now adjust the frequency controls of your frequency source until the display stabilizes and resembles a pattern in Fig. 2-14. The accuracy of the final measurement will be a function of how stable you can make the display, so make certain that the display is as steady as you can get it. It might help to let your equipment warm-up for a while if drift is a problem, but don't forget that many frequencies are not too stable. We will tell you how to check the stability of your frequency source later. Also, though it is possible to obtain stable displays that have many loops in them, it is usually best to keep the number of loops in either direction below five if possible. This is simply because they are easier to count.

Finally, referring to the examples shown in Fig. 2-14, count the number of times that the trace "touches" the left side of the display, and the number of times that the trace "touches" the top of the screen. Divide the number of "left-touches" by the number of "top-touches" and multiply the indica-

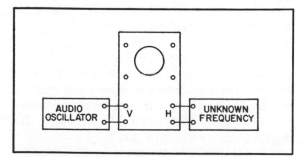

Fig. 2-13. The frequency or phase measurement set up. Frequency less than 1 Hz is usually described in terms of phase angle. When the phase has shifted 360 degrees, it has changed in frequency by one hertz.

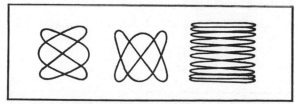

Fig. 2-14. Various vertical to horizontal frequency ratios.

tion of your frequency dial by the result. This gives you the unknown frequency:

$$\frac{\text{left-touches}}{\text{top-touches}} \times \text{frequency} = \frac{\text{Unknown}}{\text{Frequency}}$$

Couldn't be easier, and you save the cost of a frequency counter.

Since your frequency source probably makes you blush when anyone mentions calibration or accuracy, and who doesn't, let's cover how Lissajous patterns can be used to calibrate your frequency source. It is merely an extension of what you do to determine an unknown frequency, except now you "borrow" the known accuracy of your public utility line frequency. The 60-Hz power that you take from your wall socket is generally frequency controlled to within 0.1%. By using this known frequency, safely stepped down through a filament transformer, you can calibrate your signal generator frequency dial at any frequency that is a multiple of 60.

Connect the circuit shown in Fig. 2-15. Then, beginning at 20 Hz, increase the frequency of your audio oscillator and observe how closely to the correct dial indication the scope display "locks in." After a while, say about 1800 Hz, you won't really be able to count the number of loops. But if you are careful you will be able to see the display stabilize, which indicates that you have reached the next multiple of 60.

Checking the stability of your frequency source is even easier. Simply adjust the frequency dial to obtain a stable display, and watch the display. After a reasonable warm-up time for the equipment,

you should be able to obtain a display that seems to rotate very slowly, if at all. Of course, this will be a function of unit quality. But it will give you a feeling for how much drift can be expected from your frequency source. Additional amounts can be attributed to the source of the unknown frequency.

The oscilloscope has always been the most useful tool available to the experimenter. Now you can use it to measure unknown frequencies, phase shifts, calibrate oscillators, check signal stability, and many other uses that will come to mind as you become familiar with Lissajous patterns.

FRAG (FULL RANGE AUDIO GENERATOR)

If you need an inexpensive and highly portable audio test set, this Full Range Audio Generator (FRAG) is for you! Our friendly FRAG delivers variable and fixed outputs of sinusoidal waveform from 10 Hz to over 15 kHz and up to five volts peak-to-peak.

The Circuit

There are several circuit networks which can produce a sinusoidal waveform, including the Phase-Shift and the Twin-T. It is the latter which will be examined here, as it proved in application to be the most suitable for the FRAG.

As shown in the Twin-T Oscillator diagram, (see Fig. 2-16) we have a Low-Pass network of R1, R2, and C1 in parallel with a High-Pass network formed by C2, C3, and R3. The combined network is connected between the inverting input and output of a gain device, such as the familiar 741 integrated circuit op-amp. Typically, R1 = R2, while R3 is one-half to one-tenth of R1, and C1 = C2, and C3 = 2C1.

Since the phase shifts for the two networks are opposite, there exists, in theory, only one frequency where the total phase-shift from input to output will reach 180°, at which point sinusoidal oscillations will occur, provided sufficient gain is available. The approximate frequency will be

$$F = \frac{1}{2 \pi R1\ C1}$$

Varying any or all of the network elements will

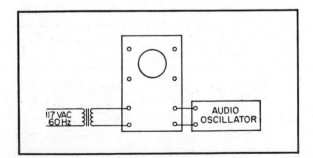

Fig. 2-15. Audio oscillator calibration set up.

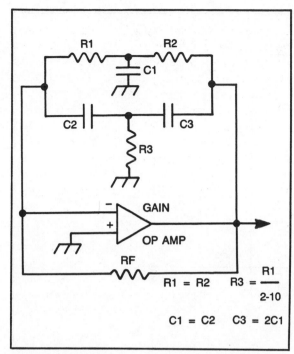

$$R1 = R2 \quad R3 = \frac{R1}{2\text{-}10}$$

$$C1 = C2 \quad C3 = 2C1$$

Fig. 2-16. This basic Twin-T circuit uses a Low-Pass network (R1, R2 and R3) in parallel with a High-Pass network (C1, C2 and C3). As the phase shifts for each circuit are opposite, sinusoidal oscillations will occur at only one frequency, given sufficient gain.

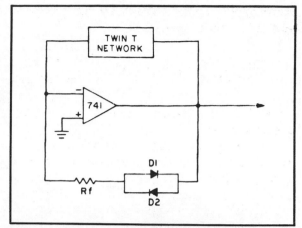

Fig. 2-17. Shunting a Twin-T network with feedback resistance (rf) yielded fair results. The addition of a back-to-back diode pair as an active feedback element greatly tended to increase the FRAG's operating range.

cause the nominal frequency to change, accompanied by a drop in output, until oscillation can no longer be sustained. Over a certain range, varying the resistive elements simultaneously, as by a ganged potentiometer, will yield a useful frequency span, provided the gain can be raised appropriately, but without causing overdriven distortion.

Shunting the Twin-T network with a fixed resistance rf yielded fair results, in experiments conducted to obtain a wide operating range consistent with simplicity. It was then found that addition of a diode back-to-back pair, forming an active feedback element, gave a considerably greater range, as shown. See Fig. 2-17. Further experimentation finally showed that even greater improvement could be obtained by connecting the feedback elements between output and the offset-null terminal associated with the inverting-input. Three switch positions give ranges of 10-100 Hz, 100-1000 Hz, and 1kHz – 10 kHz. A fixed output of about 5 VPP

and a variable output of 0-1.0 VPP were added to provide a choice of useful signal levels. See Fig. 2-18.

Put It All Together

For convenience in portability, a utility box having a five inch length by two and one-quarter inch height and width was selected (Either Bud CU-2104A or Premier 12P3886 types are suitable).

Check Fig. 2-19 to see how these components may be placed on a two inch square section of perfboard having 0.1 inch spaced holes. A pair of No. Six ground lugs are bent at right angles to serve as miniature mounting brackets. There is sufficient room for a 14-pin DIP IC socket for the 741 op-amp, should replaceability be desired. Although a mini-dip 8-pin 741 was used in this circuit, the standard 14-pin unit will do as well, paying attention to the pin connections. The nine-volt transistor battery (Eveready type 222, or equivalent) is secured in place by an S-shaped half-inch wide aluminum bracket.

The only component difficult to find is a three-gang 250K, 250K, 25K potentiometer, used for variable frequency settings. If a ready-made assembly (preferably log-taper) cannot be obtained, use a built-up unit, like Centralab Fastach components.

Optional resistors R4, R5, and R6 are included

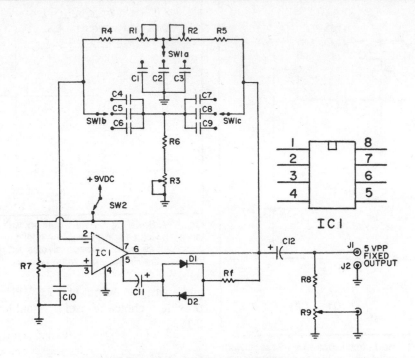

Parts List For The Friendly FRAG

IC1—Type 741C (Radio Shack 276-010 or equiv.)

C1—.22uF capacitor (Radio Shack 272-1402 or equiv.)

C2—.02uF capacitor (Allied 710R1136 or equiv.)

C3—.002uF capacitor (Allied 710R1093 or equiv.)

C4, C7—.1uF capacitors (Radio Shack 272-1069 or equiv.)

C5, C8—.01uF capacitors (Radio Shack 272-131 or equiv.)

C6, C9—.001uF capacitors (Radio Shack 272-126 or equiv.)

C10—.1uF capacitor (Radio Shack 272-135 or equiv.)

C11—10uF electrolytic capacitor (Radio Shack 272-1002 or equiv.)

C12—220uF electrolytic capacitor (Radio Shack 272-1006 or equiv.)

D1, D2—1N914 silicon diodes (Radio Shack 276-1122 or equiv.)

R1, R2, R3—250,000-ohm, 250,000-ohm, 25,000-ohm, ganged potentiometer (Centralab "Fastach")

R4, R5—10,000-ohm, ¼-watt resistor (Radio Shack 271-1335 or equiv.)

R6—1,000-ohm, ¼-watt resistor (Radio Shack 271-1321 or equiv.)

R7—5,000-ohm trimmer potentiometer (Radio Shack 271-217 or equiv.)

R8—4,700-ohm, ¼-watt resistor (Radio Shack 271-1330 or equiv.)

R9—1,000-ohm potentiometer (Allied 854-5800 or equiv.)

SW1—3-position, 3 or 4-pole miniature rotary switch (Calectro E2-168 or equiv.)

SW2—potentiometer switch (mount on back of R9) (Radio Shack 271-1740 or equiv.)

Rf—feedback resistors (see text)

J1—Pair of five-way binding posts (Radio Shack 274-661 or equiv.)

J2—RCA type phono jack (Radio Shack 272-346 or equiv.)

Misc.—9-V battery, battery clip, perf. board with .1-in. spacing (Radio Shack 276-1395 or equiv.), perf. board terminals (Radio Shack 270-1392 or equiv), DIP socket (Radio Shack 276-027 or equiv.), a 5 x 2.25 x 2.25-inch chassis (such as the Bud CU 2104A), wire, solder, etc.

Allied Electronics' address is:
401 East 8th St., Ft. Worth, Texas 76102
Calectro Electronics' address is:
400 S. Wyman St., Rockford, Ill. 61101
Centralab Electronics' address is:
P.O. Box 858, Fort Dodge, Iowa 50501

Fig. 2-18. Schematic diagram and parts list for friendly FRAG.

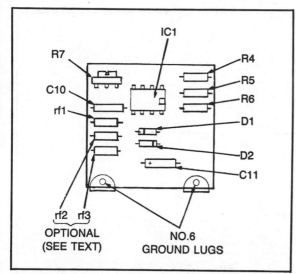

Fig. 2-19. Use this parts layout for your perfboard. rf2 and rf3 are optional, as mentioned in the text. Also, use a socket for IC1.

so that the variable frequency dial may be rotated to maximum frequency without having the circuit drop out of oscillation, as it would should R1, R2, and R3 fall too low. Temporarily omit the feedback resistor(s) rf for later adjustment. If a four pole-three position switch (such as Calectro E2-168) is available, then each range may have its own individually selected feedback resistor for maximum efficiency.

Adjustment and Operation

An oscilloscope is essential for adjustment of the friendly FRAG to determine optimum waveform and amplitude and for rough frequency determinations. A frequency-counter is also useful, although the FRAG is not intended to be a precision audio generator.

Before applying power, set the input bias potentiometer R7 for approximate midrange position and connect a decade resistance box, set at about 33K ohms, in place of rf. Set the Range Switch to its middle (X100) position and the variable frequency control to its mid position. Connect the scope (and frequency counter, if available) to the fixed output terminals.

Switch on the power by turning the Output con-

trol to mid-position. The scope should display a more or less square wave of about 200 Hz. Adjust the decade box, or individual fixed resistor, for a sinusoidal waveform of maximum amplitude, consistent with low distortion. If the wave is flattened at top or bottom, try adjusting R7 while rechecking rf. Rotate the variable frequency control from one end to the other, rechecking rf and R7 should distortion occur. Amplitude will be less at each end of the dial, and will drop out entirely at the upper end, unless the optional resistors R4, R5 and R6 have been included. A maximum output of 5 VPP should be obtainable at the fixed output terminals and up to 1 VPP at the variable output jack. If separate feedback resistors are used (with a four-pole Range Switch) recheck the other two range positions and select the correct individual resistors and mount them on the perfboard. Otherwise, a single feedback resistor will have to be a compromise for best operation over the entire span of all three ranges.

The variable frequency dial may be calibrated simply on a 1 to 10 basis, which should hold good for the three ranges. If a linear potentiometer is used (all that was available in the Fastach components at time of construction) the dial will necessarily be non-linear, which is why a log-taper pot is more desirable. Also, due to mechanical backlash in the stacked sections, it is best to move well past an over-shot frequency point before reversing to zero back in. The 0-1 VPP shielded jack is best for low-level output applications involving audio amplifiers and other high-input impedance gear. The 5 VPP fixed-output terminals are useful for general purposes, or where it may be desired to construct fixed voltage-divider networks.

Although the battery drain is quite modest, make sure to turn off the test set when not in use.

Other Applications

During development of the circuitry, additional diode pairs were tried to see how far their "dynamic feedback" operation could extend the variable frequency range. Although two pairs gave some increase, this was at the expense of waveform purity. This distortion, however, can be put to use in the

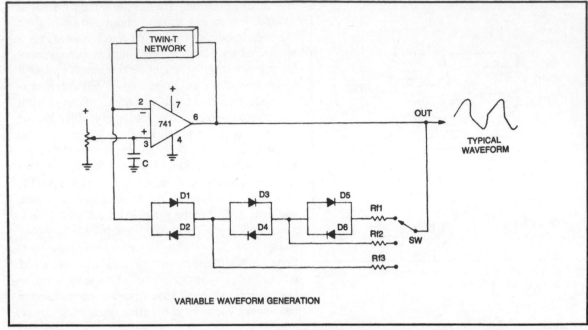

TWIN-T NETWORK

741

OUT

TYPICAL WAVEFORM

D1
D2
D3
D4
D5
D6
Rf1
Rf2
SW
Rf3

VARIABLE WAVEFORM GENERATION

Fig. 2-20. During development of the FRAG, additional diode pairs were added to see if they would further increase the variable frequency range. They did—but at the cost of adding some distortion. This, however, results in some interesting tones—music!

area of electronic music. The Fig. 2-20 shows how a chain of diodes, with individually selected feedback resistors may be switched in to provide for the generation of interesting synthetic tones . . . another benefit of this original FRAG!

QUAD-MIX AUDIO MIXER

We've got an interesting four position audio mixer, designed around in RCA integrated circuit (IC), that can be built for just a few dollars worth of parts and about one evening's worth of your leisure time.

What can you do with it? It's an excellent pre-amplifier/mixer that will let you feed four different audio signals into a single input of your power amplifier and individually adjust their volume levels. You may have organized a new rock group that owns up to four guitars that you want amplified to get that solid sound the group is capable of producing. Easy to do with Quad-Mix. Just feed the outputs from the electrical pickups on the guitars to the individual input jacks of Quad-Mix and feed

the output of Quad-Mix to the input of the PA amplifier. If your group doesn't use four guitars, you can connect one or more microphones to the unused inputs on Quad-Mix and blend the volume level of instruments and/or voices for the specific effects you want. Quad-Mix has sufficient gain to raise the low level output of musical instrument pick-ups and most microphones to drive the average PA to full power and perhaps, even beyond into distortion.

How It Works

Input jacks J1 and J2 are connected through potentiometers R1 and R2, which serve as series mixers, to feed one of the two pairs of Darlington connected transistors that make up the IC. Input jacks J3 and J4 are similarly connected through potentiometers R3 and R4, which serve as series mixers, that feed the second pair of Darlington connected transistors of the IC. See Fig. 2-21.

Resistors R5, R6, R7 and R8 were purposely made fairly high in resistance to assure freedom from interaction between the potentiometers or af-

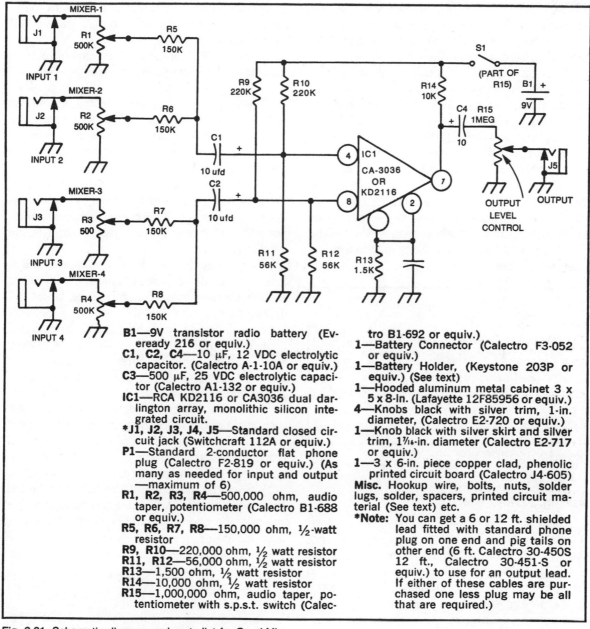

B1—9V transistor radio battery (Eveready 216 or equiv.)
C1, C2, C4—10 μF, 12 VDC electrolytic capacitor. (Calectro A-1-10A or equiv.)
C3—500 μF, 25 VDC electrolytic capacitor (Calectro A1-132 or equiv.)
IC1—RCA KD2116 or CA3036 dual darlington array, monolithic silicon integrated circuit.
*****J1, J2, J3, J4, J5**—Standard closed circuit jack (Switchcraft 112A or equiv.)
P1—Standard 2-conductor flat phone plug (Calectro F2-819 or equiv.) (As many as needed for input and output —maximum of 6)
R1, R2, R3, R4—500,000 ohm, audio taper, potentiometer (Calectro B1-688 or equiv.)
R5, R6, R7, R8—150,000 ohm, ½-watt resistor
R9, R10—220,000 ohm, ½ watt resistor
R11, R12—56,000 ohm, ½ watt resistor
R13—1,500 ohm, ½ watt resistor
R14—10,000 ohm, ½ watt resistor
R15—1,000,000 ohm, audio taper, potentiometer with s.p.s.t. switch (Calec-

tro B1-692 or equiv.)
1—Battery Connector (Calectro F3-052 or equiv.)
1—Battery Holder, (Keystone 203P or equiv.) (See text)
1—Hooded aluminum metal cabinet 3 x 5 x 8-in. (Lafayette 12F85956 or equiv.)
4—Knobs black with silver trim, 1-in. diameter, (Calectro E2-720 or equiv.)
1—Knob black with silver skirt and silver trim, 1⁷⁄₁₆-in. diameter (Calectro E2-717 or equiv.)
1—3 x 6-in. piece copper clad, phenolic printed circuit board (Calectro J4-605)
Misc. Hookup wire, bolts, nuts, solder lugs, solder, spacers, printed circuit material (See text) etc.
*****Note:** You can get a 6 or 12 ft. shielded lead fitted with standard phone plug on one end and pig tails on other end (6 ft. Calectro 30-450S 12 ft., Calectro 30-451-S or equiv.) to use for an output lead. If either of these cables are purchased one less plug may be all that are required.)

Fig. 2-21. Schematic diagram and parts list for Quad-Mix.

fecting overall gain due to variations in setting of any of the controls. If they were not a fairly high resistance, it is possible that differences in settings of the two potentiometers associated with their common amplifier would be effected. This would be particularly true in the event one of the poten-

tiometers in the pair should be set at minimum gain (near or at ground).

The RCA KD-2116/CA3036 integrated circuit (IC) contains two low-noise, wide band amplifier circuits in one package. It has two isolated inputs and a common output connection. Each of the amplifiers is comprised of Darlington connected transistor pairs arranged in a differential amplifier configuration. The IC is housed in a standard 10 lead TO-5 package. See Fig. 2-22.

When used as an audio mixer in our Quad-Mix, the IC is employed as a dual input active mixer. By combining two passive mixer circuits, one dual passive for each of the active sections of the IC, the unit can mix, and individually adjust, the level of a total of four different transducers (pickups) or microphones. Since total current drain of the IC is only 50 mA, we power Quad-Mix from a 9 V transistor radio battery mounted in Quad-Mix's cabinet. Another advantage of the battery supply is that it makes Quad-Mix portable and independent of the 117 Vac power lines. This also results in a much quieter hum free operating mixer.

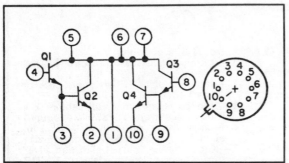

Fig. 2-22. Ever wonder what's crammed into the TO-5 case of an IC? Here's a schematic, base pin arrangement of CA3036.

Making a Quad-Mix

Since the mixer is small and designed for portable use, we housed it in an attractive hooded front aluminum cabinet that's only 3-in. high, 8-in. wide, and 5-in. deep overall. Although we haven't finished the aluminum cabinet of our model, you can, if you have a more artistic nature, paint yours an appropriate attractive color or you can cover it with pressure sensitive plastic sheeting (CONTAC or equiv.) that comes in either woodgrains, solid colors or patterned prints.

We suggest you identify each of the controls and input jacks by applying transfer letters and digits (Datak or equiv.) once the newly applied spray paint or plastic sheeting has thoroughly dried.

You should spray the letters and digits with a very light coat of clear plastic to protect them from scratches etc.

First step in fabricating your Quad-Mix is to make the printed circuit board. We have included a full sized pattern to assist you. See Fig. 2-23.

While the etching process for the printed circuit board is in progress you can spend this time in laying out and drilling the chassis. Since you are dealing with very high gain units, we suggest that you follow our layout. See Fig. 2-24. A great amount of thought has been put into it to reduce, to a minimum, input-output coupling. With this layout you are assured of maximum separation of input and output leads, which makes for a stable amplifier.

By the time the holes have been located and at least partially drilled, the etching of the PC board will have been completed. If, by chance, layout and drilling takes longer than the recommended etching time, follow those etching timing instructions explicitly in preference to completing the drilling which can be completed after the etching. Once etching is completed rinse the board thoroughly, dry it, and put it aside.

Finish the drilling and de-burring of all holes, then apply either the vinyl covering or the spray paint to the cabinet and front panel. During the time the finish is setting thoroughly, mount all components to the PC board and the chassis. See Fig. 2-25. Save the mounting of the IC on to the PC board for the last task. Double check to be sure that you have it properly oriented before applying heat from the soldering iron. Use a small, low wattage iron to avoid damage to the IC, the capacitors and the PC board from excess heat. Make certain too, that electrolytic capacitors are properly polarized before soldering them into the circuit.

A short scrap of coiled spring, extended between two solder lugs makes up the battery holder on the inside of the chassis. You may prefer to buy a standard battery holder since they are inexpensive and do a good job of holding the battery in place. We've listed one in the parts list along with a standard battery connector.

Bond the ground side of the four input jacks

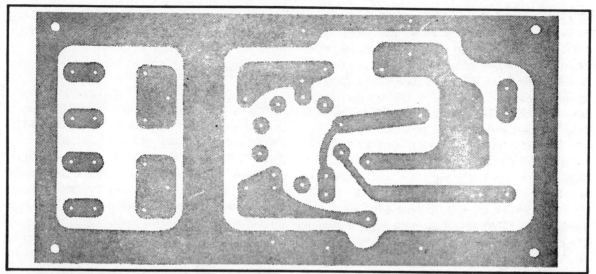

Fig. 2-23. Full-size pattern for the PC board.

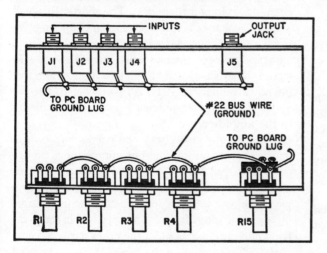

Fig. 2-24. Because an actual photo of Quad-Mix doesn't show ground buss details too clearly we had this pictorial layout drawing made. From it you can readily determine just where and how to run grounding leads between components.

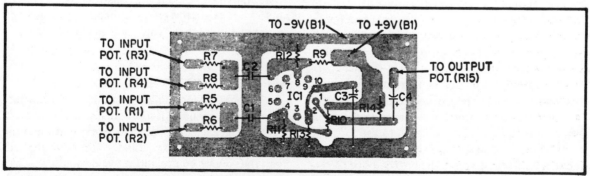

Fig. 2-25. Here's a foil side view of printed circuit board showing where each component is located. Components are mounted on top side of board and are soldered to foil on bottom.

to a common ground point on the PC board. Do the same for the ground point of the five potentiometers. Easiest way to do this is to loop a bus wire from ground lug to ground lug of each of the components involved and terminate the loop on a ground point of the PC board. Use separate loops for the jacks and potentiometers and make each loop as short and direct as possible.

A bundle, or harness, made of four different colors of insulated hookup wire connects the high side of each jack to the high side of its respective potentiometer. Clamp one end of four lengths of different colored wire, each about 2-ft. long, in the jaws of your bench vise. Clamp the other ends into the chuck of your hand drill. Twist them together to make a neat tightly twisted bundle; once removed from the vise and chuck they'll hold together. To assure their holding together you may wrap the bundle at several points with 1/8-in. wide strips of insulating tape. Locate the harness with one end centered between pots 2 and 3, fan out two leads to the right and two to the left of this center position and solder them to the high side of each potentiometer. Neatly fold the bundle to conform with the bends in the chassis, crossing under the PC board and coming inside up the rear apron of the chassis between input jacks 2 and 3. Following the color scheme used in connecting the pots match the fan out and connection to high side of the jacks so that the same color used for a potentiometer is used for the corresponding numbered jack. (i.e., Jack 1 to pot 1 etc.) Center contact of each input pot is connected to its respective resistor, mounted on the PC board, through connecting pods on the left hand side of the board (see photo). The output lead from the center of the master control potentiometer to the output jack is dressed under the PC board's right edge, close to the chassis. The lead to the high side of this pot is connected to a pod on the PC board near the right edge.

Once the four input, one output, and the battery connector leads are soldered to the PC board it can be fastened to the chassis. Use 1/4-in. spacers or extra 8-32 nuts to raise the board above the bottom of the chassis to avoid shorting any of the PC board ribbons or solder mounds. Before tightening down the board check out the circuit to be sure you've not made any mistakes. If all checks out, mount and connect the battery.

You've Done It

Now you are ready for The Big Thrill—checking the mixing action and actually putting Quad-Mix into use. You'll need a shielded lead between the output jack of Quad-Mix and the input connector of your amplifier. In all probability the plugs for both the Quad-Mix output and the amplifier input jack will be the same, standard tip-sleeve phone plugs. Before purchasing parts to hold Quad-Mix check for the correct input plug so you can add this to your parts purchase and have everything available at the same time. It is best to keep the interconnecting lead between Quad-Mix and the main power amplifier as short as possible; in any event never longer than 25-ft. The shorter this lead is the less chance there will be for picking up electrical interference. Also, by keeping the lead short capacity between ground (shield) and the hot side (center conductor) will be small to reduce high frequency attenuation. After all you want to get the widest band of frequencies from the instruments to the amplifier.

You might also check the connectors on the leads from the guitars and/or microphones you're going to use with Quad-Mix. You do want to be able to plug them into Quad-Mix after doing such a fine job of building it. If they don't match the input jacks buy suitable plugs for them as specified in the parts list when purchasing all of the other parts. So now that you've completed the construction and tested out your Quad-Mix—go ahead and surprise everyone—use it on your next performance.

U-PICK-IT GUITAR BOX

Would you spend about six bucks to tailor the sound of your guitar? Especially if you knew you'd have the great sound of that group you know is heading to the top? Or, maybe, you're not satisfied with the sounds you're getting, and want to be able to change the tone of your guitar to suit the mood of your music. We're not saying that our U-Pick-It will make a Segovia out of you. But it sure will make your guitar sound great, and who knows, maybe it will help you on to fame and fortune.

What does U-Pick-It do for your instrument? It gives you a choice of bass, treble or midrange boost just by turning a single knob. You can make that old guitar sound twangy, smooth or raunchy at the twist of your wrist. Furthermore, U-Pick-It's bass boost will allow a regular guitar to be used as a string bass by giving those low notes an extra boost.

PSO With a Difference

Check the schematic in Fig. 2-26; it will ring a bell for many of you. Basically, you'll see a phase

shift oscillator with a few necessary changes. Note the network consisting of components R1, R2, and R3 isolates transistor Q1 from the loading effect of the guitar pickup. Also, potentiometer R6 is used to lower the stage gain to the point where the transistor will be amplifying rather than oscillating. The phase shift network peaks the response within a fairly narrow range, depending on the setting of potentiometer R8.

You Pick It's Parts

We housed U-Pick-It, including its own self-contained battery power supply (a 9 V transistor battery) in a 4 × 2 1/4 × 2 1/4-in. Minibox. All of

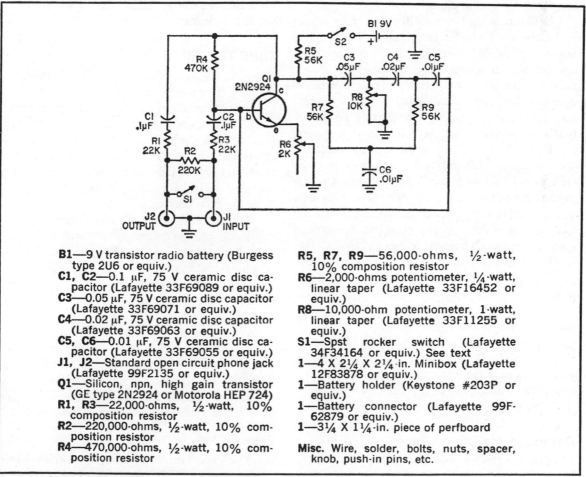

B1—9 V transistor radio battery (Burgess type 2U6 or equiv.)

C1, C2—0.1 µF, 75 V ceramic disc capacitor (Lafayette 33F69089 or equiv.)

C3—0.05 µF, 75 V ceramic disc capacitor (Lafayette 33F69071 or equiv.)

C4—0.02 µF, 75 V ceramic disc capacitor (Lafayette 33F69063 or equiv.)

C5, C6—0.01 µF, 75 V ceramic disc capacitor (Lafayette 33F69055 or equiv.)

J1, J2—Standard open circuit phone jack (Lafayette 99F2135 or equiv.)

Q1—Silicon, npn, high gain transistor (GE type 2N2924 or Motorola HEP 724)

R1, R3—22,000-ohms, ½-watt, 10% composition resistor

R2—220,000-ohms, ½-watt, 10% composition resistor

R4—470,000-ohms, ½-watt, 10% composition resistor

R5, R7, R9—56,000-ohms, ½-watt, 10% composition resistor

R6—2,000-ohms potentiometer, ¼-watt, linear taper (Lafayette 33F16452 or equiv.)

R8—10,000-ohm potentiometer, 1-watt, linear taper (Lafayette 33F11255 or equiv.)

S1—Spst rocker switch (Lafayette 34F34164 or equiv.) See text

1—4 X 2¼ X 2¼-in. Minibox (Lafayette 12F83878 or equiv.)

1—Battery holder (Keystone #203P or equiv.)

1—Battery connector (Lafayette 99F-62879 or equiv.)

1—3¼ X 1¼-in. piece of perfboard

Misc. Wire, solder, bolts, nuts, spacer, knob, push-in pins, etc.

Fig. 2-26. Schematic diagram and parts list for U-Pick-It.

the components with the exception of the input and output jacks, the IN-OUT switch, potentiometer R8 and the battery are mounted on a 3 1/4 × 1 1/4-in. piece of perfboard. Push-in clips are used for input, output, battery + and ground terminations.

Although the transistor doesn't have the usual triangular pin orientation, if you follow our layout, it can be mounted without having to cross over any of its leads. A word of caution now: this circuit won't work with low gain transistors. So please, no substitutions! Besides, the one we used isn't expensive, so there really isn't a good reason to fiddle with dime-a-dozen transistors.

In the phase section, use good quality disc capacitors rated 50 Vdc minimum or better. Seems we found that low voltage ones sometimes may leak too much for this application.

Drill mounting holes for the two jacks in one end of the bottom half of the Minibox. Whether you buy a commercial battery holder, or make one from a scrap of aluminum, locate the battery so that it will clear the other components when the Minibox is closed. Drill two mounting holes; one for the battery holder, and the other to support the perfboard that's raised 1/4-in. off the bottom with a spacer.

IN-OUT switch S1 is located in the center of the top half of the Minibox. It's a push-button ON-OFF switch that we picked up in the electrical supply section of the local hardware store. This kind of switch is normally used on desk lamps and the like. We have listed in the parts list, however, a rocker-type switch because, on second thought, we feel it is more practical since you can tell at a glance whether it's ON or OFF. Don't care to make a rectangular opening to mount a rocker type, either? Then use a regular toggle switch mounted with a marker plate to indicate its status.

After mounting and wiring all of the components on the perfboard, check your work to be sure you've wired it correctly. Then mount it in position in the bottom half of the Minibox as shown in our photo.

Getting to the Gig on Time

Connect the battery, plug your guitar into the input jack, and connect the output jack to the normal guitar input on your power amplifier. Standard patch cords in varying lengths are available with a phone plug on one end to match the input jack on U-Pick-It and a choice of plugs on the opposite end so you can match the input jack of your amplifier.

Turn both units on, and open switch S1 so that the short circuit it places across U-Pick-It's input/output jacks is removed. After the amplifier has warmed up, adjust trimmer potentiometer R6 with a small screw driver to a point just below feedback with potentiometer R8 set at its midpoint position.

Once the setting is achieved, turning the knob on R8 to the right or left of center should now change the sound of the guitar. One extreme in rotation will favor bass and the opposite extreme will favor the treble while R8's midpoint setting will favor the midrange.

TAPE TESTER

Virtually no two brands of recording tape, particularly the cassette tapes, deliver similar results at slow speeds. Even within the same price range, tape A might sound best on machine X, while tape B is the right one for machine Y. Fact is, because there is so much variation between tapes, many of the better cassette decks provide some means to optimize the bias for optimum frequency response from the tape playback.

The trouble is, not all machines have user-adjustable bias, and some models with the adjustment have no test system. The user must try for an adjustment that sounds right to the ear, a somewhat dubious method. Basically, most of us simply try a wide assortment of brands and types hoping to find the one that works best on our recorder.

With our easy-to-build Tape Tester, however, you can check out tapes in seconds to find the one that gives the best response in your sound system. And the same thing goes if your deck has a bias adjustment; again, it takes just a few seconds to find the optimum adjustment for peak performance.

Easy to Use

The Tape Tester provides two switch-selected test tones of approximately 1000 and 12,000 Hz at

0 dB reference output level—for adjustment of the recording level—and at approximately −20 dB, the standard cassette test level. (Of course, it can be used for reel-to-reel machines, though their test level is generally −10 dB.)

To determine whether you are using the best tape for your machine, or to make a bias adjustment, you simply record the −20 dB 1000 Hz signal for a few seconds, followed by 12,000 Hz. On playback, the 12,000 Hz tone should be within 3 dB of the 1000 Hz reference for "average" performance, and within 1 dB for optimum sound reproduction. If you're using metal tape and want to see how well the tape, or the machine itself, handles high-frequency high-level saturation, simply use the 0 dB output before running the standard −20 dB level test.

As an example, assume you've checked a tape and the 12,000 Hz playback is 7 dB below the 1000 Hz playback. Obviously, this isn't hi-fi, so try a tape with "hotter" highs. Alternately, if the 12,000 Hz output was 6 dB above 0 dB, you need a tape with less high frequency output—generally a less expensive tape. If your machine has a bias adjustment but no test system, simply adjust the bias until the 12,000 Hz playback level reads within 1 dB of the 1000 Hz playback level on your deck's VU record/playback meters.

Construction

The Tape Tester is assembled in a plastic cabinet sized approximately 2 5/8 by 1 5/8 by 5-inches, usually available from Radio Shack or Calectro. Some cabinets have square corners, some are round; it doesn't make any difference unless you contemplate problems in rounding the corners of a printed circuit board.

The cabinet cover (which replaces the supplied metal cover) is the printed circuit board itself. This arrangement eliminates the hassle of trying to mount the PC board inside the cabinet. Figures 2-27 and 2-28 show the printed circuit board.

Before etching the printed circuit, make certain the board is cut to the exact size of the metal cover supplied with your particular cabinet. Not only is there the problem of round or square corners, but the overall dimensions and the location of the mounting holes vary from cabinet to cabinet. The holes for the switches and jack are 1/4-inch diameter, and all other component holes are made with a #58, #59, or #60 drill.

All oscillator values have been selected so the project will work with low-cost, normal tolerance components. There is no need to go through the ex-

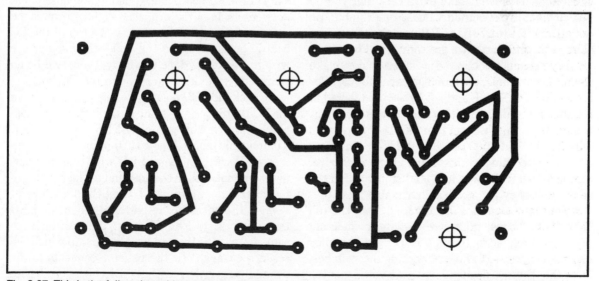

Fig. 2-27. This is the full scale etching guide for the Tape Tester's PC board. Note that the holes marked for the switches and J1 are not full-size. You will need a 1/4-inch drill bit.

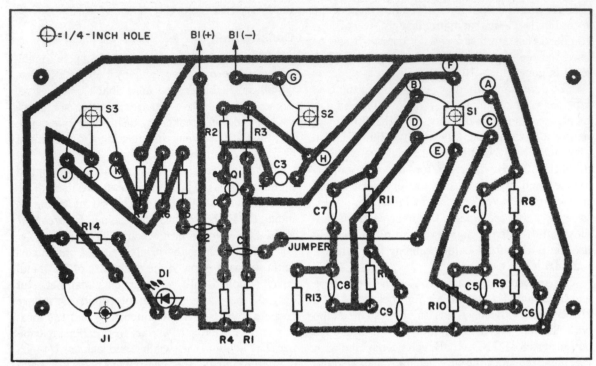

Fig. 2-28. In this expanded view of the parts arrangement on the printed circuit board, note that 1/4-inch holes are required for mounting S1, S2, S3, and J1. Be sure to remember to wire in the lone jumper between C1 and point E at switch S1. Be sure to observe polarity when installing D1 and C3 on the PC board.

tra expense of purchasing precision resistors and capacitors. However, take extra care that you do not change any specified value. For example, do not change R1 to 270K, or R13 to 1200-ohms. The schematic and parts list are shown in Fig. 2-29.

If you cannot obtain the specified values, make them. For example, the 0.003-μF capacitor used for C9 can be a 0.002-μF and a 0.001-μF connected in parallel by simply twisting their leads together. Similarly, C7 and C8 can be a 0.001-μF in parallel with a 0.0005-μF (500 pF). The 0.022-μF capacitor is a standard value available just about anywhere. Similarly, all resistor values are "standard" in the sense that they are generally available types.

Since the switches are installed from the foil side of the board, take care that the connecting wires don't extend up through the board where they can act as a hazard to fingers working the switches. Note that there is a small loop in the wire from the switch contact to the board. First, solder the wire to the switch contact (or jack). Before soldering to

the board, trim the wire flush with the top (non foil side) of the PC board. Next, using long nose pliers or tweezers, back the wire very slightly towards the switch so the end is just below the top of the PC board—but still within the hole—then solder the wire to the foil. If done correctly, there will be no sharp edges sticking up through the PC board.

Check the LED polarity before you install it on the PC board, because some of the instructions supplied with "hobby grade" LEDS are incorrect. Temporarily tack-solder a 1000-ohm resistor to either LED wire. Clip one LED wire to either battery terminal. Touch the free end of the resistor to the other battery terminal. If the LED doesn't light, reverse the wires to the battery. When the LED lights, the LED wire attached to the resistor is the same polarity as the battery terminal to which the resistor connects. (If the resistor connects to the positive battery terminal, the LED wire on the opposite end of the resistor is the ANODE.) If the resistor is connected to the negative battery termi-

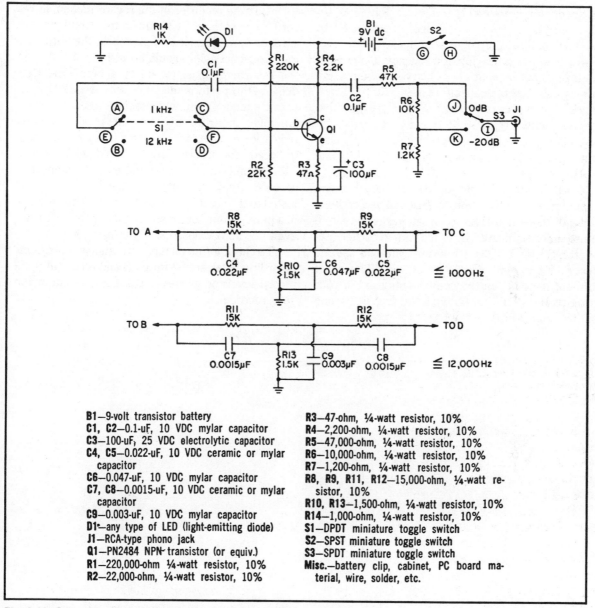

Fig. 2-29. Schematic diagram and parts list for Tape Tester.

B1—9-volt transistor battery
C1, C2—0.1-uF, 10 VDC mylar capacitor
C3—100-uF, 25 VDC electrolytic capacitor
C4, C5—0.022-uF, 10 VDC ceramic or mylar capacitor
C6—0.047-uF, 10 VDC mylar capacitor
C7, C8—0.0015-uF, 10 VDC ceramic or mylar capacitor
C9—0.003-uF, 10 VDC mylar capacitor
D1—any type of LED (light-emitting diode)
J1—RCA-type phono jack
Q1—PN2484 NPN transistor (or equiv.)
R1—220,000-ohm ¼-watt resistor, 10%
R2—22,000-ohm, ¼-watt resistor, 10%

R3—47-ohm, ¼-watt resistor, 10%
R4—2,200-ohm, ¼-watt resistor, 10%
R5—47,000-ohm, ¼-watt resistor, 10%
R6—10,000-ohm, ¼-watt resistor, 10%
R7—1,200-ohm, ¼-watt resistor, 10%
R8, R9, R11, R12—15,000-ohm, ¼-watt resistor, 10%
R10, R13—1,500-ohm, ¼-watt resistor, 10%
R14—1,000-ohm, ¼-watt resistor, 10%
S1—DPDT miniature toggle switch
S2—SPST miniature toggle switch
S3—SPDT miniature toggle switch
Misc.—battery clip, cabinet, PC board material, wire, solder, etc.

Using the Tape Tester

The output of the calibrator at 0 dB is nominal, the LED wire on the opposite end is the CATHODE. If the LED doesn't light with either polarity, it is defective (not unusual in LED hobby assortments.)

nally 0.5-volts, and should be connected to a recorder's LINE/AUX input, not to the microphone input. Because of normal component tolerance, the oscillator might not "start" when power is first applied if the frequency switch is set for 12 kHz. If this occurs with your model, rather than trying to "trim" resistor and capacitor values in the Twin-

T feedband networks-R8 through R13 and C4 through C9—simply set frequency selector S1 to 1000 Hz before applying power. The oscillator will always "start" at the lower frequency. If the oscillator does not start at all, either you have made a wiring error, or the capacitors in each Twin-T network are not approximately equal to the specified values. Generally, the C4/C5 and C7/C8 combinations don't have to be the precise specified value, but each capacitor in a pair must be close in value to the other.

Set S3 for 0 dB output, S1 for 1000 Hz, and turn power switch S2 on. Adjust the record level for a 0 dB record level, or whatever is the maximum meter-indicated level for your recorder. Set switch S3 for a −20 dB output; you will see the recorder's meter drop 18 to 20 dB. (The exact amount depends on the components used in your project. It doesn't matter what the drop is, as long as it's near 20 dB.)

Start the recorder in the record mode and record a few seconds of 1000 Hz, followed by a few seconds of 12,000 Hz. On playback, the output of the two frequencies should be within 3 dB. Adjust the recorder's bias, or select a tape type that delivers this performance. Because of the 20 dB input attenuation, you will probably need an external level indicator because the usual −20 dB indication on a recorder's meter is not all that easy to "read" for precise value on playback. Use any external indicator, such as the meters on another recorder (feed the output of the recorder being tested to the input of a second recorder), the meters of a power amplifier, or an ac/audio meter. You can even use an oscilloscope if you have one.

To check for metal tape saturation at maximum recording level, set S3 for 0 dB and record at 0 dB record level, or whatever value is maximum for your recorder.

Chapter 3

Radio Electronics

CRYSTALS AND HOW THEY WORK

Can you imagine the chaos on the AM broadcast band if transmitters drifted as much as those inexpensive table radios? The broadcast station engineer must keep his station carrier within 20 hertz of its assigned frequency. How does he do it? What about the CBer unable to contact his base station with an unstable, super-regen walkie-talkie. Lost calls don't often happen to a CBer who can keep his receiver frequency right on the assigned channel center.

This and much more is, of course, all done with a little help from a very basic material, the quartz crystal. It is the single component that serves to fill a basic requirement for precision frequency control. Quartz crystals not only fix the frequency of radio transmitters (from CB installations to multi-kilowatt-broadcast installations), but also establish the frequency of timing pulses in many modern computers. In addition, they can provide the exceptional selectivity required to generate and receive single-sideband signals in today's crowded radio spectrum. Yet this list merely touches upon the many uses of quartz crystals. No exhaustive list has ever been compiled.

A Real Gem

This quiet controller is a substance surrounded by paradox. While quartz composes more than a third of the Earth's crust, it was one of the three most strategic minerals during World War II. And despite its plenitude, several semiprecious gems (including agate and onyx) are composed only of quartz.

Unfortunately, quartz exercises its control in only a relative manner. When it's misused, the control can easily be lost. For this reason, if you use it in any way—either in your CB rig, your ham station, or your SWL receiver—you should become acquainted with the way in which this quiet controller functions. Only then can you be sure of obtaining its maximum benefits.

What Is It?

One of the best starting points for a study of

quartz crystals is to examine quartz itself. The mineral, silicon dioxide (SiO_2), occurs in two broad groups of mineral forms: crystalline and non-crystalline. Only the large crystalline form of quartz is of use as a controller.

The crystalline group has many varieties, one of which is common sand. The variety which is used for control, however, is a large, single crystal, usually six-sided. The leading source of this type of quartz is Brazil. However, it also is found in Arkansas. Attempts have been made to produce quartz crystals in the laboratory, but to date synthetic quartz has not proven practical for general use.

A property of crystalline quartz, the one which makes it of special use for control, is known as piezoelectricity. Many other crystals, both natural and synthetic, also have this property. However, none of them also have the hardness of quartz. To see why hardness and the piezoelectric property, when combined, make quartz so important, we must take a slight detour and briefly examine the idea of resonance and resonators.

Resonators and Resonance

As physicists developed the science of radio (the basis for modern electronics), they borrowed the acoustic notion of resonance and applied it to electrical circuits where it shapes electrical waves in a manner similar to an acoustic resonator. For instance, both coils and capacitors store energy and can be connected as a resonator (more often termed a resonant circuit). When ac of appropriate frequency is applied to the resonator, special things happen.

Pendulum Demonstrates

The principle involved is identical to that of a pendulum, which is itself a resonator closely similar in operation to our quartz crystals. To try it you can hang a pendulum of any arbitrary length (see Fig. 3-1), start it swinging, then time its period—one complete swing or cycle. The number of such swings accomplished in exactly one second is the natural or resonant frequency of the pendulum in cycles per second (Hertz).

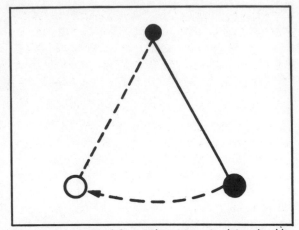

Fig. 3-1. A long pendulum swings at a rate determined by its length. To experiment at home, the arm should be made of light thread (no weight) and a small heavy mass (all the weight concentrated at one point).

You can, by experiment, prove that the frequency at which the pendulum swings or oscillates is determined by the length of the pendulum. The shorter the pendulum (see Fig. 3-2), the faster it swings (the greater the frequency). The weight of the pendulum has no effect on frequency, but has a marked effect upon the length of time the pendulum will swing after a single initial push—the heavier the pendulum, the greater the number of cycles.

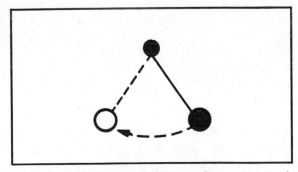

Fig. 3-2. A short pendulum swings at a faster rate no matter what the weight is. The heavier the weight, the longer the pendulum will swing at the faster rate.

A Real Swinger

Once the pendulum begins to swing, very little effort is required to keep it swinging. Only a tiny push is needed each cycle, provided that the push is always applied just as the pendulum begins to move away from the pushing point. If the push is given too soon, it will interfere with the swinging and actually cause the swing to stop sooner than it would without added energy; if the push is given too late, it will have virtually no effect at all. It is this principle—a tiny push at exactly the right time interval—which makes a resonator sustain sound or ac waves. You can prove it with the pendulum by first determining the resonant frequency of a pendulum, then stopping it so that it is completely still. A series of small pushes, delivered at the natural resonant frequency, (each too tiny to have more than a minute effect) will very rapidly cause the pendulum to swing to its full arc again. Pushes of the same strength at any other frequency will have little or no effect.

The pendulum is an excellent control mechanism for regulating a clock to keep time to the second, since the resonant frequency of the pendulum can readily be adjusted to be precisely one cycle per second. However, for control of audio frequencies from tens of hertz (cycles per second) up to tens of thousands of cycles per second (kilohertz), or for radio frequencies ranging up to hundreds of millions of cycles per second (megahertz), the pendulum is too cumbersome a device.

The Tuning Fork

In the audio range, the equivalent of the pendulum is the tuning fork. This is an extremely elongated U-shaped piece of metal (see Fig. 3-3), usually with a small handle at the base. When struck, it emits a single musical tone.

The operating principle is exactly the same as the pendulum. Each of the arms or tines of the fork

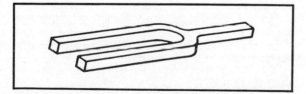

Fig. 3-3. The geometry of the tuning fork produces a continuous pure tone for a long time when struck gently. It is favored by piano tuners as a convenient way to carry a source of accurately-known tone or pitch.

corresponds to a pendulum arm. But here the arms are extremely short and much heavier in proportion to their size than the pendulum. (The shorter the arms of a tuning fork, the higher the resonant frequency in the audio range.) This greatly increased mass causes them to oscillate much longer when struck.

Not all tuning forks operate precisely like pendulums. The pendulum principle is based on a flexing of the arm upon its long dimension. While this is the most common operation, the fork may flex along any dimension.

It's even possible for a single, solid resonator such as a tuning fork to flex along several dimensions at once. A main part of the design of a good tuning fork is to insure that only a single dimension flexes or, in the language of resonators, only a single mode is excited.

Area Too

There's no requirement that the resonator be a completely solid substance. A mass of air, suitably enclosed, forms a resonator. This is the resonator that works on a classic guitar or violin. Here, single-mode operation is distinctly not desired. Instead, multiple-mode operation is encouraged so that all musical tones within the range of the instrument will be reinforced equally.

Now, with the principles of resonance firmly established, we can return to the quartz crystal and its operation.

Quartz Crystal as Resonators

Like the tuning fork or, for that matter, any sufficiently hard object, the quartz crystal is capable of oscillation when struck physically or in some other way excited.

But unlike the tuning fork, or indeed any other object except for certain extremely recent synthetic materials, the quartz crystal is not only sufficiently hard to oscillate at one or more resonant frequencies, but is piezoelectric.

Piezoelectricity

This piezoelectric property means simply that

the crystal generates an electric voltage when physically stressed or, on the other hand, will be physically deformed when subjected to a voltage (see Fig. 3-4). Other familiar objects making use of piezoelectricity include crystal and ceramic microphone elements and phonograph cartridges.

This virtually unique combination of properties (sufficient hardness for oscillation and piezoelectricity) found in quartz crystals, makes it possible to provide the initial push to the crystal by impressing a voltage across it. To provide the subsequent regular pushes, a voltage can be applied at appropriate instants.

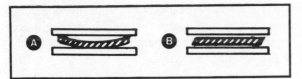

Fig. 3-4. Depending on how the crystal is cut or sliced from the mother crystal, some crystals warp or bend as in A and others shear as shown in B. Each of the many cuts have special characteristics.

Quality Factor

Almost any discussion of resonance and resonant circuits (or for that matter, inductance) eventually gets to a rather sticky subject labelled in the earliest days of radio as quality factor but now known universally as Q.

As used in radio and electronics, Q is usually defined by other means. Some of the definitions put forth at various times and places include:

- The ratio of resistance to reactance in a coil.
- The ratio of capacitive reactance in a resonant circuit to the load resistance.
- The impedance multiplication factor, and others even more confusingly worded.

All, however, come out in the end to be identical to the definitions cited above: The Q of a resonator is the ratio of the energy stored per cycle to the energy lost per cycle.

In a resonator, high Q is desirable. Q is a measure of this energy loss. The less energy lost, the greater the Q of the circuit.

Not so obvious (and rather difficult to prove without going into mathematics) are some of the other effects of Q. A resonant circuit is never completely selective; frequencies which are near resonance but not precisely equal to the resonant frequency pass through also!

An Interesting Fraction

The greater the Q, the narrower the band of frequencies which can affect the resonator. Specifically, the so-called half-power bandwidth (see Fig. 3-5) of a resonator (that band in which signals are passed with half or more of the power possessed by signals at the exact resonant frequency) is expressible by the fraction Fo/Q, where Fo is the resonant frequency and Q is the circuit Q. Thus a 455 kHz resonant circuit with a Q of 100 will have a half-power bandwidth of 455/100 kHz, or 4.55 kHz. This relation is an approximation valid only for single-tuned circuits; more complex circuits are beyond this basic discussion.

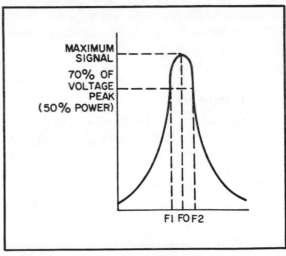

Fig. 3-5. Bandwidth characteristic of a typical tuned circuit shows the peak or maximum signal amplitude and the 70% voltage peak (50% power) points. This is the characteristic that determines overall selectivity.

The Q of Quartz Crystals

When we talk of the Q of conventional resonant circuits composed of coils and capacitors, a figure of 100 is usually taken as denoting very good performance and Q values above 300 are generally considered to be very rare.

The Q of a quartz crystal, however, is much higher. Values from 25,000 to 50,000 are not unheard of.

The extremely high Q makes the crystal a much more selective resonator than can be achieved with L-C circuitry. At 455 kHz, for example, the bandwidth will be between 10 and 20 hertz (cycles per second) unless measures are taken to reduce Q. Even in practice (which almost never agrees with theory), 50-hertz bandwidths are common with 455-kHz crystal filters.

So far as external circuitry is concerned, the crystal appears to be exactly the same as an L-C resonant circuit except for its phenomenal Q value. See Fig. 3-6.

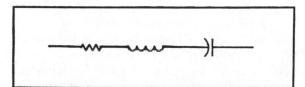

Fig. 3-6. Diagram is a typical equivalent circuit for a crystal. As resistance is lowered to near zero, crystal efficiency increases. In use, the crystal holder and external circuit add some capacitance across the entire circuit.

At series resonance, the crystal has very low impedance. You may hear this effect referred to as a zero of the crystal. At parallel resonance, impedance is very high; this is sometimes called a pole. Figure 3-7 shows a plot of pole and zero for a typical crystal. The special kind of crystal filter known as a half-lattice circuit matches the pole of one crystal against the zero of another, to produce a passband capable of splitting one sideband from a radio signal. Such filters are widely used in ham, commercial and, to a lesser extent, in CB transmitters.

When a crystal is used to control the frequency of a radio signal or provide a source of accurate timing signals, either the pole or the zero may be used. Circuits making use of the pole allow more simple adjustment of exact frequency, while those making use of the zero often feature parts economy. Later we'll examine several of each type.

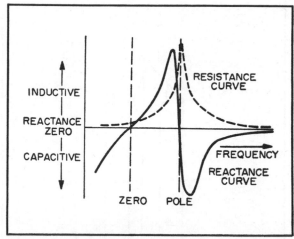

Fig. 3-7. Some characteristics of a quartz crystal. When slightly off resonant frequency (at the pole) a crystal exhibits inductive or capacitive reactance—just like an LC circuit.

From Rock to Finished Crystal

To perform its control functions properly, a quartz crystal requires extensive processing. The raw quartz crystal must be sliced into plates of proper dimension, then ground to the precise size required. Each plate must be as close to precisely parallel, and as perfectly flat, as possible. The electrodes must be in proper contact with the polished plate; in many modern units, the electrodes are actually plated directly to the crystal surface, usually with gold.

The crystal plate is known as a blank when it is sliced from the raw crystal. The blank is cut at a precise angle with respect to the optical and electrical axes of the raw crystal, as shown in Fig. 3-8. Each has its own characteristics for use in specific applications. Some, notably the X- and Y-cuts, are of only historic interest. The Y-cut, one of the first types used, had a bad habit of jumping in frequency at critical temperatures. The X-cut did not jump, but still varied widely in frequency as temperature changed.

Today's crystals most frequently use the AT cut for frequencies between 500 kHz and about 6 MHz, and the BT cut for between 6 and 12 MHz. Above 12 MHz, most crystals are specially processed BT or AT cuts used in overtone modes. These cuts are important to crystal makers and not

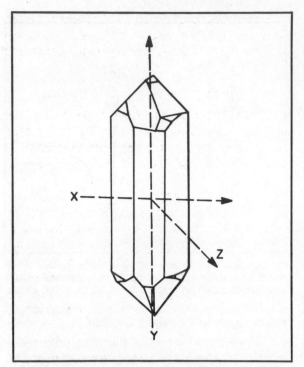

Fig. 3-8. A view of a mother crystal showing X, Y, and Z axes. Crystal is sliced into blanks, ground to frequency, polished and plated (on facing sides) to make permanent electrodes. All crystals are not made perfect by Mother Nature and must be examined optically before being sliced.

relevant to our layman's theory.

The blanks are cut only to approximate size. The plates are then polished to final size in optical "lapping" machines which preserve parallelism between critical surfaces. During the final stages of polishing, crystals are frequently tested against standard frequency sources to determine exact frequency of operation.

If electrodes are to be plated onto the crystal surfaces, frequency cannot be set precisely by grinding since the electrodes themselves load the crystal slightly and cause a slight decrease in operating frequencies. These crystals are ground just a trifle above their intended frequencies, and the thickness of the electrodes is varied by varying plating time to achieve precision.

Accuracy

The precision which can be attained in produc-

tion of quartz crystals is astounding. Accuracy of ± 0.001 percent is routine, and 10-times-better accuracy is not difficult. In absolute figures, this means an error of one cycle per megahertz. In another frame of reference, a clock with the same accuracy would require more than 11 days to gain or lose a single second.

However, such accuracy can be achieved only when certain precautions are taken. For instance, the frequency of a crystal depends upon the circuit in which it is used as well as upon its manufacture. For an accuracy of ± 0.005% or greater, the crystal must be ground for a single specific oscillator. If ± 0.001% (or better) circuit accuracy is required, it must be tested in that circuit only. Thus, CB transmitters are on the narrow edge of being critical. This is why all operating manuals include a caution to use only crystals made specifically for that transmitter.

When one-part-per-million accuracy is required, not only must the crystal be ground for a single specific oscillator, but most often the oscillator circuit must then be adjusted for best operation with the crystal; this round-robin adjustment must be kept up until required accuracy is achieved. Even then, crystal aging may make readjustment necessary for the first 12 to 18 months.

Frequency Variation—Causes and Cures

Possible variations in frequency stem from three major causes, while cures depend entirely upon the application.

The most obvious cause of frequency variation is temperature. Like anything else, the crystal will change in size when heated and the frequency is determined by size. Certain cuts show less change with temperature than do others, but all have at least some change.

For most noncommercial applications, the heat-resistant cuts do well enough. For stringent broadcast station and critical time-signal requirements, the crystal may be enclosed in a small thermostatically-regulated oven. This assures that the steady temperature will cure one cause of frequency change.

The second well-known cause for variation of

frequency is external capacitance. Some capacitance is always present because the crystal electrodes form the plates of a capacitor where the crystal itself is the dielectric. Most crystals intended for amateur use are designed to accommodate an external capacitance of 32 pF, so if external capacitance is greater than this, the marked frequency may not be correct. Crystals for commercial applications are ground to capacitance specifications for the specific equipment in which they are to be used. CB crystals also are ground for specific equipment, although many transceivers employ the 32 pF standard.

Trim a Frequency

When utmost precision is required, a small variable capacitor may be connected in parallel with the crystal and adjusted to change frequency slightly. The greater the capacitance, the lower the frequency. Changes of up to 10 kHz may be accomplished by this means, although oscillation may cease when excessive changes are attempted.

Like temperature-caused variations, frequency variations due to capacitance may be useful in special cases. Hams operating in the VHF regions obtain frequency modulation by varying load capacitance applied to the crystal in their transmitters.

The third cause for variation of frequency is a change in operating conditions in the associated circuit. This cause is more important with vacuum-tube circuits than with semiconductor equipment. As a rule, operating voltages for any vacuum-tube oscillator providing critical signals should be regulated to prevent change.

Again, this cause can be used to provide FM by deliberately varying voltages.

Crystal Aging

A final cause of frequency variation, small enough to be negligible in all except the most hypersensitive applications, is crystal aging. When a crystal is first processed, microscopic bits of debris remain embedded in its structure. These bits are displaced during the first 12 months or so of use,

but during that time the crystal frequency changes by a few parts per million. Extreme accuracy applications must take this change into account. For most uses, though, it may be ignored.

Using Quartz Crystals

After all the discussion of crystal theory, it's time to examine some typical circuits. While dozens of special crystal circuits have been developed for special applications, a sampling will suffice for discussion. Figure 3-9 shows four typical vacuum tube crystal oscillator circuits.

The simplest of these is the Pierce circuit, Fig. 3-9A. While at first glance this circuit appears to employ the crystal's zero to feed back energy from plate to grid, the pole is actually used through a mathematically-complex analysis. This circuit has one unique advantage: it contains no tuned elements and, therefore, can be used at any frequency for which a crystal is available. This makes it an excellent low-cost test signal source. The major disadvantage is that excessive current may be driven through the crystal if dc plate voltage rises above 90 or so.

The Miller oscillator (Fig. 3-9B) is almost as simple to construct and operate as is the Pierce and has an additional advantage of operation with overtone crystals. This is the circuit recommended by International Crystal Mfg. Co. for use with their overtone crystals. The capacitor shown between plate and grid is usually composed of grid-plate capacitance alone. The pole is used here also, energy feeds back through the grid-plate capacitance, and the pole selects only the parallel-resonant frequency (shorting the rest to ground).

ECO

The electron-coupled Pierce oscillator (Fig. 3-9C) is similar to the basic Pierce. The tuned circuit in the plate offers the possibility of emphasizing a harmonic—an rf choke may be used instead if freedom from tuning is desired and fundamental-frequency operation will suffice.

GPO

One of the most popular oscillators of all time

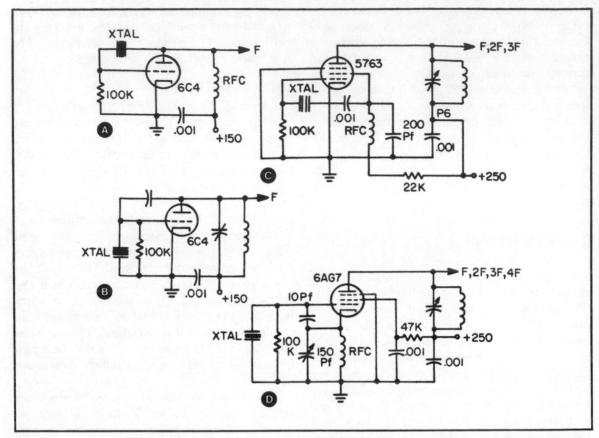

Fig. 3-9. The simplest crystal oscillator circuit (A) has no tuned circuits. To change frequency it is only necessary to change crystals, although a small variable capacitor across the crystal will cause some small frequency change. Miller oscillator (B) is nearly as simple as Pierce type shown in (A). Tuned circuit can pick out fundamental frequency or harmonics. Pierce electron-coupled oscillator (C) derives its feedback from the screen circuit, eliminating need for a buffer amplifier in most cases. Colpitts oscillator (D) gets its feedback from cathode circuit. Variable capacitor in the grid-cathode circuit can trim frequency.

is the Colpitts Crystal oscillator of Fig. 3-9D, sometimes known as the grid-plate oscillator. The feedback arrangement here consists of the two capacitors in the grid circuit; feedback is adjusted by means of the 150 pF variable capacitor (the greater the capacitance, the less the feedback) until reliable oscillation is obtained. Like the other three oscillators, this circuit employs the crystal pole frequency.

Since all four of these oscillator circuits utilize the pole for frequency control, exact frequency adjustment capability may be obtained by connecting a 3-30 pF trimmer capacitor in parallel with the crystal.

Crystal oscillators may, of course, be built with transistors, too. Two typical circuits are shown in Fig. 3-10. Feedback mechanisms differ somewhat because of the basic differences between tubes and transistors. In general, transistorized oscillators are more stable.

As a Clock

To use a crystal as the timing element of a clock, an oscillator identical to those shown in Figs. 3-9 and 3-10 is the starting point. Crystal frequency is chosen at a low, easily-checked value such as 100 kHz. This frequency is then divided and redivided

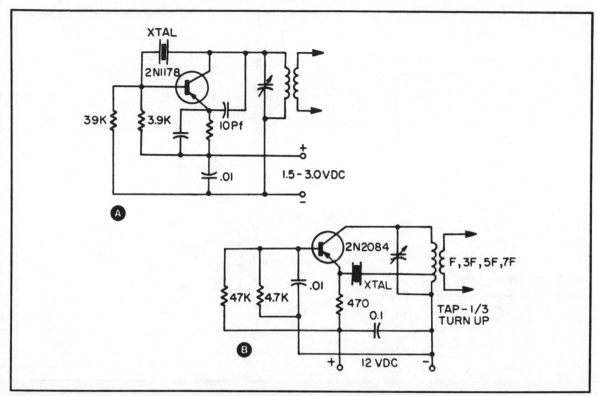

Fig. 3-10. Fundamental frequency transistorized oscillator (A) is quite similar to that in Fig. 3-9A. One difference is that tuned circuit in output replaces RFC unit. The overtone (harmonic) circuit (B) uses crystal for odd harmonic feedback. Either circuit can be used for fundamental frequency operation—just tune.

by synchronized multivibrators to produce one-cycle-per-second pulses. These may then be counted by computer counting circuits.

In addition to being used as oscillators and timing elements, crystals find wide application in filters. Figure 3-11 shows some typical crystal-filter circuits.

The single-crystal filter circuit shown in Fig. 3-11A provides spectacularly narrow reception. When the notch control is set to precisely balance out the crystal stray capacitance, the resonance curve of the filter is almost perfectly symmetrical. When the notch control is offset to one side or the other, a notch of almost infinite rejection appears in the curve (the pole). The width control varies effective Q of the filter.

More popular for general usage today is the band-pass filter, shown in Figs. 3-11B and 3-11C. Both circuits make use of matched crystals (X1

and X2)—the pole of one must match the zero of the other for proper results. When this condition is met, the reactances of the two crystals cancel over the passband. The passband is roughly equal to the pole-zero spacing.

While the two circuits shown are virtually identical in operation, the transformer-coupled circuit of Fig. 3-11C is easiest for home construction. The only critical component is the transformer. It should be tightly coupled, with both halves of the secondary absolutely balanced. This is done by winding a trifilar layer of wire (wind three wires at the same time); the center wire becomes the primary winding and the remaining two wires become the secondary. The left end of one secondary half connects to the right end of the other, and this junction forms the center tap. The remaining two ends connect to the crystals. If you have sufficient patience to wind on it, a toroid form is recommended.

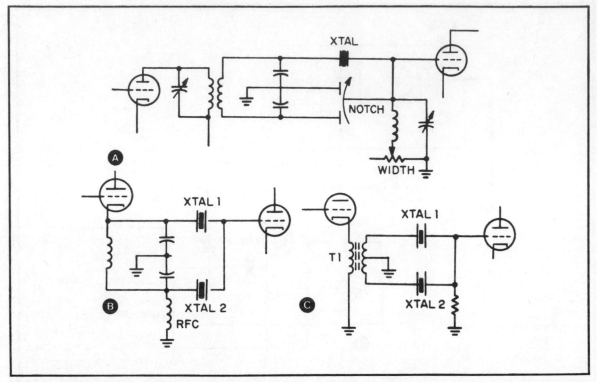

Fig. 3-11. Crystal filter used in the i-f amplifier of a receiver sharpens the selectivity. Circuit in A uses special variable capacitor to adjust notch frequency. Potentiometer varies width (selectivity) of notch. Adding resistance lowers Q of crystal circuit which increases bandwidth. Two-crystal circuits (B, C) are more expensive since specially matched pairs are required. The mechanical filter gives the crystal-type circuit a lot of competition where fixed bandwidth is wanted. Trifilar-wound transformer T1 (C) can be wound by experimenters of home-brew receivers.

ONE-TUBE REGENERATIVE RECEIVER

Many experimenters new to electronics have never worked with tubes. This is unfortunate because while transistors don't require large amounts of power, and ICs can cram huge circuits into dust grains, the vacuum tube has an aesthetic advantage over solid state components. In addition, the tube's elements are physically large and the principles involved are simpler and easier to understand. So, here is a one-tube broadcast band regenerative receiver project. The finished radio is much superior to the beginner's crystal set, yet is not much more difficult to build. It only requires a modest antenna (20 feet or so) and a good ground to perform well. Incidentally, the circuit is a real oldtimer. Lee De Forest and E. H. Armstrong simultaneously discovered it around 1912, and were involved in a long patent dispute over it.

Theory

For those of you who don't remember those two gentlemen, I'm going to give a bit of theory about vacuum tubes and this particular radio. I apologize to those of you who are well versed on these subjects, and beg your indulgence.

The simplest tube is a diode (di- two, ode- element), which is a hairpin of tungsten wire surrounded by a cylindrical metal tube. Both are sealed in a glass bulb from which all the air has been pumped. Connecting a battery across the filament wire causes it to glow red hot (much like an ordinary incandescent lamp) and the electrons in the wire are given enough energy to boil off into the vacuum.

If a battery's plus terminal is connected to the metal cylinder (the plate) and its minus terminal is connected to the filament, a current of these elec-

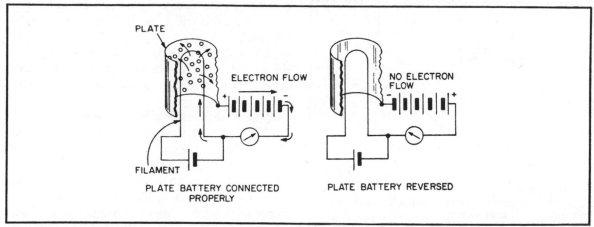

Fig. 3-12. The diode is the simplest form of vacuum tube. It is made up of a filament wire surrounded by a cylindrical metal tube. Its origins date to before World War I.

trons (electrons have a negative charge) will flow through this plate circuit. No current, however, will flow if the plate battery is connected backwards, because electrons cannot leave the plate's surface (see Fig. 3-12). Although this diode will function as a rectifier (one-way valve) or as a rudimentary radio detector, it is good for little else.

Around 1906, Lee De Forest changed this by adding a small twist of wire in between the filament and the plate. This grid can be used to control a large power (in the plate circuit) with a small power (in the grid circuit). Here's how: putting a negative voltage on the grid diminishes the plate current, because electrons traveling from filament to plate are repelled by the electrons sitting on the grid. Remember, like charges repel; see Fig. 3-13.

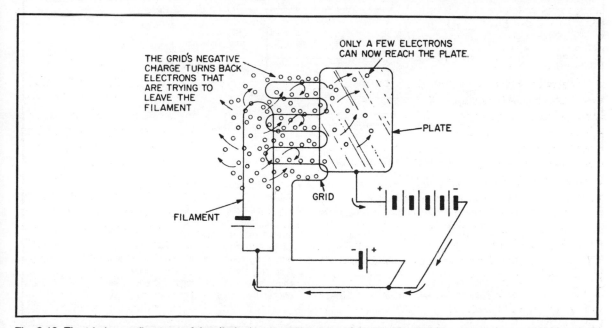

Fig. 3-13. The triode, a refinement of the diode, has a grid between the plate and filament. This made a rectifying tube into a tube with amplifying capabilities.

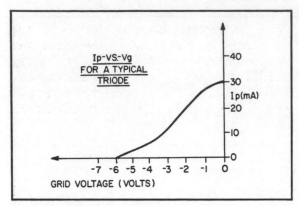

Fig. 3-14. This graph shows the relationship between the grid voltage and plate current.

There's a smooth relationship; many electrons on the grid cause a very weak plate current, or Ip, and only a few sitting there allow a stronger plate current. Figure 3-14 is a graph of just such a relationship. In this case, no plate current flows when the grid voltage is negative seven volts. Of course, the tube (a triode) is still a rectifier, but now it amplifies, too!

Okay, first diode, then triode, now radio: our simple receiver consists of a tuner, a radio frequency (or rf) amplifier, a detector, and an audio amp.

Our versatile tube is both detector and amplifier. The tuner is the parallel combination of L2 and C1. Here's the scheme: many different rf signals exist at the antenna input (see Fig. 3-15), and are coupled to L2 through the antenna coil, L1. The LC tuner (L2 and C1) looks like a short circuit for all frequencies but one, and this one is sent through C2 and R1 to the grid of V1. They make V1 act like a detector by fixing it so two signals appear: the rapidly varying rf signal (1 MHz or so) and a slowly changing audio signal (200 to 5000 cycles or so). Pretending for a moment that R2 is fully shorting L3, we see electrons flowing from ground,

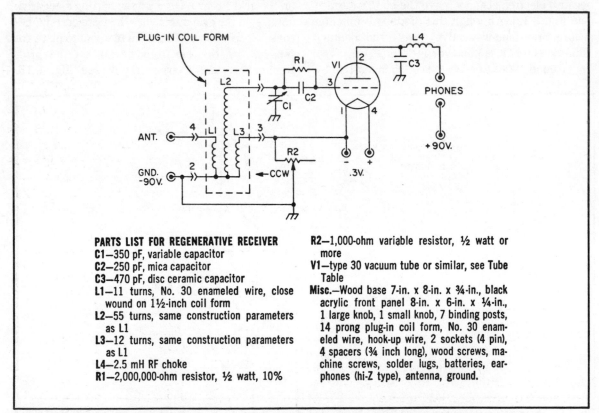

PARTS LIST FOR REGENERATIVE RECEIVER
C1—350 pF, variable capacitor
C2—250 pF, mica capacitor
C3—470 pF, disc ceramic capacitor
L1—11 turns, No. 30 enameled wire, close wound on 1½-inch coil form
L2—55 turns, same construction parameters as L1
L3—12 turns, same construction parameters as L1
L4—2.5 mH RF choke
R1—2,000,000-ohm resistor, ½ watt, 10%

R2—1,000-ohm variable resistor, ½ watt or more
V1—type 30 vacuum tube or similar, see Tube Table
Misc.—Wood base 7-in. x 8-in. x ¾-in., black acrylic front panel 8-in. x 6-in. x ¼-in., 1 large knob, 1 small knob, 7 binding posts, 14 prong plug-in coil form, No. 30 enameled wire, hook-up wire, 2 sockets (4 pin), 4 spacers (¾ inch long), wood screws, machine screws, solder lugs, batteries, earphones (hi-Z type), antenna, ground.

Fig. 3-15. The schematic diagram shows how the coil feeds the selected frequency from antenna to amplifier.

through V1, where they pick up the two signals in an amplified form, and then flow either through C3 to ground or through L4, the earphones, the 90 volt plate battery (which supplies all the electrons' energy) and thence to ground. Note, however, that the rf signal goes through C3 because that capacitor is too small to pass the low audio frequencies, and conversely the audio travels through L4 (an rf choke), which presents an open circuit to the high radio frequencies. Thus an amplified version of the audio that was once impressed on the rf carrier wave appears in the earphones.

So, what's L3 for? Well, I wasn't telling the whole truth when I said our LC tuner selected only one frequency. It tuned in on mostly one frequency, but some others sneaked in, too. The width of this tuning curve (see Fig. 3-16) determines the selectivity, or station selection ability of our radio. This bandwidth depends on the Q, or quality factor, of the LC combination. A high-Q circuit has thick wires, no energy losses, and consequently a sharp tuning curve. Unfortunately, the Q of our L2, C1 combination is low, and that's why a small amount of rf energy in the plate circuit has to be fed (via L3) back into the grid circuit to account for energy losses there.

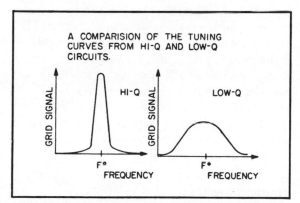

Fig. 3-16. The width of the tuning curve is the determining factor in set's selectivity.

Feeding more and more energy back (turn R2 clockwise) forces the Q sky high, along with the slectivity. The rf amplification increases, too. When we feed more energy into the tuner than is lost, the tube starts oscillating, or producing its own rf sig-

nal, at the frequency the tuner is set for. This is undesirable, because it distorts the signals and reduces the set's gain. Obviously, the best setting for R2 is where the tube almost oscillates (see Fig. 3-17). Now that some of the fundamentals are clear, we discuss next building a real live regenerative receiver.

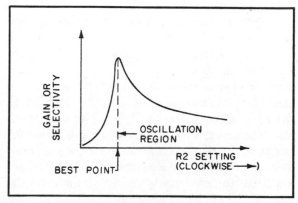

Fig. 3-17. Too much oscillation is undesirable; R2 must be set to give the minimum.

Finding the Parts

Unfortunately, few electronics shops stock battery tubes (some don't stock any tubes at all!) so here are some hints: a type 30 tube (called for in the parts list) is not necessary. Any of the tubes in Table 3-1 could be used, but just be sure to use the right filament voltage and the right pin diagrams when you wire. Obviously you will need an appropriate socket, and you may have to up the plate voltage on some tubes to obtain sufficient regener-

Table 3-1. Triode Type Tubes.

Remarks	Tube type	Filament Voltage
4 pin	199, 299	3 V
4 pin	201-A, 301-A	5 V
4 pin	30	3 V
5 pin	227, 327	2.5 V AC
8 pin octal	1LH4	1.5 V
8 pin octal	1G4GT	1.5 V
8 pin octal	1H4GT	1.5 V
8 pin octal	6C5	6.3 V AC
8 pin octal	1/2 6SN7	6.3 V AC
8 pin octal	6J5	6.3 V AC

ation. Those tubes marked ac can use alternating current for their filaments because the actual electron emitter is a metal sleeve (called a cathode) insulated from the filament. Without it, hum would be too loud. These types will, of course, use dc as well, but to save the batteries, you would use a transformer to run the filament, and connect the cathode to top of L3 and R2.

Enough about tubes. Plug in coil forms are hard to find (I don't know if they're still made) but they can be had if you scrounge enough. See Fig. 3-18. More on that later. You can salvage the coil wire from an old power transformer by pulling the laminations apart and unwinding the core—number 30 wire is about sewing thread size. The wire, along with the tuning capacitor, earphones, dials and tube sockets, came from my junk box, but any of these items could be purchased commercially (note: don't try to use the low impedance hi-fi earphones or the crystal tape, either. These won't work). Any wood will do for the base (pine is easy to work with) and the front panel doesn't have to be fancy black plastic: plywood, fiberboard, or metal would all work. My panel, however, was free, courtesy of the local plastic distributor (they even cut it to size!) and it only took a bit of abrasive paper to clean up the edges. The filament, or A battery, can be anything from number six dry cells to storage batteries to flashlight cells soldered together. The B, or plate battery, is a rather esoteric item, and while some stores still stock them, a substitute might be 9 volt transistor (yuch!) radio batteries soldered in series, or a myriad of worn out flashlight cells. Plate current (Ip) is only about 6 mA.

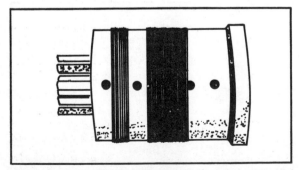

Fig. 3-18. Coil forms such as this one are becoming rare items, so you may have to substitute.

Construction

Now that all the parts are at hand, begin by cutting and finishing the wood base. A quick sanding and a coat of linseed oil or shellac will give it a glossy surface, but avoid paint, as paint often has metallic pigments that could short out connections. Then, mark and drill the front panel to fit your particular way of mounting R2, C1, and the binding posts for the earphones. Some capacitors have threaded holes on their bottoms, so you may have to fashion an L bracket to hold it to the front panel, or mount it from the base using spacers. Drill three holes 3/8-inch up from the bottom of the panel to fasten it to the base. In all cases, be sure to drill slowly and carefully to avoid splitting the plastic as the bit pops through. Drill pilot holes on the front of the base, and screw the front panel on. After mounting C1, R2, and the earphone connectors, mount the knobs and tube sockets. I mounted my sockets by passing a 1 1/4-inch long wood screw through each of the socket's holes, and slipping a 3/4-inch long spacer over each. Then I screwed the whole thing to the base about halfway between the front and the back, to allow room for wiring. At the back edge of the base, mount the binding posts or clips for the batteries, ground, and antenna. Once again, I mounted all the posts on a strip of plastic, and used the wood screw—spacer technique. Then wire according to the schematic. You probably won't need any tie points, because you can always solder an extra length of wire to a too-short lead, and slip spaghetti over the connection.

Do try to keep the wire between V1's grid and the C2, R1 combination very short. It tends to pick up noise. Finally, mark each binding post with its proper function.

Winding the Coil

As I said before, plug-in coil forms are becoming scarce, so if you can't get one (try to, because it makes the coil winding easier), you can substitute many things in its place. Tissue rollers, wood dowels, plastic tubing, or anything non-metallic will work, and it doesn't have to be exactly 1 1/2-inch in diameter if you're willing to experiment some. If the form is too narrow, you'll have to wind more turns than I've indicated, and if it's wider, less wire will be needed. If you're not sure how much to wind onto L2 (L1 and L3 aren't too critical), wind on extra, because it's easier to remove turns than to add them.

Start by marking and drilling the form as I've indicated (see Fig. 3-19), and proceed by winding the required number of turns. Scrape (using fine sandpaper) the insulation off the end of your wire, run it through the bottom-most hole you drilled on the form, and insert and solder it into pin 4. Hint: if your form is plastic, hold the pin in the middle with a pair of pliers to prevent the heat from softening the plastic. Wind 11 turns, clip the wire (leaving enough to make the other connection) and insert it into pin 2, via the hole in the form's side. Don't solder it, but just cut off the wire, leaving about 1/4 inch protruding from the pin. Pull that same end back out of the form so you can scrape 1/2-inch of insulation off, and re-insert it into pin 2. Still don't solder, but just fold that extra wire over the edge of the pin, to keep the coil from unwinding. Repeat this process for the remaining coils and pins, soldering in pins three and one, and folding two more wires over the edge of pin two. Eventually, you will have three bare wires sticking out of pin two. That's when you can solder them all in place, at once. Finally, add a bit of coil dope to the whole thing to

keep it from loosening up and unwinding (clear nail polish works well). Plug the coil into place, and the tube, too, while you're at it.

For those of you who are using a substitute coil form, just run the ends of the windings out of one end of the coil, and secure the coil to the base using L brackets or spacers.

Operation

Check the wiring against the schematic for errors. If all looks okay, attach only the filament battery. If you can see it, the tube's filament will glow orange red. If not, re-check the wiring. Don't connect the B battery if there's any chance that 90 volts will wind up across the filament—some of these battery tubes like the 99 are very fragile in this respect. Assuming all looks well, connect earphones, an antenna, and a ground. Finally, connect the B battery; doing this should cause a decided click in the earphones.

Turn the regeneration control (R2) clockwise until you hear a pop or click in the phones, and beyond that point will be a soft hissing or squealing. That means the set is oscillating. Back off on the regeneration control until the set pops back out of oscillation, and tune around until you hear a station. Alternately adjust C1 (for loudest volume) and R2 (for most regeneration without allowing oscillation). This is where a steady hand helps. If, for some reason, you can hear stations, but can't seem to get any regeneration, by turning R2 back and forth. If the signals are loudest when R2 is counterclockwise, you may have accidentally reversed the leads to L3, producing negative feedback, instead of positive. Try switching the leads.

Now is the time to see if your coil covers the broadcast band properly. Using a calibrated AM receiver set to the high end (1.6 MHz) of the band, make your regenerative radio oscillate, and tune C1 until its plates are mostly open; at some point you should hear a hiss or a whistle in the calibrated receiver as it is held nearby. Do the same for the low end (.55 MHz or so). The dials should roughly match, and if they don't, you will have to add or subtract wire from L2. Removing wire will shift your radio's range to higher frequencies, and

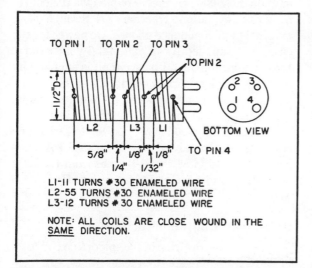

LI-II TURNS #30 ENAMELED WIRE
L2-55 TURNS #30 ENAMELED WIRE
L3-I2 TURNS #30 ENAMELED WIRE

NOTE: ALL COILS ARE CLOSE WOUND IN THE SAME DIRECTION.

Fig. 3-19. The coil winding guide shows the wiring configuration of the important coil.

adding wire will shift it downwards.

If you find that stations are too loud (which might be the case if you live nearby several transmitters) you can reduce the overload on the rf amp by inserting a small (10-75 pF) capacitor in series with the antenna lead, at the receiver. Choose a value that cuts out enough signal: the larger the capacitor, the more signal gets through.

Finally, always be super-careful when installing antennas. Stay away from power lines and avoid high dives off ladders or out of windows. B batteries can give you a small sting, but 90 volts probably couldn't injure you if you're in good shape. However, that sting could surprise you enough to make you drop your prized audion to the floor, smashing it to bits. Exercise caution.

Warnings aside, this project has many open ends that beg for experimentation: filament current might be varied with a low value (10-20 ohms) rheostat to provide volume control. The antenna coupling could be varied with a 150 pF variable capacitor in series with the antenna lead. Many different triodes are usable, or even tetrodes (double grid tubes) can be used. The coil may be re-wound for other bands, although the value of C1 might have to be lowered. Regeneration can be accomplished by varying C3 and eliminating R2, or even by physically rotating L3 with respect to L2. Try considering what negative feedback does to any amplifier.

A good book to help the experimenter is the ARRL's *The Radio Amateur's Handbook*, which has tips on safety, construction, theory, and it even has a complete index of tube types and pin diagrams for all your junk box tubes. Even if you are somewhat of an advanced hobbyist, you can still delight in an antique technology as you listen to the radio by the glow of your venerable vacuum tube.

SPIDERWEB RECEIVER

In the old days of radio, back when grandpa was building his first one tube radio, the spiderweb coil was the "cat's pajamas." This type of tuning coil was very popular with the home-constructors, and with good reason; the spiderweb coil is a high Q type, wound with interleaved turns for minimum residual capacity. Many of the old timers made long

distance reception commonplace with this type of tuning coil in their radios.

The spiderweb coil is a type of coil in which the wire is wound on a flat form so that the radius of successive turns increases from the center outward. You can experiment with this type of coil by building our receiver model which combines the old spiderweb coil with present day solid state circuitry. The receiver covers from 550 kHz to 14 MHz, with three plug-in spiderweb coils in a FET regenerative-detector circuit. A stage of audio is included with a pnp transistor directly coupled for good headphone volume.

The Spiderweb Coil Receiver Circuit

Signals from the antenna are coupled through J1 and C1 to L1 and the tuning capacitor C3. The bandspread capacitor C2 is used to fine-tune crowded SW bands and the resultant signals are fed via C4 to the gate-leak R2 and the gate of FET Q1. The rf signals are detected and amplified by Q1 and a portion of the rf is fed back into L1 from the source circuit of Q1. This feedback rf is detected and further amplified by Q1. The regen control R1 varies the amount of rf feedback to L1.

The detected audio signals in the drain circuit of Q1 are coupled through T1 to the AF Gain control R5 and to the audio amplifier circuit of Q1. The amplified signals are direct-coupled via the collector circuit of the pnp transistor Q1 through J4 to external high impedance phones. Dc power for the circuits is supplied by an external 6 volt battery. Bias current for the Q1 base circuit is supplied by the R6-R7 divider circuit, and R8-C7 acts as the interstage decoupling network to minimize audio feedback between the stages via the dc power bus.

Three plug in coils are used for L1, each one covering a different band of frequencies. L1 A tunes from 7 MHz to 14 MHz, L1 B tunes from 1.7 MHz to 5 MHz, and L1 C tunes from .55 MHz to 1.6 MHz.

Spiderweb Coil Construction

Look at the drawing of the spiderweb coil form in Fig. 3-20. There are seventeen "vanes," 7/8-inch long and approximately 1/4-inch wide, positioned

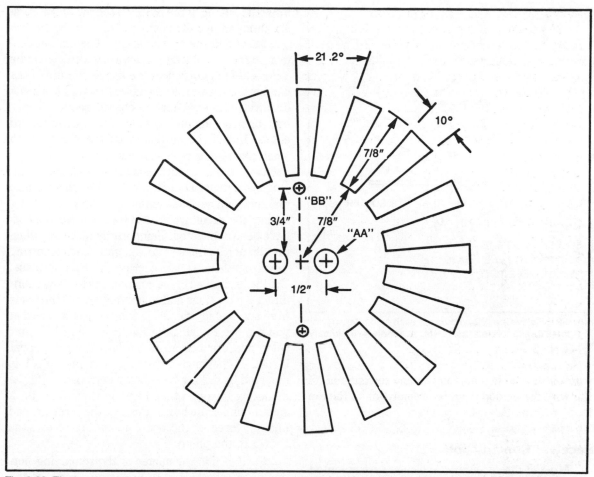

Fig. 3-20. The best material for the coil is the plastic used for making printed circuit boards (approx. 1/16-in. thick). There are 17 vanes, each about 7/8 inches long and about 1/4-in. wide. Trace this diagram with thin tissue paper then glue the paper to three pieces of plastic sheet that have been temporarily glued together. Then cut them with a jig saw and pry apart.

around the perimeter of a 1 1/2-inch disc. A good quality plastic should be used for the coil form; the coil forms shown in the receiver model photo are made from the type of plastic sheet used for printed circuit boards (approx. 1/16-inch thick).

The easiest way to start construction of the coil forms, is to trace the outline of the spiderweb coil form drawing and temporarily cement the tracing onto a sheet of plastic. Then cut out the coil form with a hack saw. If desired, three sheets of plastic can be temporarily cemented together with rubber cement and the coil forms for all three bands can be cut out at the same time. After cutting out the

forms, carefully pry apart the spiderweb coils.

Brass eyelets (available at notions counters in department stores) are soldered to lugs and P2-P3 as shown in Fig. 3-21. Carefully drill holes to fit the eyelets, positioned 1/2-inch apart, for each of the three spiderweb coil forms, and mount the phono plugs (P2-P3).

Refer to Table 3-2 and wind the coils with the turns indicated for each band. Start winding on the inside of each coil form and wind to the outside of the form. Allow enough wire at each end of the coil to solder to P3A-B as shown in the schematic in Fig. 3-22. After winding the coil, make the taps as indi-

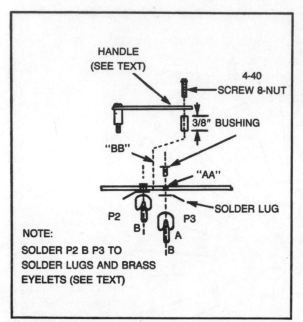

HANDLE
(SEE TEXT)

4-40
SCREW 8-NUT

3/8" BUSHING

"BB"

"AA"

SOLDER LUG

P2   P3

NOTE:

SOLDER P2 B P3 TO
SOLDER LUGS AND BRASS
EYELETS (SEE TEXT)

Fig. 3-21. Solder the phono plugs to each spiderweb by using small brass eyelets as rivets. A handle will simplify plugging-in.

cated in the table; carefully scrape the enamel off the wire for a good soldered connection to the tap leads to P2A-B.

Receiver Construction

Most of the receiver components are mounted on a 3- by 4 1/2-inch perfboard section installed on a cut-out portion of a 5- by 7- by 2-inch aluminum chassis. As shown in Fig. 3-22, the perfboard is installed on one half of the top of the chassis to leave enough room for the plug-in spiderweb coils. The tuning capacitor C3 and the bandspread capacitor C2 are mounted on a 5- by 7-inch section of copper-clad printed circuit board used as the front panel. A similar section of sheet aluminum would also be suitable for the front panel. The panel is held by the mounting nuts of the regen control R1, audio gain (volume) control R5, and the phone jack J4 that are mounted in holes drilled through the front of the chassis and the lower half of the panel.

Begin construction of the receiver by cutting the perfboard section to size and then temporarily positioning it upon the top of the chassis. Lightly

draw the outline of the board on the top of the chassis, then remove the board and lay out the chassis cut-out within the board outline. The cut-out section on the model shown is approximately 2 1/2 by 4-inches. Drill holes near the inside corners of the cut-out section and use the holes to start a hack saw or jewelers saw. After the chassis section is cut-out, drill six mounting holes for the perfboard edges. Install the perfboard on the chassis with small machine screws and nuts.

Locate and install the board components with perfboard clips. Do not install Q1 at this time to minimize any possible damage to the FET; solder Q1 into the circuit when all of the other components have been connected. Temporarily place an alligator clip across the source and gate leads (shorting them together) while soldering the FET in place. Cut the leads of all of the components to allow short, direct connections and to prevent any of the leads from accidentally coming in contact. Make sure that you remove the alligator clip from the FET after soldering. For best results follow the component layout of the model shown in the photo. T1 is mounted by drilling holes in the perfboard to fit the mounting tabs and then bending them over for a snug fit under the board. Position the three ground lugs on three of the board mounting screws, as shown in the photo.

Cut holes in the center of the remaining portion of the chassis top to fit J2 and J3. Space the two jacks to fit the plugs P2 and P3 mounted on the plug-in spiderweb coils. A dual jack was used

Table 3-2. Spiderweb Coil Winding Table.

	Wire Size	Total Turns	Ant Tap (P2A)	"S" Tap (P2B)
Band A 7 MHz to 14 MHz	#18 Enam.	4	1/2-Turn from end	1-turn from start
Band B 1.7 MHz to 5 MHz	#24 Enam.	17	1 1/2-turns from end	2-turns from start
Band C .55 MHz to 1.6 MHz	#28 Enam.	52	10-turns from end	1-turn from start

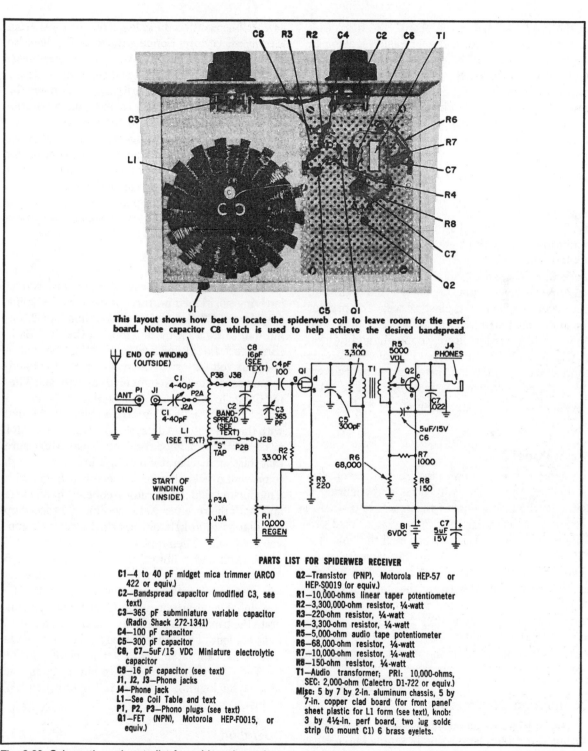

This layout shows how best to locate the spiderweb coil to leave room for the perf-board. Note capacitor C8 which is used to help achieve the desired bandspread.

PARTS LIST FOR SPIDERWEB RECEIVER

C1—4 to 40 pF midget mica trimmer (ARCO 422 or equiv.)

C2—Bandspread capacitor (modified C3, see text)

C3—365 pF subminiature variable capacitor (Radio Shack 272-1341)

C4—100 pF capacitor

C5—300 pF capacitor

C6, C7—5uF/15 VDC Miniature electrolytic capacitor

C8—16 pF capacitor (see text)

J1, J2, J3—Phone jacks

J4—Phone jack

L1—See Coil Table and text

P1, P2, P3—Phono plugs (see text)

Q1—FET (NPN), Motorola HEP-F0015, or equiv.)

Q2—Transistor (PNP), Motorola HEP-57 or HEP-S0019 (or equiv.)

R1—10,000-ohms linear taper potentiometer

R2—3,300,000-ohm resistor, ¼-watt

R3—220-ohm resistor, ¼-watt

R4—3,300-ohm resistor, ¼-watt

R5—5,000-ohm audio tape potentiometer

R6—68,000-ohm resistor, ¼-watt

R7—10,000-ohm resistor, ¼-watt

R8—150-ohm resistor, ¼-watt

T1—Audio transformer; PRI: 10,000-ohms, SEC: 2,000-ohm (Calectro D1-722 or equiv.)

Misc: 5 by 7 by 2-in. aluminum chassis, 5 by 7-in. copper clad board (for front panel' sheet plastic for L1 form (see text), knob: 3 by 4½-in. perf board, two lug solder strip (to mount C1) 6 brass eyelets.

Fig. 3-22. Schematic and parts list for spiderweb receiver.

on the model shown in the photo. But, it may be easier to use separate jacks for easier spacing in the front and rear of the chassis to fit the components to be installed; R1, R5 and J4 on the front and J1, C1 and the rubber grommet for the dc power leads on the rear chassis. C1 is mounted on a two lug terminal strip with a small access hole drilled in the chassis to allow adjustment.

Bandspread Capacitor Construction

The bandspread capacitor C2 is a modified tuning capacitor that originally had a 365-mmf capacity. The model in the photo utilizes a Radio Shack miniature type with plastic dielectric. In this particular make of capacitor, the stator blades are made from thin sheet metal and are fastened with only one screw and nut. Carefully remove the end nut (after removing the plastic cover) and pry out the stator blades one by one with small pliers until only one blade is left. Replace the nut and tighten it. Check with an ohmmeter to see if the blade is shorted to the rotor blade assembly. If so, remove the nut and readjust the stator blade. The rotor blades should be able to rotate freely as the shaft is turned.

Front Panel

Mount the panel on to the front of the chassis by drilling the appropriate holes and securing it with the mounting nuts of the panel controls. After the panel is mounted with the copper clad surface facing outward, locate and drill the holes for C2 and C3. Install the two variable capacitors and then connect them to the circuit board with short leads. C8 is mounted between the stator of C2 and the stator of C3. The exact value of C8 is best determined by experiment after the receiver is operational for the desired bandspread. A good starting value is 16 mmf (as on the model shown in the photo).

Completing Construction

Complete the construction of the receiver by wiring the underchassis components. Make sure that the leads to J2 and J3 are as short and direct

as possible; position these leads up and away from the chassis bottom. Connect the dc power leads to the circuit and mark them with the proper polarity. Or, a red lead can be used for positive and a black lead for negative polarity. Make a knot in the power leads before putting them through the rubber grommet on the rear of the chassis.

Install knobs on the shafts of the front panel controls. If necessary, cut shafts of the controls for a uniform appearance. Cement a 1-in. length of Number 18 wire on the rear of the C3 knob. Or, a shaped section of clear plastic with a black line drawn down the center can also be used for a pointer.

Dial Calibration

The front panel dials are marked with rub-on lettering positioned on three concentric India-ink lines for the C3 dial, and one inked line for C2. Begin dial calibration by plugging in the "C" Band (Broadcast Band) coil and connecting earphones and a six volt battery to the receiver. Set the Bandspread capacitor C2 to minimize capacity and Tuning Capacitor C3 to maximum capacity. Connect a signal generator to J1 and then calibrate the dial with the generator. Adjust the AF Gain R5 and R1 as necessary for a good received signal. Make sure that the signal generator output is kept low enough to prevent overloading of the receiver. Begin with a modulated signal generator frequency of 550 kHz and mark the receiver dial accordingly. Proceed up the dial to 1600 kHz and mark the scale at convenient points. Then replace the "C" with the "B" plug-in coil and calibrate the scale from 1.7 to 5 MHz with the signal generator. Also, calibrate the "A" plug-in coil with a generator from 7 to 14 MHz. If a signal generator is not available, you can calibrate the bands with markings noted from received radio stations of known frequency. The Bandspread dial is not calibrated, but a set of points can be marked over the range of C2 to aid in tuning the dial, or for logging purposes in the crowded SW bands.

Operation

For best results a good antenna and ground are

required. Also high impedance earphones (2000 ohms or more) are needed. If a dc power supply is used in place of the 6 volt battery, make sure that the supply does not have any hum in the output as this will affect the receiver sensitivity. Tune C3 for a received station, while at the same time adjusting the Regen control R1 for a whistle. If the station is AM, back off R1 until the station is received clearly. If the received station is CW, adjust R1 for a convenient "beat note." Many strong side-band stations can also be received by experimentally tuning R1 and C2 for best reception. Adjust the AF Gain control for good earphone volume. Adjust C1 for best reception for each coil. The position of the "S" tap can be experimented with (moving up or down on L1) for best regeneration over the band. Also, try several FET's as Q1 for maximum sensitivity over the higher SW frequencies.

UNDERSTANDING SUPERHETS

Born out of necessity during World War I, the superheterodyne receiver circuit toppled all existing conventional receiver types on electronics' popularity chart. And, to this day, none of the "conventional" radios of that era have been able to recapture electronics' limelight. Stranger yet, every branch of electronics is still being swept along the path of Progress by a circuit that should have gone the way of the flivver and the flapper. From military and industrial to commercial and consumer—everybody who's ever seen a radio, and certainly a television set, has found himself staring face to face with a superheterodyne receiver. The fact is, you'd be hard-pressed to find any up-to-date radio—even the integrated-circuit-and-ceramic-transformer variety—that doesn't somehow utilize the superhet circuit.

After the First World War, the "All-American Five," as it was dubbed, took its place in living rooms and parlors from coast to coast. And it continues to be built today as its inventor generally conceived of it, way back when the circuit was made to track and help locate enemy aircraft spitting fire over French skies.

Narrow Squeeze

The superheterodyne found itself ruling the re-ceiver roost largely because it had a redeeming quality no other receiver of that vintage era could boast. Called *selectivity,* this hitherto unheard-of quality endowed the superhet with the ability to select the particular station a listener wanted to hear (and later see), and reject all others. Indeed, it was a revolutionary step forward in receiver design. But selectivity was hardly a quality needed back in grandfather's day. Why?

First, grandpop used to listen to signals sent by spark-gap transmitters. The primitive spark signals generated by those common-as-apple-pie transmitters were extraordinarily broad. It was like listening to the lightning crashes you can pick up as you tune across the dial of an AM radio during a thunderstorm. More important, though, there were fewer signals on the air. So selectivity wasn't too important.

The year 1922 saw the meteoric rise of radio for entertainment and communication. As hundreds of stations took to the air it became apparent that the primitive receiving gear capable only of broad-bandwidth reception couldn't even begin to handle the impending traffic jam beginning to build on the airwaves. And the problems of receiving only one station, without an electronic cacophony drowning it out, takes us back even further into electronics' primeval time.

Cat's Whiskers and TRF

Digging through to the bottom of the twentieth century, we uncover two electronic fossils: the cat's whisker crystal receiver, and the tuned radio frequency (TRF) receiver. These were popular predecessors of the superhet circuit.

The crystal set (see Fig. 3-23) had the least selectivity of either circuit, and what it did have was obtained mostly from one measly tuning circuit. Consisting of a coil and a homemade variable capacitor, these crude tuning devices could barely pick out a desired radio signal and, hopefully, reject all rf intruders trying to elbow their way into the listener's headphone on either side of the signal. The cat's whisker consisted of a strand of fine wire for gently probing, or tickling, the crystal's natural galena surface in order to locate its most

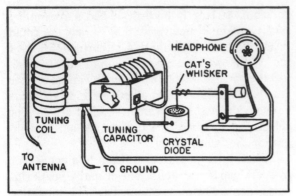

Fig. 3-23. Schematic representation of crystal radio shows how cat's whisker gently contacted diode surface in order to achieve demodulation of rf signal. Earliest semiconductor diodes made were miniature crystal diode/cat's whisker affairs encased in glass package.

sensitive point. Though the cat's whisker detector could extract audio signals from the amplitude-modulated radio frequency signal, the galena detector decreases the listener's chances of picking up stations other than the desired one.

Matters improved with the TRF receiver (see Fig. 3-24). It aimed for, and hit, sharper reception dead center, by adding more tuned circuits. This feat wasn't practical with crystal sets, because this circuit's inherent losses ran too high to gain any benefit from any additional coils.

The invention of the triode vacuum tube gave engineers the perfect amplifying device. Circuit losses could now be overcome with ease; the TRF

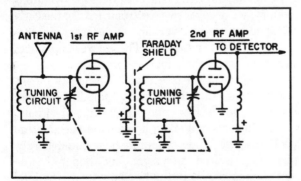

Fig. 3-24. Our schematic shows relatively advanced tuned radio frequency receiver. First TRFs had individually adjusted tuning capacitors; ganged units were still to be invented. By adjusting battery voltage twist ground, tuning circuit, radio gain's varied.

took over where the cat's whisker left off, dooming the crystal set to mantelpiece and museum.

Three or four amplified radio-frequency stages were customarily added prior to the TRF's detector, all the while adding to selectivity's cause. However, all wasn't perfect in TRFville.

The amount of noise introduced by the tubes limited the number of TRF stages. So the Silver-Masked Tenor's strains could still be heard with those of the Clicquot Club Eskimos—but not by his choice, or that of the listener.

Pitching the Low Curve

The public soon learned that these newfangled TRF receivers weren't exactly the living end. The TRFs, as a rule, failed to perform satisfactorily as frequencies inched higher into kilohertz land. Seems that as the frequency of the signal went up, the TRF's tuned circuit efficiency for that frequency dropped almost proportionately.

To demonstrate this, look at Fig. 3-25. The bell-shaped curve represents response of a tuned circuit selecting some low-frequency station. The circuit delivers good selectivity, and interference on a slightly higher frequency is rejected.

But examine what happens when a similar tuned circuit is operated on a higher frequency. Although the curve's proportions remain the same, it's actually responding to a much greater span of frequencies. Now it's possible for two closely spaced stations to enter the response curve and ultimately be heard in the speaker.

Since tuned circuits grow more selective as frequency is lowered, wouldn't it be to our technical advantage to receive only low-frequency signals? This idea probably occurred to Major Edwin Armstrong, because his invention, the superheterodyne circuit, does just that.

Superselectivity

By stepping signals down to a lower frequency than they were originally, the new circuit could deliver neat-as-a-pin selectivity on almost any band. The fact is, this development helped open the high-frequency bands, and by the 1930s virtually every receiver adopted the Major's superheterodyne idea.

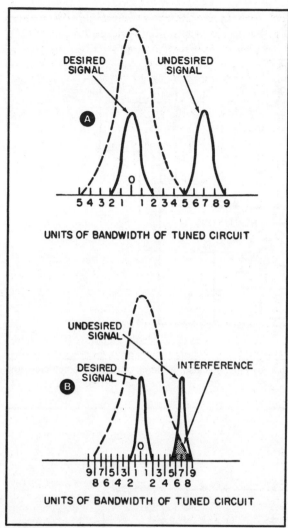

Fig. 3-25. Tuned-circuit bandwidth varies proportionally with frequency. Tuned circuit A, working at low frequency, rejects unwanted signal. Tuned circuit B, working at high frequency, can't completely reject undesired signal; interference results.

Major Blocks

You can get a good picture of the superhet in its natural habitat if you look at our block diagram (see Fig. 3-26). Though our schematic (see Fig. 3-27) shows a tubed receiver, all equivalent stages tend to do the same job regardless of whether the receiver is transistor or tube. (See Fig. 3-28.) Now that you know what the superhet does and how it looks, let's take a peek at how it works.

For sake of illustration, assume a signal of 1010 kHz in the standard BC band enters the antenna, and from there is sent down the line to the mixer. But what, you ask, is mixed?

Our frequency mish-mash consists of the different frequencies made up of the desired station on 1010 kHz, and a second signal generated internally by the local oscillator. This oscillator perks at a frequency of 1465 kHz, for reasons which you'll understand in a moment.

True to its name, our mixer combines both signals from antenna and oscillator. And from these two frequencies, it delivers yet another frequency that is the difference between them—namely 455 kilohertz. So far, our superhet circuit changed, or reduced the desired signal to a frequency having an intermediate value. Beating two frequencies together in order to produce a third signal is known by members of the Frequency Fraternity as mixing, heterodyning, or beating. And some engineers prefer to call the lowly mixer a converter; this term

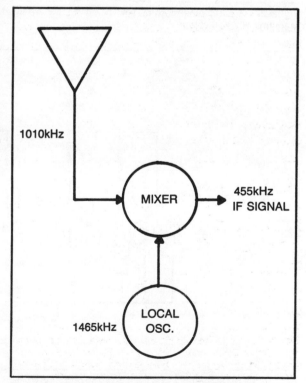

Fig. 3-26. Block diagram of basic superhet circuit.

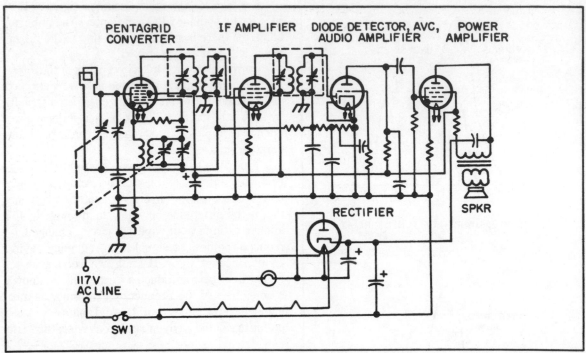

Fig. 3-27. Virtually all superhets sold commercially are five-tub rigs; most are also, in terms of design, electrically and mechanically equivalent.

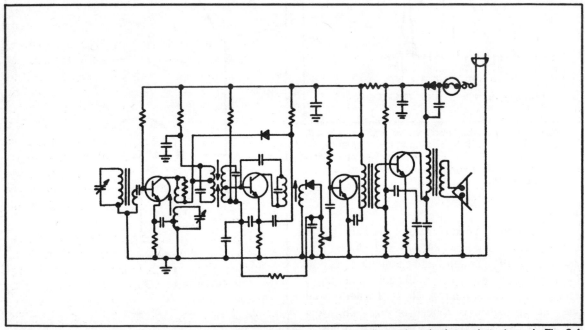

Fig. 3-28. Our schematic of a transistorized superheterodyne receiver is similar to the tubed superhet shown in Fig. 3-4. Biggest differences between the two are semiconductor diodes found in audio detector, AVC loop, and power rectifier stages.

often appears in schematics. But whatever name you throw its way, the result is the intermediate frequency.

There's something else you should know about the intermediate, or i-f, frequency. It always remains the same no matter what station you tune to. If you sweep the dial across the broadcast band in one continuous motion, the i-f frequency remains constant. How's this accomplished?

It's done by tuning the incoming signal simultaneously with the local oscillator. That's something akin to the mechanical rabbit which paces greyhounds at a race track. In the superhet a ganged tuning capacitor performs this dynamic-duo feat.

Take a close look at the tuning capacitor in any superhet radio, and you'll see physically smaller plates assigned to the local oscillator. Since these plates are smaller than the antenna stage capacitor plates, the effect is to lower the capacity, and raise the frequency of the oscillator stage. That's how the oscillator stage consistently produces a signal which is 455 kHz above the incoming frequency. But why bother, you ask?

More Muscle, Too

When we convert each incoming station's frequency to the same i-f, we gain another advantage besides better selectivity. A fixed-tuned amplifier always operates at higher efficiency than one which needs to muscle a multitude of frequencies. There are fewer technical bugaboos in a one-frequency amplifier, so our tubes or transistors can operate more effectively at this lower frequency. And, last but not least, circuit layout and wiring are less critical. All of this is well and good, but how do we actually extract our Top-Forty tunes, news, and weather from our super-duper-het?

Sound Sniffing

The detector stage recovers original audio voltage from the station's signal. Since we're cranking the rf voltages through a superhet circuit, the rf signal did a quick disappearing act, only to appear as an i-f frequency of 455 kHz. Though the original carrier (1010 kHz) is converted downward in frequency to 455 kHz, any audio voltage variations impressed upon the carrier remain the same. So if a musical note of 1000 Hz was sounded back in the radio studio, the note still remains that value in both rf and i-f circuits, despite the mixing process.

Like a ladle skimming heavy cream off the top of a jug of fresh milk, the detector rectifies either the positive- or negative-going portion of the carrier, skimming off the audio signals from the carrier. Though audio modulation appears during both positive and negative swings of an amplitude-modulated carrier, only one half of the available signal is used. If both positive and negative portions of the rf signal were detected simultaneously, the audio signals would cancel each other at the output!

Now let's look at the stages of an ordinary solid-state superhet circuit that might be found in a common table radio or transistor portable.

Simplified Schematic

Figure 3-29 is pretty typical of transistorized superheterodyne circuits. Of course, there may be variations on this circuit's theme, like the addition of an rf amplifier ahead of the mixer to improve sensitivity. The number of i-f stages also varies with receiver quality, and specialized items such as filters may appear in ham and SWL rigs.

Leading the pack on our superhet speedway is the antenna tuning circuit. Loopstick antenna L1 grabs the rf signal out of the ether, and also serves in partnership with the tuning capacitor in the tuning circuit. You sharpies will also notice that the antenna tuning capacitor is mechanically joined to the oscillator tuning capacitor. (This is represented schematically by a dotted line.) Remember now, we want to develop the i-f frequency. This ganged antenna/oscillator capacitor ensures the necessary tracking of the local oscillator with the radio-frequency signal.

The oscillator frequency is developed by the oscillator portion of our variable capacitor, and coil L2. In our superhet's schematic, the oscillator signal is capacitively coupled from the oscillator transistor base and sent on its way to the mixer stage. The mixer, therefore, "sees" both oscillator and incoming station frequencies. The electrons from oscillator and antenna circuit get it all together in the

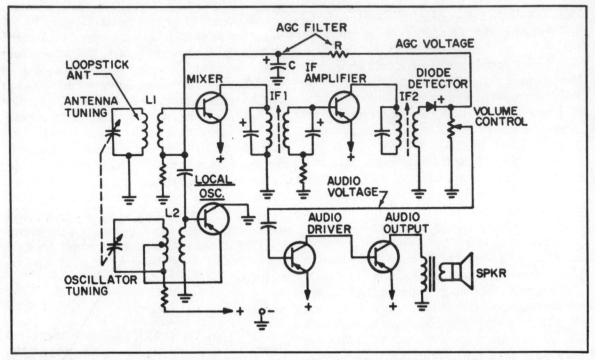

Fig. 3-29. Most superhets don't have separate local oscillator, mixer function; this schematic is more typical of BCB set. Communications-type receiver needs added usefulness of separate stages—it's easier to suppress images.

mixer's base, producing our intermediate frequency.

If you could look at the mixer's output, you'd see more than just the i-f signal. In fact, the mixer's load contains a jumble of frequency byproducts. As signals combine in this circuit, they add, subtract, and recombine in many ways. It's as if you had to separate the wheat from the chaff with a pair of tweezers!

Only the desired signal emerges from the mixer stage because intermediate-frequency transformer i-f1 picks the proper signal to the exclusion of all the others. Now our freshly-created signal passes through a stage of i-f amplification, and receiver selectivity is further whipped into shape by the second intermediate-frequency transformer, i-f2.

As we've already described, the detection process takes place at the diode, regaining the radio station's original audio signal. This audio voltage is fed from the volume control to both audio stages where they're further amplified and sent to the loudspeaker.

The detector diode doesn't merely extract soul sounds from the ether; it also delivers a second voltage output. Called AGC (Automatic Gain Control), this voltage controls our mixer's amplification, preventing the speaker from blasting when you suddenly tune your radio to a strong station. In our simplified schematic, the AGC voltage is a positive-going voltage which increases proportionately with rising signal strength. But before AGC can control receiver gain, it's filtered for pure dc in a resistor and capacitor network.

The result is a dc signal which can be used to control the gain of the mixer transistor. Thus, if a strong rf signal tries to muscle its way through this stage, the mixer is subjected to a higher bias voltage on its base terminal, which tends to put the brakes on our mixer's gain.

Pitfalls, Yet

Let's not lionize the king of receivers, though, for sometimes its growl turns to a puny purr. The biggest problem, and the most annoying, is a form of interference peculiar to the superhet known as an *image*. Produced by a mathematical mixup, images are all of those undesired signals finding easy routes to travel through your receiver. Take a look at our image explanation in Fig. 3-30; you'll see the receiver is tuned to a desired signal of 8000 kHz.

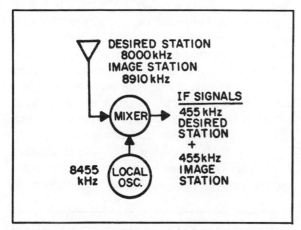

Fig. 3-30. Mixer is superhet's weakest link as signal handler. Too strong input signal can develop image frequency. Too much local oscillator signal pumped into mixer has same effect.

The local oscillator generates a frequency of 8455 kHz, which places it exactly in our i-f signal ball park. But note that a second station on 8910 kHz also happens to be 455 kHz away from the local oscillator. For each oscillator frequency there are now two station frequencies giving identical i-f frequencies. It's up to your receiver to strike out the image station.

You might expect the receiver's antenna tuning circuit to completely reject the image signal. After all, it's supposed to be tuned to generate a very high i-f frequency, positioning any images developed by the mixer well outside the tuning range of the antenna circuit. Looking at our example of a double superhet in Fig. 3-31, you'll see one i-f amplifier perking at 5000 kHz and another working on 455 kHz. Now if we receive an incoming signal on 8000 kHz, the local oscillator, now called a high-frequency oscillator, generates a frequency at 13,000 kHz, so the first i-f signal works out to 5000 kHz. Your receiver would have to pick up a signal

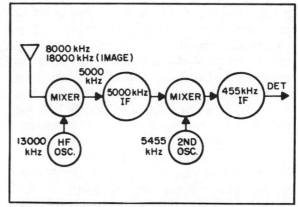

Fig. 3-31. Any superhet worthy of warming an amateur shack works around image problem with dual conversion. Combination of i-fs puts image out of range of either stage.

falling on 18,000 kHz to produce any image. Naturally, the image frequency in this instance is significantly removed from the antenna circuit, so the image is greatly attenuated.

While high i-f frequencies work well against image interference, they also revive Nagging Problem Number One: the higher the frequency of a tuned circuit, the poorer its selectivity. Since this situation also applies to i-f stages, a second conversion is required, bringing the first i-f signal down to 455 kHz, where we can sharpen our receiver's selectivity curve. That's how the double-conversion receiver solves both image and selectivity hassles. Any ham or SWL rig worthy of an on/off switch is sure to have this feature. But don't think of dual conversion as a receiver cure-all.

Dual conversion is not usually found in entertainment receivers—radio broadcast and TV for example, because it's too sharp! High selectivity could easily slice away sidebands in an FM stereo program and kill its multiplexed channel, or rob a TV image of its fine picture detail.

But, for all its faults, the basic superhet circuit we've been talking about must be doing something right. Every year several million superhets are sold in the U.S. Not bad for a circuit that might have gone the way of the hip flask, eh?

AM/FM RECEIVER ALIGNMENT

The words "receiver alignment" often conjure

up a mysterious and complicated procedure which can be performed only by an expert. While it is true that receiver alignment should not be attempted by anyone who does not have the necessary skills and equipment, it is not a very difficult procedure if you have some basic guidelines. This article will explain the various procedures for aligning AM, FM, and AM/FM receivers using a minimum of equipment.

Before getting into the mechanics of receiver alignment, it is important that the service technicians understand the basic operation of the receiver, and why proper alignment is necessary. To this end, a discussion of the modern superheterodyne receiver will follow.

Receiver Fundamentals

Virtually every AM and FM receiver manufactured today is a superheterodyne receiver. They utilize a built-in rf oscillator and mixer circuit to convert the received signal to a lower frequency called an intermediate frequency (i-f). In a given AM or FM receiver, the i-f remains the same frequency regardless of which radio station is being received.

The basic advantage of this type of circuit is that the greatest part of the rf gain, and bandpass characteristic of the receiver, is provided by the i-f stages, and is a constant for all received frequencies. Thus, the manufacturer of the receiver can precisely determine the sensitivity and selectivity of the receiver. Proper alignment ensures that the receiver performs exactly the way the manufacturer intended. Refer to Fig. 3-32, which is a simplified schematic diagram of the rf and i-f sections of a typical modern day AM receiver.

In Fig. 3-32, simplified AM radio schematic, you will note a combination mixer-oscillator stage, and two stages of i-f amplification. This circuit is

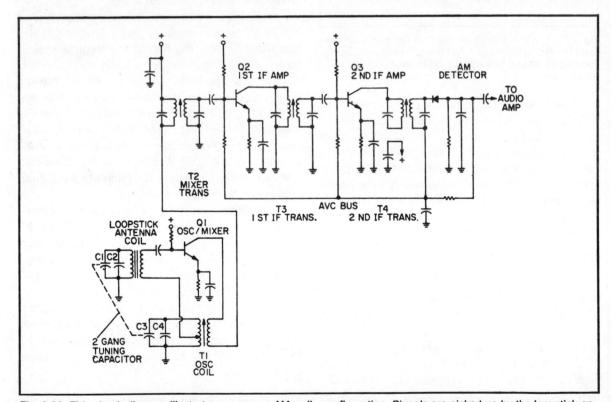

Fig. 3-32. This circuit diagram illustrates a common AM radio configuration. Signals are picked up by the loopstick antenna and then fed to the base of transistor Q1, which is used as a combination local oscillator and mixer; signals are parallel to base.

typical of a minimum cost AM receiver which has a two gang tuning capacitor and no rf amplifier. Such a circuit might be used in the common pocket-sized AM transistor radio. More expensive receivers will use a similar circuit with the addition of a transistor stage for rf amplification.

In the circuit of Fig. 3-32, the received signal is picked up by the loopstick antenna and is fed to the base of Q1. This transistor stage is used as a combination local oscillator and mixer, and is actually a Hartly oscillator with the received signal being placed in series with the base drive of the oscillator. The frequency of oscillation is determined by C3, C4, and T1. At the same time C1, C2 and the loopstick antenna are tuned to the received signal frequency. The output of T2 contains several frequencies: the radio station frequency, the local oscillator frequency and two new frequencies equal to the sum and difference of the local oscillator and received frequency.

It is the function of the two i-f stages, Q2 and Q3, to amplify the difference frequency (i-f) and reject all others. This is accomplished by tuning all i-f transformers, T2, T3, and T4, to the specified frequency. For most AM receivers, this is 455 kHz. The tuning of these transformers is performed during alignment of the receiver.

FM Circuitry

Figure 3-33 is a simplified schematic of a typical FM receiver. In this diagram you will note the similarity with the AM receiver schematic of Fig. 3-32. This basic difference, aside from the higher operating frequency, is that the FM receiver employs an rf amplifier stage, Q1.

Most FM receivers have at least one rf amplifier, since it is the nature of FM transmission that weaker signals than AM are usually encountered. Good FM reception requires a solid signal in the i-f amplifier, so that effective limiting takes place. Note also the requirement of a three gang variable capacitor instead of the two gang as appears in Fig.

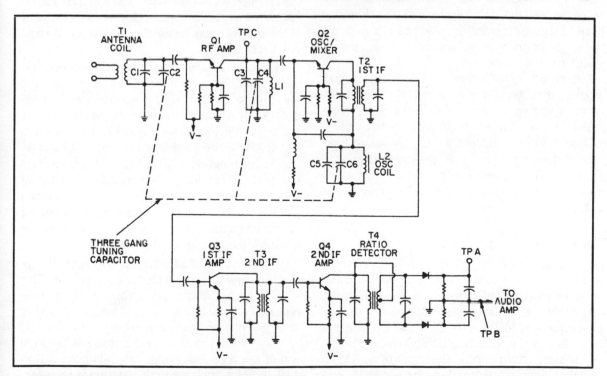

Fig. 3-33. While there are similarities between FM and AM circuitry, the most obvious difference shown in this FM circuit schematic is an rf amplifier stage to boost signals.

3-32. The additional cost and size of this capacitor is one reason why most AM receivers have no rf amplifier stage.

Although the i-f amplifier stages of the AM receiver and FM receiver appear to be similar, there is a substantial difference in the way in which they are designed. The bandwidth of an AM radio station is just 10 kHz, and the receiver must be designed to have an i-f bandwidth no greater than this. Such a narrow bandwidth is easily controlled by the design of the i-f transformers which, when tuned to the same frequency such as 455 kHz, will provide the desired bandwidth of 10 kHz.

In the case of FM reception, and especially Stereo Multiplex FM, good reception requires a receiver with at least 150 kHz bandwidth. It is the nature of FM to have significant sidebands on either side of the carrier frequency, as far away as 75 kHz. Such a wide bandwidth in the i-f stages of an FM receiver cannot be attained by tuning each stage to the same frequency. What is done is to stagger tune each stage, so that the resultant overall response has the required bandwidth. Note that each i-f transformer in Fig. 3-33 has separate tuning slugs for primary and secondary which permit stagger tuned alignment.

Because of the problem of attaining proper alignment in the i-f stages of an FM receiver, the more expensive designs utilize special filter circuits which are tuned at the factory and require no adjustments in the field. You will find that many modern stereo receivers are designed this way. However, these types of receiver still require alignment of the rf and local oscillator sections of the unit as you would expect.

AM Receiver Alignment

Alignment of an AM receiver is a relatively simple procedure, and can actually be performed by using existing radio stations as a signal source instead of a signal generator. However, if a signal generator is available, it is always best to use it as described in the following paragraphs.

When performing the alignment of an AM receiver, connect a few loops of wire across the output cable of the signal generator and loosely couple the loops to the AM antenna coil. Use the smallest rf output from the generator that will produce a reliable meter reading. For a tuning indicator you can connect a VTVM or VOM set to measure ac volts across the voice coil of the speaker.

An alternate method is to measure the dc voltage level on the AVC (Automatic Volume Control) line of the receiver. This requires a high impedance dc voltmeter such as a VTVM.

The alignment procedure will, of course, depend upon the number and type of adjustments in the specific receiver under test. If possible, obtain the manufacturer's alignment procedure. In the absence of such information you can use the following procedure.

I-F Alignment. The first adjustment to be performed is the i-f alignment. Set the signal generator at 455 kHz with about 30% to 90% amplitude modulation. Loosely couple the output of the generator to the antenna coil of the receiver and listen for the audio modulation in the receiver speaker as the rf generator is varied about 455 kHz. If you do not obtain any audio around this frequency, the i-f of the receiver may be another frequency, such as 262 kHz.

Once you have determined the proper frequency, set the generator at 455 kHz or whatever the specified intermediate frequency may be. Connect the VOM across the voice coil of the receiver and adjust the i-f transformers (T2, T3, and T4 in Fig. 3-32) for the maximum reading of the meter.

As you progress with the i-f alignment, you may find that you can lower the rf output of the signal generator to prevent overload of the receiver. When you are satisfied that all i-f transformers are tuned so that no further increase in meter reading can be attained, the i-f alignment is complete.

The next set of adjustments will align the upper and lower settings of the tuning capacitor. This is accomplished in two steps, which will have to be repeated several times, since the adjustments have some interaction with each other.

The initial adjustments are made at the high end of the broadcast band. Set the tuning dial to a silent point (where no radio station is received) near 1600 kHz. Set the rf signal generator to the same frequency. Adjust the two trimmer capacitors (C2 and C4 in Fig. 3-32) for maximum meter reading.

Then set the tuning dial of the receiver to a silent point around 600 kHz, and set the signal generator to the same frequency. Adjust the oscillator tuning coil (T1 in Fig. 3-32) for maximum meter reading.

Repeat the adjustments for 1600 kHz and 600 kHz as described above until no further improvement can be made. Once you have done this, the AM alignment will be completed.

FM Receiver Alignment

Proper FM alignment requires the use of a sweep generator and oscilloscope, unless the receiver under test has a fixed tuned i-f section which is permanently aligned at the factory. The generator may be coupled to the antenna terminals of the receiver using the circuit of Fig. 3-34, which matches the 50-ohm impedance of the generator to the 300-ohm input impedance of the FM receiver.

Some receivers may have highly selective front ends which make injection of the 10.7 MHz i-f through the rf stages difficult. In these receivers you may couple the output of the signal generator to the input of the first i-f amplifier stage through a 10-pf capacitor. This point is shown in Fig. 3-33 as test point C. Use only sufficient signal strength to achieve a usable display on the oscilloscope. Figure 3-35 is a typical connection diagram of the receiver, generator and oscilloscope.

The first section of the FM receiver to be aligned is the i-f amplifier. Set the signal generator to a center frequency of 10.7 MHz and a sweep width of about 450 kHz. An FM sweep generator should have a marker system which allows you to identify the important frequencies of interest, such as 10.6, 10.7, and 10.8 MHz. These markers indicate the desired bandwidth of the i-f amplifier.

Connect the Y input of the oscilloscope to test point A of Fig. 3-33, and adjust the scope controls to obtain a display similar to Fig. 3-36. Adjust all i-f transformers (T2, T3, & T4 in Fig. 3-33) so that

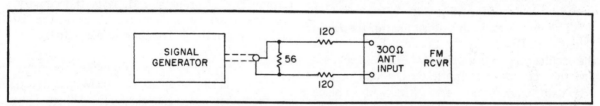

Fig. 3-34. A matching circuit must be used when attaching sweep generators to FM sets.

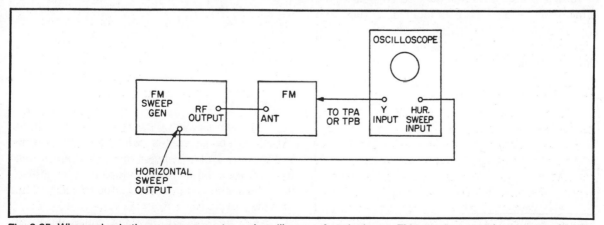

Fig. 3-35. When using both a sweep generator and oscilloscope for aligning an FM set, they must be connected in the manner shown in the diagram on the right side.

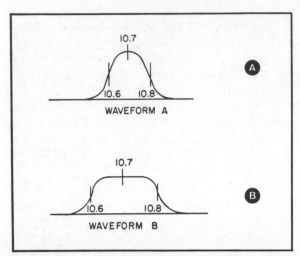

Fig. 3-36. The lower-quality FM receivers will have a waveform resembling A; while better sets will show something more like B.

the amplitude of the display is maximum, while preserving the symmetry of the waveshape at about 10.7 MHz. Bear in mind that low cost FM receivers will have a waveshape similar to that of waveform A, while high quality receivers will have the preferred waveshape B of Fig. 3-36.

The next step is the adjustment of the Ratio Detector or Discriminator. Connect the Y input of the oscilloscope to test point B of Fig. 3-33, and adjust the secondary of the Ratio Detector or Discriminator transformer (T4 of Fig. 3-33) to place the 10.7 MHz marker at the center of the S curve, as shown in Fig. 3-37. Readjust the primary of the same transformer for maximum amplitude and straightness of the line between the positive and negative peaks. This completes the alignment of the i-f section of the receiver.

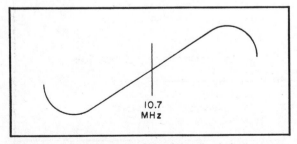

Fig. 3-37. Adjust the secondary of the discriminator transformer 'til it centers 10.7 MHz.

Trimmer Adjustments. The final adjustments to the FM receiver are made to the trimmer capacitors, which are connected in parallel with the main FM variable capacitors. These are shown in Fig. 3-33 as C1, C3 and C5. Note that some FM receivers, especially the higher quality ones, may have four such trimmer capacitors. These adjustments are made with the FM tuning dial set to near the high end of the range, (108 MHz).

Set the FM dial to a silent point near 108 MHz. Set the signal generator to the same frequency as the dial setting, and couple the output of the generator to the antenna terminals of the receiver as shown in Fig. 3-34. Connect a dc voltmeter to test point A as shown in Fig. 3-33, and use only enough signal output from the generator to attain a reliable meter reading. Adjust C1, C3, and C5 as shown in Fig. 3-33 for maximum meter reading.

As a final check, set the receiver dial to a silent point near the low end of the range, 88 MHz, and set the generator frequency to the same frequency. Now, by varying the generator about 88 MHz while watching the dc voltmeter, you can determine how accurate the FM dial is. If necessary, you may adjust the oscillator coil L2, or slip the dial pointer so that the dial reading agrees with the signal generator frequency.

Keep in mind that if you do make this adjustment you will have to go back to 108 MHz and readjust the trimmer capacitors again. In addition, if you are working on an AM/FM receiver slipping the dial pointer will also require a realignment of the rf section of the AM receiver. For these reasons it is not recommended that the dial be slipped unless it already has been placed far out of calibration through some previous servicing procedure.

SUPER DXER

Can you remember the early days of TV—back to the mid- and late-1940s—when the Joneses, who had the only TV in the neighborhood, would strain to clean up a snowy, flickering picture by adjusting a "booster" that sat on the top of their 12-in. phosphor cyclops?

Well, more often than not those outboard boxes, with their 6J6s in push-pull tunable circuits, didn't amount to the proverbial hill-of-beans. Those World War II vintage tubes were not at all well suited to the new-fangled wide-band requirements of TV. But later on as the technology advanced, and more powerful transmitters were built, good, solid pictures became the rule.

Unlike the old TV boosters, today a good booster for short wave receivers—a preselector—can be designed with all the advantages of the latest solid-state devices; and, to boot, it can be simple and very easy to build. It's the easiest way to turn any receiver into an even hotter signal sniffer. You use a booster (a very high gain rf amplifier) between the antenna and the receiver antenna terminals. A good one will also provide sharp image rejection by adding a relatively high-Q circuit to the receiver input. Image signals (which often take the pleasure out of receivers with low frequency single-conversion i-f amplifiers by jamming desired sig-nals) vanish as if by magic when passed through a high-Q booster or preselector. In short, a top quality super booster such as the Super DXer, will add another dimension of performance to any short-wave receiver.

What It Can Do

The Super DXer provides from 20 to 40 dB of signal boost—the exact amount is determined by the particular input characteristics of your receiver. Figuring on 6 dB per S-unit, that's an increase of better than 3 to 6 S-units. In plain terms, the Super DXer will bring in stations where all your receiver will pick up running barefoot is its own noise.

The Super DXer's input is a diode protected FET (field effect transistor); the protection diodes are built into the FET so that excessively strong input signals, and even static discharges, will not destroy Q1. See Fig. 3-38. Since the FET's input

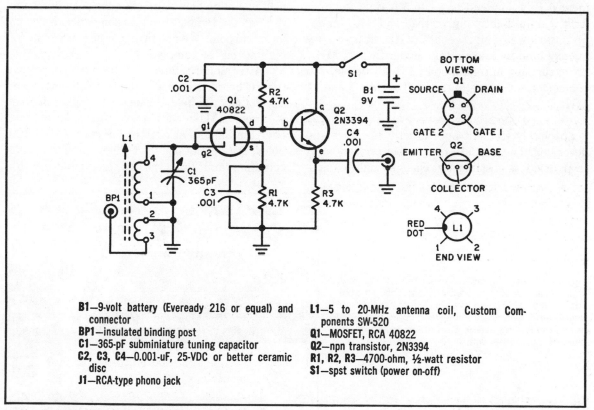

B1—9-volt battery (Eveready 216 or equal) and connector
BP1—insulated binding post
C1—365-pF subminiature tuning capacitor
C2, C3, C4—0.001-uF, 25-VDC or better ceramic disc
J1—RCA-type phono jack

L1—5 to 20-MHz antenna coil, Custom Components SW-520
Q1—MOSFET, RCA 40822
Q2—npn transistor, 2N3394
R1, R2, R3—4700-ohm, ½-watt resistor
S1—spst switch (power on-off)

Fig. 3-38. Schematic and parts list for Super DXer.

impedance is many thousands of meg-ohms, there is virtually no loading of the L1/C1 tuning circuit; its "Q" remains high and provides a very high degree of image-signal attenuation.

The Super DXer output circuit is a low impedance emitter follower, and it will match, with a reasonable degree of performance, just about any receiver input impedance. As long as your receiver has two antenna terminals, one "hot" and one ground, you can use the Super DXer.

Optimum performance will be obtained if your receiver is equipped with an antenna trimmer. Just as the antenna trimmer peaks the receiver for use with any type of antenna, it also adds something extra when matching the Super DXer.

Set Bandpass

The Super DXer has a tuning range of slightly more than 3-to-1 between 5 and 21 MHz. That means if the low end is set to 5 MHz, the upper limit will be slightly higher than 15 MHz (3 times 5). If the lower limit is set at 7 MHz, the upper frequency limit will be slightly higher than 21 MHz. Since the slug in tuning coil L1 is adjustable, you can select any operating range between 5 and 21 MHz.

Super DXer, though a very high gain device, is absolutely stable if built exactly as shown and described. There will be no spurious oscillations or response. It is possible that changes in the component layout or construction will result in self-oscillation at certain frequencies; hence, make no modifications or substitutions unless you are qualified.

Getting Started

Your first step is to prepare the printed circuit board. Using steel wool and a strong household cleanser such as Ajax or Comet, thoroughly scrub the copper surface of a 2 1/4-in. × 3 1/4-in. copper-clad board. Any type will do—epoxy or fiberglass; the type of board is unimportant. Rinse the board under running water and dry thoroughly.

Cover the copper with a piece of carbon paper—carbon side against the copper—and place under the full-scale template we have provided in Fig. 3-39. Secure the PC board in position with masking tape. Using a sharp pointed tool such as an ice pick, indent the copper foil at each component mounting hole by pressing the point of the tool through the template and carbon paper. Next, using a ball point pen and firm pressure, trace the foil outlines on the template.

After all foil outlines have been traced, remove the PC board from under the template and, using a resist pen, fill in all the desired copper foil areas with resist. Make certain you place a dot of resist over the indents at each of the corner mounting holes. Pour about one inch of etchant into a small container and float the PC board—copper foil

Fig. 3-39. Exact PC board size. Transfer image to copper-clad board using carbon paper. This is the bottom (copper) side of your board. Mount it to the front panel with 1/4-in. spacers between board and panel at each mounting screw. Secure the battery to the back of the cabinet with tape.

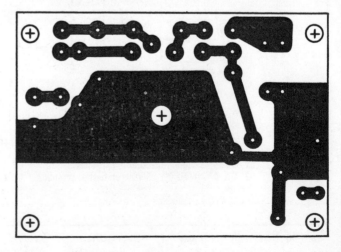

down—on top of the etchant. Every five minutes or so gently rock the container to agitate the etchant. After 15 or twenty minutes, check the PC board to see if all the undesired copper has been removed. When every trace of the undesired copper is gone, rinse the board under running water, and then remove the resist with steel wool or a resist "stripper."

Drill out all the mounting holes marked by an indent with a #57, 58, or 59 bit—this includes the corner mounting and C1 mounting holes. Then drill the corner mounting holes for a #6 screw, and use a 5/16-in. bit for the C1 mounting hole. Then install the parts as shown in Fig. 3-40.

Install tuning capacitor C1 first. It has a plastic dust cover and a long shaft. Do not use the type supplied with a short shaft to which a tuning dial for the broadcast band can be attached. Remove the mounting nut and ground washer from C1's shaft. Then make certain the shaft's retaining nut is tight. It is usually supplied loose. Discard the ground washer and secure C1 to the PC board with the mounting nut. Then install tuning coil L1. Make note of two things about L1: the terminal end of L1 has a large red dot (ignore any other marks); L1 must be positioned so the red dot faces the bottom edge of the PC board—the edge closest to the coil. Also note that the lug connected to the top of the fine-wire primary is adjacent to the bottom of the heavy-wire secondary. When the red dot is facing the edge of the PC board, both these lugs are against the board. Solder the lugs to the matching holes in the PC board. Use the shortest possible length of wire to connect the remaining primary (fine-wire) terminal to the antenna input, printed foil. Connect the remaining L1 terminal (heavy wire) to its matching hole with solid, insulated wire—form a right angle bend in the wire so it doesn't touch L1. Now mount the remaining components.

Orienting Q

Note that Q1 is positioned properly when the small tab on the case faces the nearest edge of the PC board. Also note that the round edge of Q2 faces the nearest edge of the PC board. The flat edge of Q2's case should face C1.

Because the printed copper foil faces the front panel when the assembly is mounted in the case, and is therefore inaccessible for soldering, the connecting wires to front panel components should be installed at this time. Solder 6-in. solid, insulated wires to the antenna, output, and output ground, and +9 V foils. Solder the negative (usually black) wire from the battery connector to the ground foil.

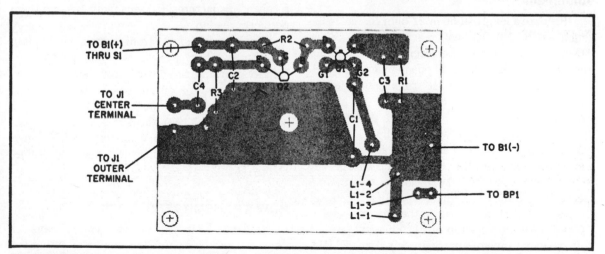

Fig. 3-40. For exact part placement on PC board, see diagram above. View is from component (top) side of your Super DXer board.

131

The Super DXer is mounted in a standard plastic or Bakelite case approximately 6 3/8-in. × 3 3/16-in. × 1 7/8-in. The front panel must be aluminum. If the cabinet is not supplied with an aluminum panel, obtain an optional or accessory metal panel. Do not use a plastic panel.

Drill a 3/8-in. hole in the center of the front panel. Position the PC assembly over the hole with C1's shaft fully inserted through the hole, and mark the locations for the four PC board mounting screws. Drill the panel and temporarily secure the PC board to the panel. Then locate the positions for power switch S1, antenna input binding post BP1, and output jack J1. Make certain J1 is as close to the PC board output terminals as is possible— within 1 1/2 inches.

Remove the PC board and drill the holes for the panel components. Power switch S1 can be any inexpensive spst type such as a slide switch. Install the panel components and then the PC board. To prevent the copper foil on the underside of the PC board from shorting to the panel, place a 3/8-in. plastic or metal spacer, or a stack of washers, between the PC board and the panel at each mounting screw. Connect the panel components to the appropriate wires extending from the PC board and the Super DXer is ready for alignment.

Alignment

Prepare a length of 50 or 52-ohm coaxial cable (such as RG-58) that will reach from the Super DXer's output jack to the receiver antenna input terminals. Solder a standard phono plug to one end. Take care that you do not use ordinary shielded cable such as used to interconnect hi-fi equipment; coaxial cable is a must.

Connect the coax between the Super DXer and your receiver. Rotate the C1 shaft fully counterclockwise and install a pointer knob so that the pointer extends to the left (9 o'clock position). Connect your antenna to binding post BP1. Then, set L1's slug so that the bottom of the screwdriver slot is level with the very top of L1. This will provide a frequency range of approximately 5 to 15 MHz. If you back out the slug 1/4 inch, the frequency coverage will be from approximately 7 to 21 MHz.

You can use any in-between slug adjustment.

Turn on the receiver and booster, and set the receiver tuning to 5 MHz, or whatever frequency you selected for the "bottom end." Adjust C1 for maximum received signal or noise and mark the panel accordingly. Repeat the procedure at approximately 7, 10, 14, and 15 (or 20) MHz. The panel markings are important because the Super DXer's tuning is so sharp it must be preset to near the desired frequency or you'll receive nothing—neither signal nor noise. The panel markings complete the adjustments.

Pull 'em In

To prevent self-oscillation, you must keep the antenna wire as far as possible from the coaxial output cable. To receive a signal, set C1 to the approximate desired frequency and then tune in the signal on the receiver. Finally, peak C1's adjustment for maximum signal strength as indicated on your receiver's S-meter, or listen carefully for an increase in speaker volume. Keep in mind that, if the signal is sufficiently strong to begin with, the receiver AVC will "absorb" the Super DXer's boost, and the speaker volume will probably remain the same, though the S-meter reading will increase. Super Dxer's boost will be most apparent on very weak signals, digging out those signals below the receiver's usual threshold sensitivity, making them perfectly readable.

Don't worry about strong signals overloading your Super DXer; it is virtually immune to overload even from excessively strong signals. However, the booster's output can be so high as to overload the input of some budget receivers. If this occurs simply reduce the booster's output by detuning C1 just enough to drop the overall signal strength below the receiver's overload value. Happy DXing!

HOW TRANSMITTERS WORK

One if by land, and two if by sea . . .'' says the famous poem by Longfellow commemorating the midnight ride of Paul Revere in April of 1775. Revere's fellow patriot, who hung the two (if by sea) lanterns in the steeple of the Old North Church of Boston 200 years ago, was engaged in communicating by modulation, just as surely as today's CBer who presses the PTT switch on his microphone. For modulation simply means variation, or change—and it's modulation, whether you're changing the number of lanterns hanging in a church steeple, or using electronic circuitry to change the radio wave emitted by an antenna in accordance with your voice.

All communication is by modulation. For centuries, the American Indians sent messages by "modulating" a smoke stream with a wet blanket, and primitive tribes have long communicated by modulating the beat of their jungle drums. Later, semaphore flags were used to send messages by modulating their position. Even these words you are reading can be considered modulation of the surface of a piece of paper with spots of ink.

But almost all of today's long-distance instantaneous communication is carried out by modulating radio waves. In fact, this means of communicating is now so commonplace that even the man in the street unknowingly refers to modulation when he speaks of "AM" and "FM." These familiar abbreviations stand for Amplitude Modulation and Frequency Modulation, respectively, and refer to the two common methods of changing a radio wave to make it broadcast words or music from one place to another.

Introducing the Carrier

A radio wave broadcast from the antenna of a transmitter is, in the absence modulation by speech or music, an unchanging, constant sine wave, as shown in Fig. 3-41. It is as constant and as unchanging as the steeple of the Old North Church, and con-

veys no more information than a steeple. It simply gives you something to monitor for the possible later appearance of a signal.

Just as the steeple was a support or carrier on which to hang the information-giving lanterns, so the radio wave becomes the carrier upon which the speech or music is "hung." In fact, the unmodulated wave is usually referred to as the carrier.

The height, or amplitude of the wave, indicates the strength of the signal, while the time it takes the wave to complete a certain number of cycles determines the spot on the radio dial where the signal will be received. For example, as shown in Fig. 3-42A if it takes only a millionth of a second for the carrier to complete seven cycles, then it will complete 7,000,000 cycles in one second, and the signal will appear on a receiver's dial at the 7,000,000-cycle-per-second (7-megahertz) point, which is on the edge of the 40-meter ham band. Such a carrier has a frequency of seven MHz.

On the other hand, a carrier taking longer to complete the same number of cycles—say, seven cycles in 10 millionths of a second (Fig. 3-42B)—would complete only 700,000 cycles in one second,

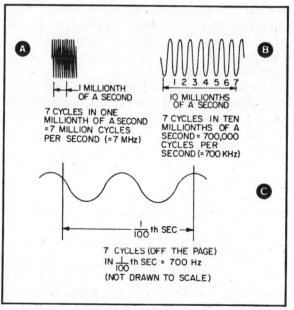

Fig. 3-42. Three, different frequency waves. 700 Hz (bottom) is partial, not drawn to same scale as the two higher frequencies.

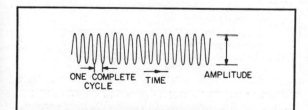

Fig. 3-41. Unmodulated carrier (rf) wave.

and would be found on the dial at 700 kHz (700 thousand hertz), which is in the standard broadcast band.

As can be seen from the above numbers, carrier frequencies are normally very high—much higher than the speech or music (audio) frequencies which we will cause the carrier to carry. For example, when a flutist plays the note F above middle C, he produces vibrations in the air which can be visualized as in Fig.3-42C. Here, the time for 7 vibrations is only one fiftieth of a second, which is a frequency of only 350 cycles per second (350 hertz).

But a constant (unchanging) carrier wave conveys no information. Something about the wave must be varied (modulated) to convey information to the listener. What can be changed, so that the listener can recognize that a signal has been sent to him?

AM and FM

Looking again at the Fig. 3-41, you can see that a carrier has two obvious characteristics—its height, or amplitude, and its frequency. Changing either of these can cause a receiver to recognize that a message has been sent. If the amplitude is changed, we call it amplitude modulation, or AM. If the frequency is changed, we call it frequency modulation, or FM.

A very simple type of AM is shown in Fig. 3-43. Here the amplitude of the carrier wave has been changed suddenly to half its former value.

This change in amplitude is a simple form of AM, and can convey simple messages. If Paul Revere had been a CBer, he could just as easily have prearranged a code signal which said ". . . one drop

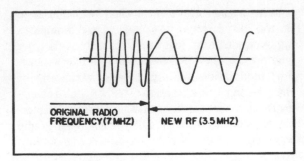

Fig. 3-44. Simplified frequency modulation of the rf carrier wave.

in carrier amplitude if by land; two drops in carrier amplitude if by sea . . ." and served the American cause just as well (though Longfellow's poetry might have suffered).

The other obvious characteristic of the carrier wave of Fig. 3-41 is its frequency. We can also modulate this characteristic, as shown in Fig. 3-44. Here, instead of a sudden change in amplitude, there is a sudden change in frequency, from 7 MHz to 3.5 MHz. This is a very simple form of FM, and can also be used to convey simple messages. Since the drop in frequency represents a shift in the carrier's location on the dial, as shown in Fig. 3-45, two receivers, one tuned to 7 MHz and the other to 3.5 MHz, could detect this shift in frequency, and the listener could interpret it as a signal, according to a pre-arranged code.

What's PM?

While the man in the street has made AM and FM household phrases, these modulation methods are only two of the three ways a radio frequency carrier wave may be modulated. The third method, Phase Modulation, or PM, although virtually un-

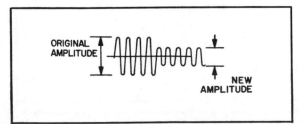

Fig. 3-43. Simplified amplitude modulation of the rf carrier wave.

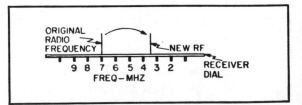

Fig. 3-45. If the frequency modulation were a simple change from one rf carrier frequency to another, an AM receiver could receive it if retuned.

134

known to most people, is nonetheless extremely important in such fields as data transmission and color television.

Phase modulation can be visualized as in Fig. 3-46. Here, neither the amplitude nor the frequency is varied, but the carrier is made to pause for a moment, and then to continue as a sine wave slightly delayed from the original. This delay is called a phase shift. Phase shift is usually measured in degrees. A phase shift equal to the time needed for an entire cycle is 360°. In Fig. 3-46, a sudden phase shift of about 70° (less than a quarter cycle) is indicated. By suitable receiver circuitry (found in every color TV receiver), this sudden change in phase can be interpreted as a signal. In color TV, it might represent a shift in hue from green to yellow.

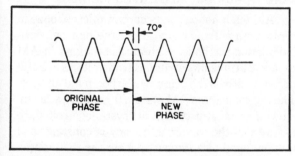

Fig. 3-46. Simplified phase modulation of the rf carrier wave.

Amplitude Modulation—A Closer Look

The sudden drop in amplitude shown in Fig. 3-43 is a good way to show the general scheme of AM, but it fails to tell us very much about how AM is used, every day, in our AM receivers and CB rigs. Here there are (hopefully) no sudden shifts in carrier amplitude, but instead, there is a remarkable recreation of speech and music from a distance transmitter. How is this done?

To explain, let us assume that our flutist stands before a microphone in a broadcasting studio, ready to play his 350-Hz F-above-middle-C. Let's also assume that the broadcasting station is assigned a carrier frequency of 700 kHz. Figure 3-47 shows how the carrier wave will appear just before the flutist plays, and just after he begins.

As you can see, the 350-Hz audio tone from the flute causes the amplitude of the carrier to rise or

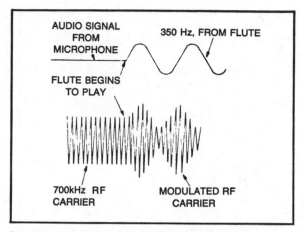

Fig. 3-47. The audio signal (sound) modulates the rf carrier wave.

fall in accordance with the rise or fall of the flute wave. Note that both the top and bottom of the carrier wave are affected by the flute waveform. It is as though the carrier had been squeezed into a snug-fitting envelope, forcing it to conform to the waveform of the flute sound. The shape thus formed by the tips of the modulated carrier wave is often called the envelope.

The envelope of an amplitude-modulated carrier is therefore a good replica of the audio waveform coming from the studio microphone. Every shading, every change, in the sound striking the microphone will be faithfully traced out by the tips of the carrier wave. For example, if the flutist were to play more softly, the result will be as in Fig. 3-48.

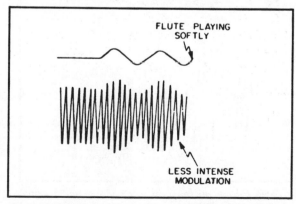

Fig. 3-48. Smaller audio signal modulates the rf carrier wave less.

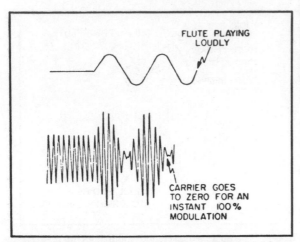

FLUTE PLAYING
LOUDLY

CARRIER GOES
TO ZERO FOR AN
INSTANT 100%
MODULATION

Fig. 3-49. Louder audio signal (sound) modulates the rf carrier wave to maximum.

If he plays more loudly, Fig. 3-49 is the result. You will note that in Fig. 3-49 the amplitude modulation is so intense that, at one point, the carrier's amplitude goes to zero for an instant. This is called 100% modulation, and represents the loudest sound AM can handle. If the flutist plays even more loudly, the result is as shown in Fig. 3-50. As the figure shows, the envelope is no longer a faithful replica of the original audio waveform, so the listener will receive a distorted sound. This condition is called overmodulation, and is undesirable.

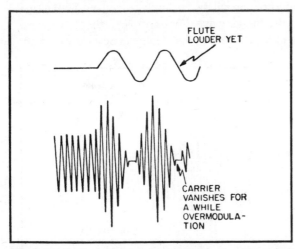

FLUTE
LOUDER YET

CARRIER
VANISHES FOR
A WHILE
OVERMODULA-
TION

Fig. 3-50. Further increase in amplitude of audio signal causes overmodulation.

Hardware for AM Systems

One of the most-straightforward methods of producing AM is the method invented by the Canadian Reginald Fessenden, in 1905. In his system, a radio frequency generator produced the carrier wave, which was fed to the antenna through a carbon (variable-resistance) microphone. See Fig. 3-51.

Since a carbon microphone varies its resistance in accordance with the speech or music, the microphone in this primitive system acted as a valve to allow more or less of the rf carrier wave to pass to the antenna. In this way the carrier wave broadcast by the antenna was amplitude modulated by the sound waves striking the microphone.

More Up-to-Date Modulation Methods

Although nobody puts carbon microphones in series with antennas any more, the more modern modulation methods, such as those found in AM broadcast transmitters or CB transmitters are still rather similar to the primitive carbon-mike method. The typical modern AM system (Fig. 3-52), still employs an oscillator (which is crystal-controlled, to ensure that the carrier frequency is constant, and thus is found at a known spot on the dial), and a power amplifier to strengthen the carrier before feeding it to the antenna. The amount of "strengthening" is controlled by the audio signal.

Receiving the Signal

At that distant point, we all know that the carrier power delivered to the antenna is in this way amplitude-modulated and the radiated carrier will convey the speech or wave may be intercepted by a suitable antenna and applied to a receiver. A simple receiver is shown in block diagram form in Fig. 3-53. Here, the weak signal from the antenna is first amplified in a carrier-wave amplifier, an rf (radio frequency) amplifier, and applied to a detector which can extract the original audio signal from the amplitude-modulated rf carrier. This audio wave is further amplified and then fed to a loudspeaker, which re-creates the original speech or music.

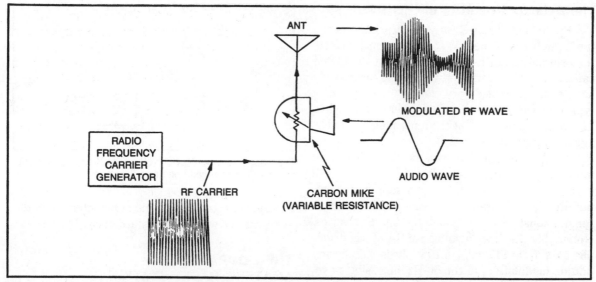

Fig. 3-51. The first radio telephone broadcast transmitter, invented by Canadian Reginald Fessenden, who broadcast voice and music to a few ships at sea on Christmas Eve, 1905. It worked, but was very noisy.

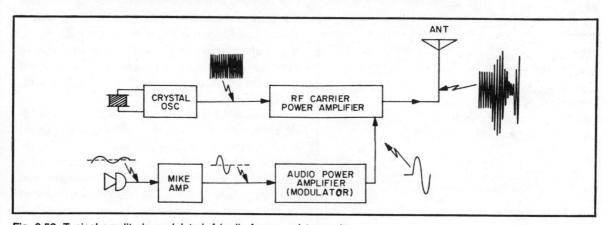

Fig. 3-52. Typical amplitude-modulated rf (radio frequency) transmitter.

Fig. 3-53. Block diagram of receiver for amplitude-modulated radio frequency (rf) signals.

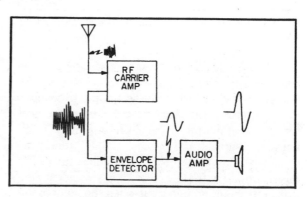

The Detector—Heart of the Receiver

By looking at Fig. 3-54, you can see the detector is the heart of the AM receiver which extracts the original signal from the amplitude-modulated carrier. The circuit that does this job is surprisingly simple. It resembles very closely the circuit of a typical power supply. In an ac power supply, when 117-volts ac is applied at the input plug, a dc voltage appears at the output. If, because of a brownout or for some other reason, the 117 volts at the input drops to, say, 105 volts, the dc output will drop correspondingly. In a power supply, this output drop is undesirable—we want the dc output to remain constant even though the input ac varies. Notice that the drop in voltage of the 60-Hz power line input from 117 volts to 105 volts is actually amplitude modulation, of the 60-Hz input sine wave, and the drop in the output dc has "detected" the AM that occurred at the input! This is shown in Fig. 3-55.

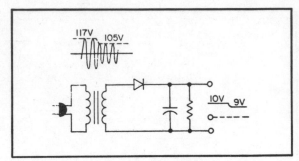

Fig. 3-55. Changing amplitude of voltage input to power supply provides changed (modulated) output.

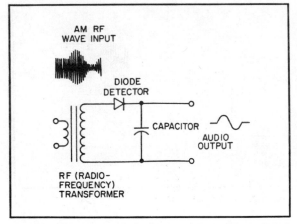

Fig. 3-54. Simple receiver of amplitude-modulated (AM) rf signals.

So a simple AM detector may be thought of as a power supply arranged to change its output very quickly in accordance with the amplitude changes in the ac (carrier) at its input. And, since these fluctuations in amplitude of carrier represent the original audio signals, the "power supply" (detector) output will be the same as the original audio. It's interesting to note the power supply's undesirable trait, unsteadiness in output when the input is un-

steady, is the useful operating characteristic of the same circuit when used as a detector!

THE COMPANION 40 AMATEUR RADIO STATION

Round-the-clock activity on the 40-meter band that includes a lively segment for the Novice Class licensee, makes this combo just right for you if you're just beginning to study for your license or if you already have a Novice license and wish to improve your ability as an operator. You can work both local DX stations on the Novice band with our terrific Companion-40.

Basic units of the Companion-40 are a hot little receiver and a matching 40-watt transmitter. Each unit can be operated independently. However, you must be licensed to put the transmitter on the air. Even if you don't have your license yet, you can build these units. There's nothing to prevent you from using the receiver to become more familiar with procedure and live reception, and then you're ready to go on-the-air when your ticket arrives.

Companion-40 Receiver

First at bat for the Companion-40 team is the nifty receiving unit that's sure to get you off to a good start on 40 meters. See Fig. 3-56. The receiver is a simplified, two-tube superhetregen with a bandspread covering the 7 to 7.3-MHz range. There is plenty of dial space for the Novice portion of the band (7.15 to 7.2 MHz). A dual-function pentode/triode tube is used as a tuned mixer-oscillator

C1, C5, C6, C15—100-pF, 500-V ceramic disc capacitor

C2—9- to 23-pF dual variable capacitor (J. W. Miller 1461-2)

C3, C4—Trimmer capacitor (part of C2)

C7, C19—47-pF, 500-V ceramic disc capacitor

C8, C9, C11, C14, C16, C21, C24—.001-uF, 500-V ceramic disc capacitor

C10, C12, C18—.005-uF, 500-V ceramic disc capacitor

C13—10-pF, 500-V ceramic disc capacitor

C17, C22—.01-uF, 500-V ceramic disc capacitor

C20—10-uF, 15-V electrolytic capacitor

C23—80-, 50-, 20-uF, 150-V, triple-section electrolytic capacitor

D1, D2—1N2071 silicon diode

F1—1-A fuse (Radio Shack 270-365 or equiv.)

I1—#51 pilot lamp (Radio Shack 272-318 or equiv.)

J1—Phono jack

J2—Phone jack (Radio Shack 274-293 or equiv.)

L1—550-uH RF choke (J. W. Miller 4649 or equiv.)

R1, R10—1,200,000-ohm, ½-watt 10% resistor

R2—33,000-ohm, ½-watt, 10% resistor

R3, R13—18,000-ohm, ½-watt, 10% resistor

R4, R8—100,000-ohm, linear-taper potentiometer

R5—15,000-ohm, ½-watt, 10% resistor

R6—2,000,000-ohm, ½-watt, 5% resistor

R7—1,500,000-ohm, ½-watt, 10% resistor

R9, R12—180,000-ohm, ½-watt, 10% resistor

R11—2700-ohm, ½-watt, 10% resistor

R14—2200-ohm, 1-watt, 10% resistor

S1—Spst switch (part of R4)

T1—Antenna transformer (J. W. Miller C-5495-A or equiv.)

T2—Oscillator transformer (J. W. Miller C-5495-RF or equiv.)

T3—455-kHz IF transformer (J. W. Miller 12-C30 or equiv.)

T4—Power transformer, 117-VAC pri., to 250-V (CT), 25-mA and 6.3-V, 1-A sec. (Allied 54B2008 or equiv.)

TS1—2-screw terminal strip

V1, V2—6U8A vacuum tube

Misc.—Vernier dial (Millen 10039, Allied 47B3242), knobs (Radio Shack 274-391 or equiv.), terminal boards (Erie 3976-228-2), 9-pin sockets, ¼-in. metal spacers, rubber grommets, RG-58A coax, AC line cord, green bezel, socket for #51 lamp, fuse holder, metal cabinet 5 x 6⅛ x 8½-in. (LMB W-1C or equiv.)

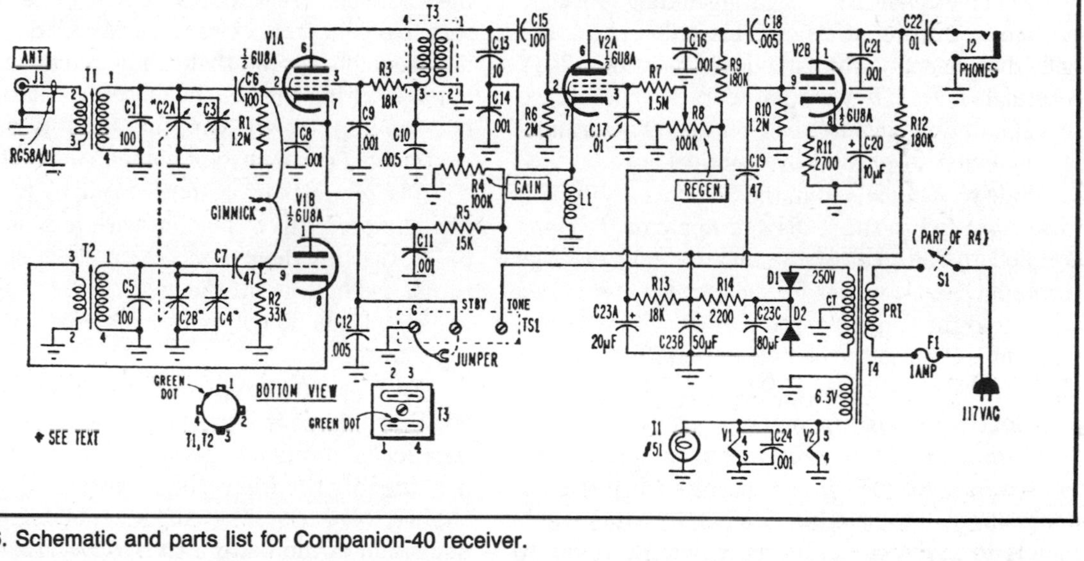

Fig. 3-56. Schematic and parts list for Companion-40 receiver.

on the front end and as a feeder for a similar tube which acts as a regenerative detector and audio amplifier to drive a set of high-impedance phones.

Circuitry is included for receiver blanking during transmitting periods and for a side tone input from the transmitter so you can monitor your keying. The Companion-40 transmitter has the proper switching and side tone circuits to feed this receiver. In spite of the receiver's small size and compact appearance, the inside of the cabinet is not crowded and is equipped with its own built-in power supply.

Signals from the antenna lead at J1 are coupled to the control grid of V1A through T1 and C6. The secondary of T1 is tuned by C2A to the 40-meter band. Local oscillator V1B and T2 are tuned by C2B to a frequency which is always just 455 kHz above the incoming 40-meter signals (C2A and C2B are ganged).

The rf output of V1B is coupled to the grid of V1A by a gimmick capacitor (explained later). The resultant 455-kHz i-f signal is amplified by V1A and picked off by T3. Transformer T3, which is tuned to 455 kHz, passes the signal on to the regenerative detector circuit of V2A.

Potentiometer R8 controls the regenerative action by varying the screen voltage of V2A. Control R4 adjusts the screen voltage on V1A for desired gain and to prevent overloading of V2A. The ensuing detected audio signals from the plate circuit of V2A are coupled by C18 to the audio-amplifier stage (V2B). After the signals are amplified, they are passed on to phones via C22 and J2.

Receiver blanking while transmitting is accomplished by cutting off V1A. This is done by externally disconnecting the cathode circuit at the STBY terminal on TS1. For normal operation without external standby transmitter circuitry, this terminal is connected to ground by a jumper lead.

Side tone signals from the Companion-40 transmitter are fed to the TONE terminal on TS1 and coupled to the grid of the audio amplifier stage through C19. Dc power for the receiver is supplied to T4 and the full-wave rectifier circuit of D1 and D2, and is filtered by the two-section RC filter consisting of C23A/B/C, and R13 and R14.

Setting It Up. A cowl-type grey aluminum 5 × 6 1/8 × 8 1/2-in. cabinet and built-in chassis houses the receiver. (The transmitter is housed in a similar cabinet.) This cabinet has removable panels to make construction easier. Best way to start building is to remove the back, top, and bottom panels. Tape a sheet of graph paper on top of the chassis, study the photos, and then position the parts.

Rest C2 on the chassis, centered on the front panel, and mark the panel to locate the hole for the capacitor's shaft. Drill a 3/8-in. hole and temporar-

ily mount the tuning dial on the capacitor's shaft. Position the front panel controls, pilot light, and J2, and mark their locations. Drill small pilot holes where needed, and remove the front panel if necessary and drill all holes to correct size.

Next, mount the controls and front panel on the chassis. You may find it necessary to make a paper template of the bottom of C2 to locate its mounting holes on the chassis. Position the capacitor approximately 1/4 in. from the front panel. When mounting the capacitor, be particularly careful not to short the stator plates to the mounting screws. Locate the position of the remaining components on the chassis, cut the holes, and mount the parts. Install rubber grommets (7) to protect wires going through the holes in the chassis. A short could prove disastrous.

Two terminal boards are used to simplify the wiring. They are mounted on 1/4-in. metal spacers to provide clearance between the terminals and the chassis. Mount and solder the components. Keep the leads short. Bend C23's mounting strap if necessary to obtain proper clearance. Watch out for cabinet assembly screws that can pierce the capacitor when securing the panels. Observe polarity of diodes and electrolytic capacitors. A reversed connection can cause instant component destruction.

The gimmick capacitor is made by connecting two short lengths of hookup wire to pins 2 and 9 of V1, twisting them together for about one or two turns, and cutting off the excess wire. Make sure the bare leads do not touch each other or the bottom cover.

Even though the operating frequency isn't high, good lead dress is important. Use spaghetti over bare leads in order to prevent shorts. Decals will help identify the front panel controls and the rear chassis connections. Install four rubber feet on the underside of the bottom chassis cover.

Alignment. Insert the tubes, plug in the power cord, and allow the receiver time to warm up. Check for signs of overheating and other indications of trouble, then plug in a pair of high-impedance phones.

Connect a signal generator to J1 and set the generator for a modulated 455-kHz output. (Don't overlook the need to connect a jumper between the chassis and the STBY terminal on TS1!) Adjust R8 to a position just below the point of detector oscillation and tune the top and bottom slugs of T3 for maximum signal. Adjust R4 for minimum signal to prevent overloading of the detector. As T3 approaches resonance you'll have to lower R4's level some more, and maybe reduce the generator's output signal, or both.

Set the signal generator output frequency to 7 MHz and adjust C2 to a bit less than full capacity. To tune the local oscillator, turn T2's tuning screw all the way out, then turn it back in slowly until you hear the generator signal. Note: the signal can be heard at two positions of the tuning screw. Set the screw at the position furthest from the chassis. Adjust T1's tuning screw for maximum signal output.

To obtain proper tracking, set the signal generator to 7.3 MHz and tune C2 until you hear the signal. Then adjust C3 for maximum signal. Repeat the 7 and 7.3 MHz adjustments until you are satisfied that you have this band pretty well centered on the dial.

Dotting the Dial. Now use your signal generator to calibrate the dial. Mark the dial at 10-kHz intervals from 7 to 7.3 MHz. Ink or decals can be used. However, you should pencil in the markings before using either.

Before disconnecting the signal generator, adjust R8 until you hear the generator signal as a beat note. This indicates the regenerative detector circuit of V2A can receive CW.

No Signal Generator? If you don't have a signal generator, set the tuning capacitor C2 to the center of the dial, and connect a good antenna to J1. Adjust T2 (starting with the tuning screw all the way out from the chassis) until you hear 40-meter Novice Band signals. Then adjust the tuning screws of T1 and T3 for maximum signal.

Tune C2 towards the maximum capacity position (fully meshed) until you hear the ham CW signals near the edge of the band. Adjust T1 for maximum signal. Now tune C2 towards the minimum capacity position until you hear the sideband or AM phone stations at the upper edge of the band. Adjust C3 for maximum signal. Finally, repeat the adjustments at the low and high ends of the band.

Operation. For best results, use a dipole antenna cut to resonate at the center of the 40-meter band. The same antenna can be used for the transmitter. However, a longwire antenna erected as high as possible and a good ground will also provide good reception.

Practice using the gain control (R4) and the regeneration control (R8) as you tune in the CW signals. Remember to adjust the GAIN control to prevent overloading the detector. Adjust the REGEN control for a beat note having a pleasant pitch. For speaker operation, you can connect a small transistorized amplifier to J2.

Companion-40 Transmitter

Here's the ideal mate for the Companion-40 40-meter novice receiver. Its 40-watt input is designed to match the receiver's performance. The transmitter is a simplified one-tube crystal oscillator and power amplifier, powered by a voltage-regulated power supply for clean keying. Crystal-controlled operation over the 7 to 7.3 MHz range is possible.

Circuits are included for receiver blanking during transmit, antenna switching from receiver to transmitter, and side tone monitoring of the transmitter keying. Also included is a simple way to "spot" the transmitter frequency on the receiver. With its own built-in power supply, the rig is compact and fits into a small aluminum cabinet that matches the receiver in size and appearance.

Fancy Colpitts. A 40-meter crystal plugged into J1 is hooked up with C1, C2, and L1 to form an rf Colpitts-oscillator circuit with V1's cathode, control grid, and screen grid. (See Fig. 3-57.) The oscillator output is electron coupled to the plate of V1 and tuned by the pi-network (C8, L4, and C9). This tuned circuit matches the high-impedance output of V1 to the approximately 50- to 75-ohm 40-meter antenna. Meter M1 monitors the plate current and is used to indicate correct tuning and loading of the transmitter's final stage.

Neon Lamp I3, along with R3, R4, and C6 works as a relaxation oscillator to provide a side tone when the transmitter is keyed. Capacitor C5 couples the tone to one of the terminals on TS1.

C1—10-pF, 1000-V NPO ceramic disc capacitor

C2—100-pF, 1000-V NPO ceramic disc capacitor

C3, C4, C6, C13, C14, C15, C17—.005-uF, 1000-V ceramic disc capacitor

C5—47-pF, 1000-V ceramic disc capacitor

C7, C16—.001-uF, 3000-V ceramic disc capacitor

C8—9- to 140-pF variable capacitor (Hammarlund MC-140-M or equiv.)

C9—Dual 10.3- to 365.7-pF variable capacitor (Lafayette 32H1102 or equiv.)

C10—Dual 20-uF, 450-V electrolytic capacitor (Allied 43B9379 or equiv.)

C11, C12—20-uF, 450-V electrolytic capacitor (Allied 43B4015 or equiv.)

D1, D2, D3, D4—1N2071 silicon diode

F1—3-A fuse and holder (Radio Shack 270-365 or equiv.)

I1, I2—#51 pilot lamp (Radio Shack 272-318 or equiv.)

I3—NE2 neon lamp

J1—Crystal socket

J2—Phono jack

J3—Phono jack

J4—SO-239 chassis mount coax connector

L1, L5—1-uH RF choke (Miller 4662 or equiv.)

L2—6 turns #22 bus wire spaced over R2 (see text)

L3—2.5-uH RF choke (Miller 6302 or equiv.)

L4—25¾ turns of AIR DUX 816 T coil stock

M1—150-mA panel meter (EMICO RF-2C, Allied 52B7620 or equiv.)

R1—47,000-ohm, 1-watt, 10 % resistor

R2—120-ohm, 1-watt, 10 % resistor

R3, R4—1,200,000-ohm, ½-watt, 10 % resistor

R5—5000-ohm, 11-watt resistor (Allied 45D6123C or equiv.)

R6—100-ohm, 2-watt, 10 % resistor

R7, R8—82,000-ohm, 2-watt, 10 % resistor

S1—4-pole, 2-position rotary switch (Mallory 3242J, Allied 56B4356 or equiv.)

S2—Spst 3-A, 120-V rotary switch

T1—Power transformer, 117-VAC pri. to 480-V (CT), 70-mA, 6.3-V, 3-A sec. (Allied 54B1463 or equiv.)

TS1—2-screw terminal strip

V1—6GJ5A vacuum tube

V2—OA2 regulator tube

Xtal—40-meter, FT243 transmitting crystals (see text)

Misc.—5 x 6⅛ x 8½-in. aluminum metal cabinet (LMB W-1C or equiv.), knobs (Radio Shack 274-392), terminal board (Radio Shack 274-737), metal spacers, rubber grommets, zip cord, terminal strips, 7-pin miniature and 9-pin novar sockets, RG-58A coax, plate cap for V1, 300-ohm twin lead, pilot lamp sockets, red and green bezels, panel mount fuse holder, wire, solder, hardware, etc.

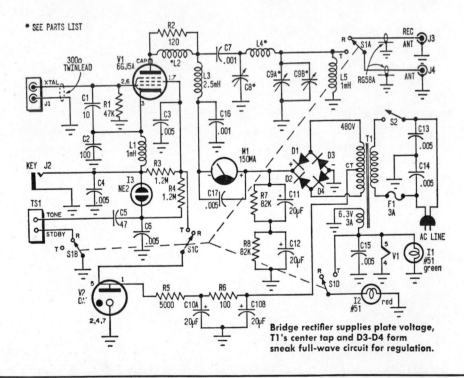

Fig. 3-57. Schematic and parts list for Companion-40 Transmitter.

Switch S1 (A/B/C/D) simultaneously connects four circuits when switched from REC to TRANS positions. Section S1A connects the antenna lead from J4 to either the transmitter or the receiver. S1B controls the receiver standby circuit, blanking the receiver while the transmitter is operating. S1C connects the regulated B+ supply to V1's screen grid when in the transmit position.

When tuning (zero beating) the receiver to the transmitter operating frequency, screen voltage is disconnected to keep the power input to V1 at a minimum. A low-powered rf signal is generated when the key (plugged into J2) is closed. S1D switches the red pilot lamp (I2) on when the transmitter is in operation.

Diodes D1, D2, D3, and D4 form a bridge rectifier and with the aid of T1 produce both a high and low B+ voltage. The high B+ voltage is filtered by C11 and C12 (in series) and connected to the plate of V1 through M2. The low B+ voltage is filtered by R6 and C10 (A/B) and fed through R5 to the voltage regulator tube V2. The regulated voltage from V2 is connected by S1C to V1's screen grid.

Building Blocks. A combination cowl type 5 × 6 1/8 × 8 1/2-in. grey aluminum cabinet and chassis is recommended. This cabinet has removable front and rear panels, as well as top and bottom covers. Remove the covers and rear panel before starting construction.

Tape a sheet of graph paper onto the top of the chassis and front panel. Temporarily position the meter on the front panel. Mark the outline for the meter cutout on the graph paper. Position C8 and C9 on the chassis. Mark the locations of the shaft holes on the panel. Then mark the location of the remaining front panel components.

Be sure that S1's terminals clear the top of the chassis and the bottom cover. Drill small pilot holes at the hole locations to guide and position the larger drills. It may be easier to separate the front panel from the chassis when cutting the holes to the necessary sizes.

Position the tube sockets, C8, C9, C10 and T1 on the chassis as shown in the photo. Mark their locations and size of holes. Remove the components and make the necessary holes. Do the same for the components to be mounted on the rear of the chassis. Space the parts closer together if necessary to fit through the precut opening on the rear panel.

Place the green bezel (For I1) on the left side of the front panel (looking at the front of the panel) and the red bezel (for I2) on the right side. Mount the sockets for I1 and I2 on the chassis directly behind and close to the bezels, but leave enough room for the lamps.

If necessary, trim the mounting flange on J4 to clear the bottom cover and the top of the chassis. Install the hardware as shown in photo. Use rubber grommets as necessary to protect the wires passing through the holes in the chassis. Mount the components on the terminal board, but observe polarity. The anode leads of D3 and D4 are connected to a ground lug which is held in place when the board is installed. To install the board, place a 3/8-in. metal spacer or standoff under each end of the terminal board to prevent shorting the components on the board to the chassis.

Capacitors C11 and C12 are mounted along the sides of the terminal board with a single-lug terminal strip as a tie point. Run secondary leads from T1 between C11 and the single-lug strip to prevent C11's can from shorting to the lug-strip mounting screw. These leads act as a physical barrier. Place spaghetti over the positive leads from C11 and C12, as well as any other leads in need of protection from shorts.

Crystal and Coil. Use a short length of 300-ohm twin lead to connect the crystal socket (J1) to pin 6 of V1 and a ground lug. Dress the twin lead up and away from all the other wiring. Neon lamp I3 is mounted on terminal strip as shown in photo. Use short leads to provide support for the lamp.

Install a cable clamp on top of the chassis to hold the RG-58A coax going from S1 to J3 and J4. On the same mounting screw that holds the clamp, install a ground lug for the lead from L5. Connect the other lead from L5 to C9A, and jump C9A and C9B with a short length of bus wire.

Cut a section of Air Dux 816 T coil stock to 25 3/4 turns, leaving short leads for a connection to C9A and C8's stator lug, as shown in photo. To form L2, wind 6 turns of #22 bus wire spaced over R2 and connect L2/R2 to the plate connector on V1. Connect L3, C7, and L2/R2 together as shown using short leads. Keep the assembly high above L4 to prevent shorts. The remainder of the wiring of the transmitter is straightforward, but be careful not to damage the coax cable insulation when soldering. Finally, mount the knobs on the front panel controls.

Decals on the front and rear panels to identify controls and jacks will give your project a professional look. Install four rubber feet on the bottom cover of the unit and drill a few ventilation holes in the bottom cover just below the terminal board.

Peaking the Power. *Caution! High voltage is present on the plate of V1 at all times, so don't touch the plate cap while ac power is connected.* Do not depress the key unless a 40-meter crystal is in J1. Set S1 to REC position and connect a 100-watt lamp (to serve as a dummy load) to J4. Connect a key to J2. Be sure that the frame of the key is wired to the chassis side of J2. Set C8 and C9 to full capacity. Plug in a crystal for that portion of the 40-meter band desired (7.15 to 7.2 MHz for the novice portion of the band).

Connect the transmitter power cord to the ac line and set S2 to the ON position. Allow the transmitter to warm up for a few minutes. Set S1 to TRANS position, close the key, and quickly adjust C8 (PLATE) for a sharp dip in plate current reading as indicated on M1. Adjust C9 (LOAD) for an increase in plate current, and readjust C8 for a dip in plate current.

Repeat this procedure until M1 indicates approximately 65 to 70 mA when C9 is adjusted for a dip. The lamp should be glowing to indicate rf output. Release the key and set switch S1 to REC position. The red pilot lamp should light up only when S1 is in the TRANS position. The green pilot light should remain lit to indicate that S2 is in the ON position. The same transmitter tuning sequence of C8 and C9 should be used for on-the-air operation when an antenna is connected to J4. Do not turn on S1 when the key is closed, unless you want to risk burning out the switch contacts.

On the Beam. To tune the receiver to the transmitter frequency, connect a lead between the transmitter and receiver chassis. Then connect leads from the TONE and STBY terminals of the transmitter to corresponding points on receiver's TS1 terminal strip. Make sure that the jumper wire is disconnected between the receiver chassis and STBY terminal. Use a short length of coax to connect the receiver antenna input to the transmitter jack J4 centered on rear apron.

Key the transmitter, with S1 in the REC position, and tune the receiver until you hear the beat note. (The receiver's rf gain control may have to be adjusted to keep the receiver from overloading.) The zero beat note indicates that the receiver is tuned to transmitter frequency.

Set the transmitter S1 switch to TRANS position, and key the unit. You should hear the transmitter side tone in the earphones connected to the receiver. If desired, a separate amplifier can be connected to the transmitter TONE terminal and chassis to obtain a speaker output of the side tone. The side tone note can be varied by changing the value of R4 or C6.

For best performance, the transmitter should be used with a coax-fed, 40-meter dipole cut for the center of the band.

ANTENNAS FOR TWO-WAY RADIO

If you happen to be a two-way radio enthusiast and are interested in "getting out" in the CB slang sense of the phrase, then you have come to the right place, for here you will find everything you need to know in order to squeeze every last inch of range out of your two-way radio.

Here are six things to think about while trying to boost your CB's range.

Antenna Height

First, for maximum range your antenna should be as high as legally possible. It is said that you can talk about one-third farther than the line-of-sight distance between the tip of your antenna and the tip of the other fellow's antenna, and the higher the antennas, the greater the line-of-sight distance. This effect comes from the fact that although light travels in a straight path, radio waves tend to follow the shape of the earth's surface somewhat. Therefore, although someone's antenna may be below the horizon so you can't see it, your radio signals may still reach him if he isn't too far below.

The question, then, is what is the legal maximum height? For omnidirectional antennas (those which radiate equally in all horizontal directions), the height limit for the tip is 60 feet. The limit for directional antennas is 20 feet.

But it is possible to do a lot within these limits if you want to increase your range badly enough. For example, put your antenna on top of a nearby hill instead of right next to your house. But of course, you will need a lot of line for this trick.

Another thing you can do is put your antenna on top of a tall building. If the building is more than 40 feet high, you are allowed 20 feet above the top of it. Obviously, mounting your antenna on top of a good-sized building can put it well above what a neighbor could achieve working from the ground up.

Standing Wave Ratio

Second, there is the matter of SWR or standing wave ratio. A good way to visualize this is through a physical analogy. See Fig. 3-58. Imagine a ball bearing rolling along. Since it is moving, it possesses some energy of motion (kinetic energy). Suppose this ball bearing were to collide with another ball bearing which had equal mass and was stationary. Upon collision, the rolling bearing's kinetic energy will be totally transferred to the formerly stationary bearing. The transfer of kinetic energy will be 100 percent, but only because the bearings are of the same mass. It reminds one of head-on collisions between billiard balls.

In electronics, impedance (like resistance) plays the role that mass played in the ball bearing analogy. Ideally you want 100 percent energy transfer from the transmitter to the antenna, but this can happen only if the impedance of the transmitter and that of the antenna match. Otherwise, some of the energy is reflected back from the antenna to the transmitter.

What you have then is waves traveling from

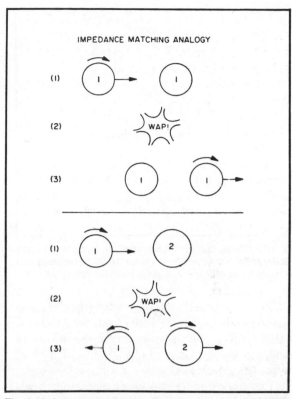

Fig. 3-58. Impedance matching can be represented by the transmission of energy from one rolling ball to another stationary one. If both have equal mass the first will stop and the second take off at equal speed (in a frictionless system). If the second ball is more massive, as illustrated in the three bottom drawings, the first ball will bounce back just as rf will bounce back if an antenna is improperly matched to the transmitter and line.

your transmitter to your antenna and from your antenna to your transmitter, both at the same time. The two sets of waves interact to form standing waves, which decrease the efficiency from maximum and could damage your radio to boot. See Fig. 3-59.

The presence of such waves can be detected by an instrument which measures standing wave ratio. This quantity is a number which you want to be as low as possible. Some sample SWR readings together with what they will do to your radiated power are shown in Table 3-3. 3:1 generally is considered to be the highest SWR a CB radio can live with. And really, that is too high, too. 1.5:1 or less is more like it.

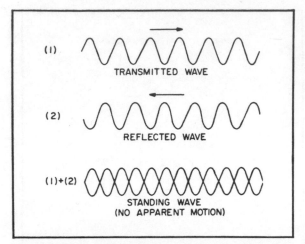

Fig. 3-59. These diagrams show how the transmitted wave and the reflected wave interact to form a standing wave that decreases the efficiency of your transmission.

So buy yourself an SWR meter (they're inexpensive) and check your radio from time to time. If the SWR is too high, getting it down to size usually is just a matter of changing the length of the antenna, provided it is not a fiberglass one.

The procedure for checking a mobile antenna's SWR goes like this: Check the SWR on the highest channel, and then check it on the lowest channel. Ideally, these two numbers will be the same and as low as possible. If the SWR on the highest channel is higher, this indicates the antenna is a bit too long and must be shortened. If the SWR on the lowest channel is higher, then the antenna is too short and must be extended a little. When the two SWR's are identical, then the SWR on the middle channel should be as low as it is going to get, hopefully near 1:1.

Table 3-3. The Effects of SWR.

SWR	Percent Reflected Power	Radiated Power
1:1	0%	4.00 watts
1.5:1	4%	3.84 watts
2:1	11%	3.56 watts
2.5:1	18%	3.28 watts
3:1	25%	3.00 watts
∞:1	100%	0.00 watts

Changing the SWR of a base antenna is another story. There is no convenient little screw to allow you to manipulate the length. If a base antenna's SWR is too high, there is probably something wrong with it or the line leading to it, like bad or wet connections or broken wires. Use your own ingenuity to figure out just what is messed up.

Antenna Gain

Third, there is the fact that all antennas are not created equal. There are those which radiate the legal 4 watts and that's it, and there are those which radiate 4 watts but seem as though they have more effective radiated power (ERP). By mathematically relating the real power output with the ERP we can derive the antenna gain which is normally measured in dBs or decibels.

An easy way to visualize this is to try the following simple experiment: Look at a low-power electric lightbulb, say 10 watts. Your eyes are perceiving 10 watts of light power. Now, hold up a mirror next to the bulb so that you now see two bulbs side by side. Your eyes perceive 20 watts of light power. If you put up a second mirror to see three images you will see 30 watts even though the bulb is still only putting out 10 watts. The ratio of ERP to power is three to one and the ERP multiplication factor is three.

All antenna gain measurements work in much the same way but instead of a 10-watt bulb we use a "standard dipole" antenna. The power received from a test antenna is compared to the power received from the "standard dipole" and the ERP multiplication factor and gain is determined by applying the mathematical equation that is explained elsewhere in this section.

This equation, if reduced to a more readily useable graph form, looks like Fig. 3-60. The graph can be used to find an antenna's multiplication factor (and hence ERP) whenever its dB gain is known. If you know the dB gain, just go up to that number on the dB gain axis, then go straight across until you hit the curve, and then drop down to the multiplication factor axis and read off the antenna's multiplication factor. That number times 4 will get ERP.

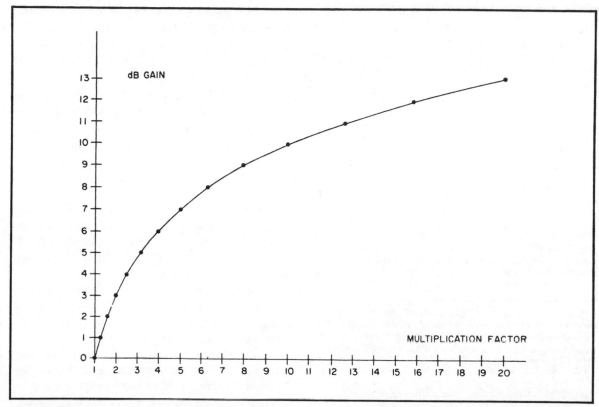

Fig. 3-60. This graph can be used to determine the dB gain if you know the multiplication factor or the multiplication factor if you know the gain. For example; a 12 dB gain will equal a multiplication factor of 15.5. This is much more convenient than the formula.

ERP and Range

So now you know just what your ERP is. What does this mean in a practical sense? If your ERP is, say, three times the basic 4 watts, does this mean you can talk three times as far?

No, it doesn't. You will be able to talk farther, but not three times as far. To find out exactly how much farther, consider the following:

Suppose that at some distance R some radio signal comes in just as strong as some other radio signal at some other distance r. For the two signals to come in at the same strength, their intensities (power per unit area) must be the same, but the ERP must be greater for the signal to travel distance R. By turning this all around mathematically it is possible to discover how much farther a signal will reach (in terms of r) if you know the ERP. Again the mathematics are shown elsewhere in this

section and can be reduced to the graph form as shown in Fig. 3-61.

On the graph, the range of an antenna whose ERP is only 4 watts is taken as 1. The range of other antennas will then be so many times this distance.

For example, the original question was, if an antenna's ERP is 12 watts, how much farther should you be able to talk than with just the basic 4 watts? The answer is readily attained using the graph. Go up the ERP axis until you find 12, then go straight to the right until you hit the curve, and then drop down to the range axis and read off the relative range. In the case of 12 watts you get 1.73, which means you can talk 1.73 times as far as with an antenna with no dB gain.

If you don't mind doing a little math you can derive your dB gain and the range that gain should

147

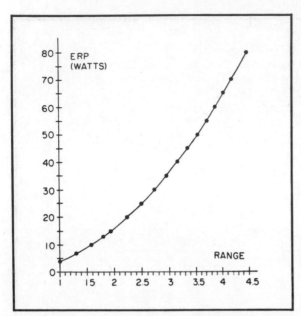

Fig. 3-61. By using this graph your probable range can be determined if you know your effective radiated power (ERP). For example: If your set has a range of 5 miles with no gain (ERP 4 watts for CB), increasing the ERP to 35 watts will up your range to 15 miles (Range factor of 3, times 5 miles).

give you by using the following equations.

dB Gain

This factor can be determined by using the antenna multiplication factor and a logarithm table or the log button on your calculator, and applying the following formula, where ERP = Effective Radiated Power and P = Power:

$$dB\ gain\ =\ 10\ \log\ \frac{ERP}{P}$$

or

$$dB\ gain\ =\ 10\ \log\ (multiplication\ factor)$$

Range

In the diagram below two transmitters put out signals that are received at equal strength at distances R and r respectively. That is, the power per unit area is the same at each point of reception.

From these geometrical relationships we can derive the following formula.

$$R\ =\ r\ \sqrt{\frac{ERP}{P}}$$

In this equation R represents the larger range provided by an antenna with a dB gain, and r represents the range of an antenna with no dB gain.

Beams

But there is just so much dB gain which can be built into an omnidirectional antenna, no matter how clever the designer is. If you want more than five or so dB gain, then you have to move on to a directional antenna, a beam.

A beam gets its super dB gain from taking the idea behind omnidirectional antennas with gain and taking it one step further. An omnidirectional antenna with no gain takes your 4 watts and sprays it all over the place, a lot of it skyward. The skyward part is of no use to anyone, so if it could be eliminated, there would be more to spray out parallel to the ground where it is needed—there would be a gain in useful power, a dB gain.

But even if all your power were sprayed out parallel to the ground, a lot of it still would be wasted. Since generally you are interested in being heard in only one horizontal direction at a time, why waste a lot of power in all the other horizontal, non-skyward directions, too? Why, indeed. So a beam more or less eliminates all wasted energy and radiates in one and only one direction at a time. See Fig. 3-62.

It is a neat trick and is accomplished like this: The simplest beam antenna is composed of three parts or elements. The radio signal is fed into the driver element, which radiates in the usual way. But the reflector element tends to bounce back any waves radiated towards it. This tends to strengthen the signal in the other direction. On the other side of the driver is a director element. It tends to reradiate any energy which is passing by it, narrowing the radiated energy into a stronger, more concentrated beam. More than one director will

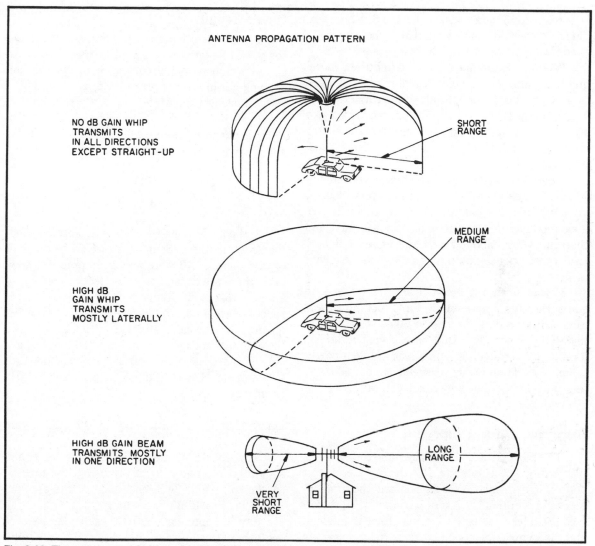

Fig. 3-62. These three drawings are simplified illustrations of antenna propagation patterns. The top diagram is of a unity gain whip antenna—rf propagates equally in almost every direction. The middle antenna is a whip with some gain such as a 5/8 wave VHF antenna or an antenna with an effective ground plane. It will transmit more of its radiation horizontally rather than waste it trying to reach birds. There are thousands of different types of beam antennas but they all try to achieve the results shown in the third drawing—to put the rf out in one direction with as little wasted energy as possible. These antennas also receive directionally. At short ranges they transmit and receive in all directions.

increase this effect, so there are beams with more than three elements.

The only problem is that if someone is trying to talk to you from a direction other than the one in which your beam is pointed, you may never even notice him. Therefore, a beam is seldom used all by itself. An omnidirectional antenna is usually used with the beam as a stand-by antenna. You listen for callers on the stand-by antenna and then point the beam at them to talk.

Power Mikes

And finally, there are power mikes. When a microphone is keyed, a carrier wave is sent out. It is a steady kind of radio wave, having the same amplitude always. (On a wave diagram, the amplitude is represented by the height of the wave.)

When a microphone is keyed and then someone talks into it, the voice signal causes changes to take place in the amplitude of the carrier wave. These changes are called modulation. Given two signals of equal strength, the one with the better modulation will be clearer, louder, and more easily understood.

There are various ways to increase your modulation. You can hold the microphone very close to your lips and talk loudly into it, and this will give good modulation. Or you can buy a power mike and then not worry about where the mike is or how loudly you speak—the power mike will take care of it.

If you do want to buy a power mike, there are some things to remember. First, not all power mikes fit all radios. Second, it takes some skill to install a power mike. And third, if your radio has a mike gain knob on it, you already have a power mike. Now, I don't want to offend you or make you feel unwelcome, but why don't you take your radio and get out?!

UNDERSTANDING DIPOLES

The most critical part of any radio transmitting installation is the antenna. It is the last element of control in transmission of signals, and the first element in reception. As a cost-saving device, the dipole provides an inexpensive, yet efficient antenna, and the knowledge needed to construct one serves as the basis for understanding all types of radio antennas, whether you build your own, or purchase a ready-made one.

What Is a Dipole?

The horizontal dipole is a simple, effective antenna. Antenna wire and accessories for its construction are inexpensive and readily available. It is of a length that makes for efficient use as a receptor of an incoming radio wave. When used as a transmitting antenna, it radiates efficiently and, at the same time, displays a proper impedance to the output of the transmitter.

Dipole Length

The physical length of the antenna is related to the wavelength of the signal frequency to be received or transmitted. Frequency in megahertz, and wavelength in meters are related as follows:

Wavelength in Meters = 330/Frequency in MHz.

For example, the wavelength of a 3.75 MHz signal frequency would be:

$$\text{Wavelength} = \frac{300}{3.75} = 80 \text{ meters}$$

A dipole is a half-wavelength antenna and, therefore, its theoretical length would be one-half of this value, or 40-meters long. In practice, however, there are capacitive end-effects which cause a dipole that is cut to exactly the so-called "free-space" wavelength to be resonant on a lower frequency than the calculated value. In fact, to make the antenna an exact "electrical" half-wavelength long, it is necessary to shorten the physical length by 5-percent. Hence the dipole length for 3.75 MHz resonance would be:

Diople Half-Wavelength = $0.95 \times 40 = 38$ meters

Since the dipole antenna is fed at the center and separated into two quarter-wavelength segments, as shown in Fig. 3-63, each side of the antenna would be 19 (38/2) meters long.

Physical antenna length for each quarter-wave segment of the dipole can be obtained by multiplying the 19 meters times the meters-to-feet conversion constant of 3.2808, obtaining a value of 62.34 feet.

A conversion from metric to linear length results in a very simple equation that can be used to determine the length of the quarter-wavelength segment of a dipole:

$$\text{Length in Feet} = \frac{234}{f(\text{MHz})}$$

A hand calculator is an aid if you wish to make your own antenna calculations.

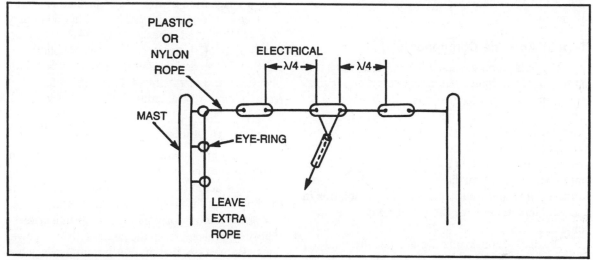

Fig. 3-63. The basic dipole.

Dipole Directivity

The horizontal dipole is directional. As a transmitting antenna, it sends out maximum radio energy (radiation) in the two directions broadside (perpendicular) to the antenna wires (Fig. 3-64). As a receiving antenna, it displays maximum sensitivity to radio signals arriving from the same two directions. Radiation and sensitivity taper off at angles away from the perpendicular, declining to a minimum in the direction along the line (parallel) of the antenna wire. The response pattern of Fig.

3-64 is a theoretical one. The antenna does radiate energy at other angles and is sensitive to incoming signals as well. The extent of the differential depends upon a number of variables including type of antenna, proximity of ground, nearby metallic structures, propagation conditions, transmission line system, etc. It is a fact though, that maximum radiation and sensitivity occur perpendicular to the antenna wire and minimum in the direction of the antenna wire. The figure-eight pattern is itself rather broad, and it is only at angles near to the an-

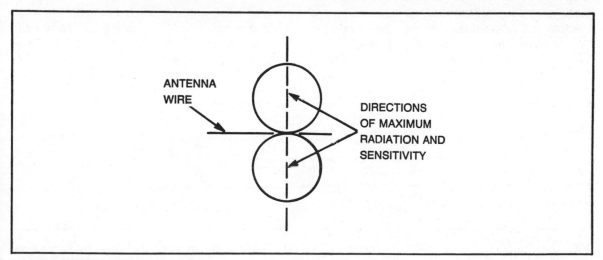

Fig. 3-64. Radiation pattern of a dipole.

gle of the antenna wire that the response is sharply down.

Dipole Antenna Components

Essential components of the dipole antenna are: antenna wire, dipole center connector, end insulators, support rope, transmission line, and other accessories as needed. The antenna wire can be the popular 7-strand, #22 type, which is common and inexpensive. When it can be found at low cost, our personal preference is for #14 or #16 solid, insulated wire. A good-quality, insulated wire gives you added safety and weather protection. Insulation in no way interferes with the radiation or pick-up of signal.

Available end insulators are usually made of porcelain and are 1.75 to 3-inches long. They are oval-shaped or rectangular, some having a ribbed construction. Two holes are provided, one for the antenna wire itself and the other for the support line. Support line can be nylon rope or strong plastic clothes-line with a nonmetallic core. To make it easy to lower the antenna, for cleaning or experimentation, the support line at one end can be fed down through eye-bolts to ground level, as shown in Fig. 3-63.

A coax-to-dipole connector, Fig. 3-65, is the ideal method of linking the dipole antenna to the coaxial transmission line. This connector provides a durable and reasonably weather-proofed connection, providing for convenient connection and detachment of transmission line. An alternative plan is to use an end insulator at the center. The two conductors of the transmission line can be attached firmly, soldered and taped to the antenna wire on each side of the center insulator.

Use good quality coaxial line, either 50-ohm or 70-ohm. Preferred types are RG-58A/U (50 ohms) or RG-59A/U (70 ohms) for low power applications. RG-8A/U is recommended for higher-powered applications, and installations where a long feed line, from antenna to transmitter, is necessary.

Erection of Dipole

Plan your installation according to length, height, and directional orientation. You must consider the space required by the antenna, and where the line must be brought into the house.

Safety and performance are important criteria. For safety reasons, keep the antenna clear of power lines. Be certain that if the antenna falls when erected, or while under erection, it cannot fall across electrical wires. Make certain that under no circumstances, can mast or wire come in contact with power lines if you lose control of the mast or antenna. Keeping clear of power lines also improves the antenna performance. You will pick up less power line noise on receive. On transmit, you will radiate the least signal into the power lines, minimizing loss and possible interference with home entertainment units such as television receivers and high-fidelity amplifiers.

Tuning With an SWR Meter

An SWR meter connected between transmitter and transmission line, Fig. 3-66, can be used to measure the resonant frequency of a dipole. To go a step further, the antenna can now be trimmed or extended if it does not resonate to the desired fre-

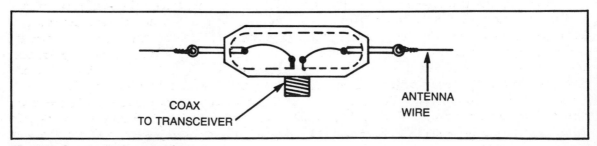

Fig. 3-65. Coax-to-dipole connections.

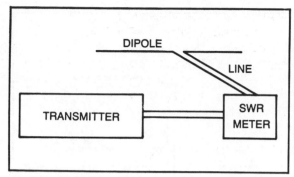

Fig. 3-66. SWR meter in line.

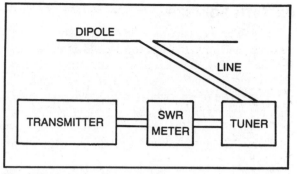

Fig. 3-67. Antenna tuner in line.

quency. The results can be observed on the SWR meter, as the antenna resonant frequency is moved up or down the band. Since it is easier to trim off rather than to add on wire length, cut the initial antenna wire longer than specified value for the particular frequency, in order to catch up with any variables that might influence resonance. A practical example will demonstrate an acceptable procedure.

Assume an antenna is to be cut for 7150 kHz in the 40 Meter Amateur band. This suggests a dipole length of 32-feet, 9-inches. Cut each dipole element to 33-feet, which would be for a resonant frequency of 7100 kHz. Erect the antenna on a temporary basis.

Measure the SWR every 25 kHz between 7025 and 7225. Set the readings down in a table form of frequency vs. SWR. Determine the precise frequency at which the SWR reading is minimum. This would be the resonant frequency. Then, trim accordingly.

Antenna Tuners at Work

The primary function of an antenna tuner, Fig. 3-67, is to provide a proper match between your antenna system and transmitter. In so doing, your transmitter sees a proper load and is able to operate at the optimum conditions of its design. The tuner does not alter the performance of the antenna or the SWR on its transmission line. Rather, it makes certain that an improper SWR does not result in unfavorable operation or possible damage to your transmitter.

A tuner makes the dimensioning of a horizontal dipole antenna less critical. It extends the range of operation of the antenna that will provide an ideal match to the transmitter. For example, an 80 Meter dipole cut to 3750 kHz, will be made operable over the entire 80 Meter band from 3500-4000 kHz. The electrical performance of the antenna will not differ greatly from an antenna cut precisely to some specific frequency on the band. Even though the SWR on the transmission line might be rather high at the band extremes, the transmitter itself will look into an optimum load.

Conclusion

The horizontal dipole, as we mentioned earlier, forms the basis for most of the other modern types of antennae. If you were to examine the driven element of a beam, you would find it to be nothing more than a simple dipole with adjustable tuning tips at both ends. It is even possible to make a three or four-element beam by paralleling several dipoles with fractional wavelength spaces between them. Of course, if you are not in the position to "grow" your own antenna farm due to space limitations, a single dipole's performance is not to be laughed at.

The dipole itself can take on other physical configurations, such as a "vee;" and "inverted vee;" a "sloper;" or even a "vertical" dipole.

The horizontal dipole is indeed a versatile antenna, giving good performance at low cost. It should be dimensioned properly, and should be used with an SWR meter to evaluate its performance.

DX WITH BOINGER

If you're an apartment-dwelling DXer, you've no doubt had your share of the age-old antenna hassle. Sad to say, few landlords sympathize with a shortwave listener's need for a good skyhook.

For those of you whose nerves are just about shot from the continual carping about your antenna (". . . that confounded wire of yours was crudding-up Kung Fu last night!"), the "Boinger" will bring fast relief.

What's the Boinger

Simply put, it's an inconspicuous *canned* antenna that'll sit on your windowsill, drawing about as much attention as yesterday's newspaper. Fact is, people just don't notice this little marvel. That's the beauty of it! But at the push of a button, this DX-dangler literally springs into action for you, as it accordions out to a fully-expanded shortwave longwire antenna. "Boinger" will be music to your ears. That's the sound made by the key to this antenna, a super-long spring. And as it unravels, it'll also unravel your aerial problems. And when you're ready to call it quits for an evening, just a few turns of the crank retracts the Boinger back into the hardly-noticeable case, ready for another day. It's been suggested we call this unit the "Candestine" (clandestine can antenna), since it does incorporate a bit of the old cloak-and-dagger. Call it what you may, it works in even the most impossible antenna conditions.

How It Works

Our Boinger is essentially an end-fed helically-wound longwire. The only big difference between it and the longwire most SWLs use is that it is vertically-oriented.

How do you find helically-wound wire? Believe it or not, the first place to check is in Junior's toybox! Or, head for the local five-and-ten and ask for "the spring that walks down stairs by itself." Right—a "Slinky!"

Since the coil is vertical, gravity will help pull it down for you. Rigging it to a fishing reel will take care of pulling it back up again. You don't have to

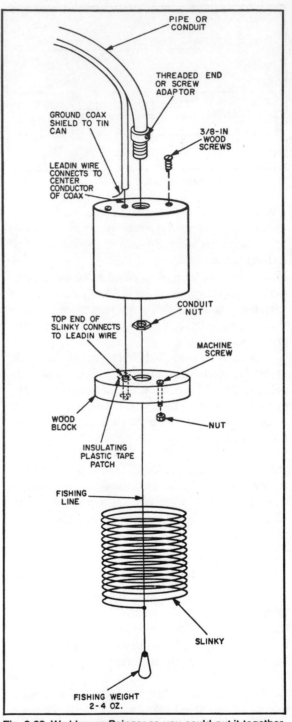

Fig. 3-68. We blew up Boinger so you could put it together. Electrical connection of Slinky to antenna leadin wire should be insulated from tin can and pipe or conduit.

154

be 20 stories up to take advantage of this antenna since the helical winding allows you to pack tremendous wire length into a short distance.

How to Build It

You'll need the following items, all of which shouldn't run more than $6 to $10:

Slinky. Actually it's a highly stretchable coil which folds down to only a few inches, but can stretch clear across the street.

Tin can to house the spring, about four-inches in diameter by five-inches deep. A salted peanut tin is perfect.

Some odds and ends from your fishing gear—a handful of lead weights, and a fishing reel with heavy-duty line. Now don't panic, the cheapest reel available will do. We've seen, and used in our own Boinger, a plastic reel that goes for about $3.

1/2-in. Conduit Pipe. Aluminum electrical conduit is easy to bend, and you'll need a screw-end adapter to secure it to the can. If you use iron pipe, it can be threaded at the can end, but it's hard to bend. However, elbow pieces are available. Look at 1/2-in. copper tubing. It's easy to work with and can be soldered to the tin can.

Miscellaneous Hardware: clamps, screws, and a piece of 1/2-inch-thick wood to fit in the can.

Construction

See diagram in Fig. 3-68. Solder an insulated leadin wire to the top end of the Slinky coil—or secure it with a machine screw. Any way you do it is okay so long as it's mechanically secure. Be sure not to let the antenna leadin wire contact the can or the conduit.

The conduit pipe serves double-duty in the Boinger. It is both the support for the unit and the feeder channel for the fishing line that controls the antenna's ups-and-downs. Bend the pipe into a flattened-out Z, with the center strut at right angles to the ends. Then, lay the pipe down flat and bend one end so it points straight up.

Put the wood-coil assembly into the can, and drill a hole through both, big enough for the pipe to fit through. Slip the end of the pipe (the end you made the last bend in) through the hole in the top of the can and through the wood, clamping both below and above with epoxy glue or threaded pipe and nut so it is solidly joined. Slip the wire through a hole in the can top, and tape it along the length of the pipe. It's a good idea to liberally apply putty or silicone sealer to the can top to seal the cracks—the Boinger will withstand some pretty rough weather.

Now, thread the fishing line into the far end of the pipe and pull it through the coil. Make a cross-hatch with two wires across the bottom loop of the Slinky (opposite end from the solder), and tie the fishing line, along with a few weights, here.

Mount the fishing reel on your inside window sill, and bolt the pipe to the outside wall. Depending upon the type of window, you may have to cut a small piece of glass out of the corner to feed the pipe through. We found that closing the window on the pipe and then trimming a wooden "stopper" to size for the crack is one good way.

Attach the leadin wire to your receiver and let out some line on the reel. Boing! Gravity and the weights will stretch out your mini-antenna as far as you need. When you're finished, the coil will reel up and fit neatly in the can. Paint it a dull black, draw as little attention as possible when you install it and, believe it or not, you'll be surprised when nobody notices all the trouble you've gone to!

Chapter 4

Digital Electronics

UNDERSTANDING LOGIC CIRCUITS

The first mistake made by people trying to explain digital logic is their insistence on name dropping. They confuse a reasonably simple subject with technical terms such as CMOS, TTL, PMOS and so on and so on. There's plenty of time to learn about these later, but first we must learn what a digital logic circuit is.

A digital logic circuit is, for all intended purposes, a solid state relay network. After a statement like this there are probably a few engineers out there grinding their teeth and pulling out their hair, but this basic definition will help you more than any explanation of "electron movement through silicon substrates."

All digital logic circuits can be broken down into combinations of three basic logic gates. These gates receive information in the form of one or more inputs of a high- or a low-voltage level—usually +5 volts dc and 0 volts (ground potential). Depending on what type of gate it is, an appropriate voltage level appears at the output. The three basic gates

are called NOT, AND and OR. Their operation can be simulated by using plain old-fashioned mechanical relays.

NOT Gates

Now we will see where the relays come into action. Look at the diagrams of the NOT gate in Fig. Fig. 4-1. When there is no input voltage the relay is not energized and the relay contact connects the output to the high voltage level. In other words, a low input is inverted by a NOT gate. When a high voltage level is applied to the input, the relay energizes and connects the output to ground potential. The gate has inverted the high input to a low output. No matter what the input is, it is NOT the output.

The next two gates, the AND and OR gates, are a bit more complicated since they have two or more inputs. When you think of them try to think of the AND gate as a series gate and the OR gate as a parallel gate. This may not be clear yet but it will help you to keep things straight in the future.

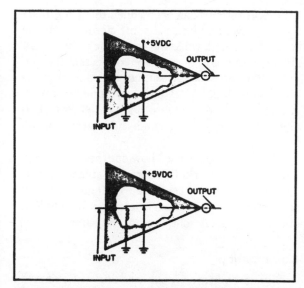

Fig. 4-1. This is the magnetic-relay equivalent of a logical NOT gate. When the input is too low to energize the magnet the relay contact is connected to the 5-volt dc power source. So, when the input is low the output is high. In the second diagram the input is high enough to energize the relay and the contact is grounded. When input is high, output is low.

AND Gates

In order for the output of an AND gate to be high all inputs must be high. If any of the inputs are low the output will be low. Look at the first of the AND gate diagrams in Fig. 4-2. Both inputs are low and neither relay is energized. The relay contacts connect the output to ground and therefore the output is low.

In the next two diagrams in Fig. 4-2 we try putting a high on one or the other inputs. In each situation the output is still connected to ground and the output is low.

When all of the inputs are high the relay contacts connect the output pin to 5 volts dc and the output of the gate is high. Any number of relays could be added in a similar manner and the output would be high only when all inputs were high, hence it is a series gate.

OR Gates

An OR gate is a parallel gate and its output is high if any of its inputs are high. In the first dia-

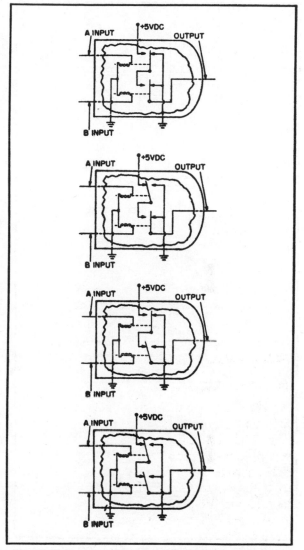

Fig. 4-2. When both inputs to an AND gate are at a low level, as is shown in the first diagram, the relays are de-energized. Each set of contacts connects the output to ground. In the second diagram input A is at a high voltage level (typically 5 volts dc) and the upper relay is energized, yet the output is still low. Now, in the third diagram, we put a high on the B input. The lower relay is energized but the output pin is still grounded. In the last diagram we see what happens when both input are high. The two relay contacts connect the output to 5 Vdc. The output will be high only if both inputs are high.

gram in Fig. 4-3, all the inputs are low and none of the relays are energized. The contacts of the relays connect the output pin to ground and the out-

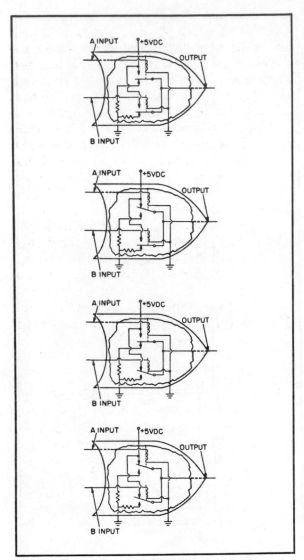

is high. A resistor has been added to each ground line to prevent an internal short circuit when one contact is on high while the other is low. In the last sketch both relay contacts are connecting the output to the high-voltage source, and the output is high. As with the AND gate, any number of relay circuits could be added in this parallel format. If any number of inputs are high then the output will be high.

Now we have learned how our three basic digital logic gates work. Of course, in an actual logic circuit the relays are replaced by integrated circuit transistors that switch the levels from high to low, but the inputs and outputs are the same.

Combinations

By now you are probably asking why this article has ignored all the other gates you've probably heard about—the NAND and NOR gates for example. The reason is that these and all other logic gates are combinations of the three basic gates. A NAND gate is really a NOT/AND gate since it is a combination of the two. In the diagram in Fig. 4-4 of the NAND gate you will see that it is an AND gate whose output is inverted by a NOT gate. For example: When any of the AND gate's inputs are low the output is low, but now the input of the NOT gate is low so its output is high. If all AND gate inputs are high then the input to the NOT gate is high and its output is low. Therefore the output of a NAND gate is high unless all inputs are high, and

Fig. 4-3. In the relay-equivalent circuit of an OR gate we have added a couple of resistors to prevent an internal short circuit. Note that when both inputs are low both relay contacts connect the output to ground. In the second OR gate diagram the upper relay is energized by a high voltage level at the A input. This connects the output to the 5 Vdc contact of the relay. In the third diagram the B input is high while A is low. Again you can see by tracing out the current flow that the output will be high. By now the last diagram should need little explanation. Both relays are energized and the output is connected to 5 Vdc through both relay contacts.

put is low. In the next two diagrams in Fig. 4-3 one of the inputs is high while the other is low. Now the output is connected to 5 Vdc and the output pin

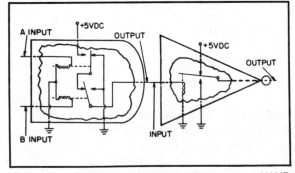

Fig. 4-4. An AND gate in series with a NOT gate is an NAND gate. It is normally shown as an AND symbol with a circle to represent an inverted output. Trace out the current flow with different inputs.

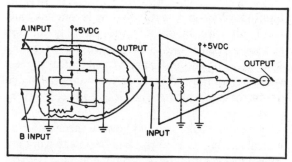

Fig. 4-5. A NOR gate is an OR gate with its output inverted by a NOT gate. It is represented as an OR symbol with a small circle at the output. Again, trace out the circuit for all possible input combinations.

then the output would be low. The output of a NAND gate is always the opposite of an AND gate if the inputs are identical.

A NOR or NOT/OR gate works in much the same way except that its output is the opposite of an OR gate. See Fig. 4-5. A NOT gate is added to the output of the OR gate turning the lows to highs and the highs to lows. A NOR gate's output will be high when both inputs are low, and its output will be low when one, or both, are high.

Exclusive Gates

Two more important gates are the exclusive OR and exclusive NOR gates. See Fig. 4-6. The exclusive OR gate has a low output when the inputs are either all high or all low. If one input is high and the other low then the output is high. An exclusive NOR gate, as you might have guessed, has a high output if the two inputs are the same and a low output if they are not the same. An exclusive OR or NOR gate can only have two inputs.

Making an exclusive OR gate is a little more tricky. It comprises two NOT gates, two AND gates and an OR gate. Study the diagram of this gate and see what happens. When both inputs are the same the two NOT gates cause each AND gate to receive a high and a low. They will, in turn, put a low on each input of the OR gate and its output will be low. Now, if we put different signals into the two inputs the NOT gates will criss-cross the signal levels so that one AND gate receives two lows and the other two highs. This will put a high on the OR gate's input and its output will also be high. To make this an exclusive NOR gate we just add a NOT gate to the final output.

Flip-Flops

You now have a pretty-good understanding of how digital logic circuits work, but there is one more type of device that needs some explaining—the flip-flop. The best way to understand about flip-flops is to think back to your childhood when you used to play a game called "Red Light—Green Light." One kid was "it" and the others could only

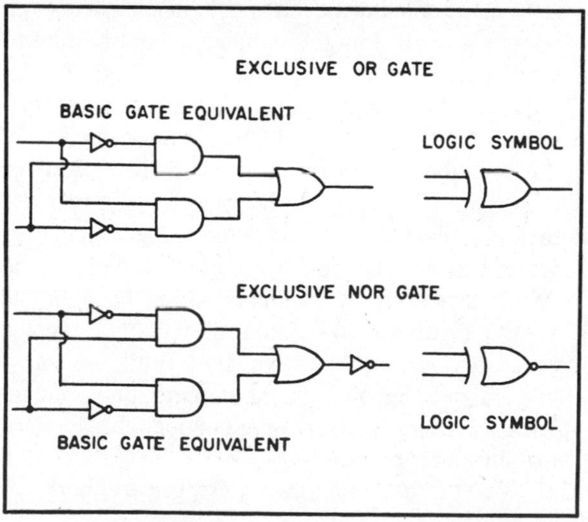

Fig. 4-6. Exclusive Gates are special combinations of logic gates. Use your knowledge of the three basic gates to see how the exclusive OR gate and exclusive NOR gate operates. First, see what happens when both inputs are low; then make A high and B low; then B high and A low; then try it with both A and B at a high level. See how the two gates are opposites.

sneak up on him when he turned his back and said "green light." If he said "red light," everyone had to freeze in whatever positions they were in before he turned around and stay that way until he gave another "green light." A flip-flop works just like that. When the circuit gets the "red light" its output freezes at whatever level is on the input at that moment. An actual flip-flop may have a few more frills but if you remember red light, green light you should have no problems with these handy devices.

To see how a flip-flop works we have to put our collection of logic gates together in a more-complex fashion. There are actually two main sections in a flip-flop, the gating network and the flip-flop itself.

First, let's take a look at the gating network. There are two inputs—the data input and the latch (red light—green light) input. Now, consider what happens under green-light conditions when the latch input is high. This input is connected to one input on each of 2, two-input AND gates. (Refer to the gating network diagrams in Fig. 4-7). The data input is split into two lines, one goes straight into one AND gate and the other goes through a NOT gate to put the opposite signal on the other AND gate. These two inputs are referred to as D and $\bar{D}$ ("data bar" is how "$\bar{D}$" is said), D being the data and $\bar{D}$ being its opposite or complement.

The outputs of the AND gates are called set and reset. When D is high, set is high and reset is low. When D is low then reset will be high and set low. The levels on these two lines will toggle back and forth with the level of the input data.

The set and reset lines, known as S and R, feed into the two NOR gates that make up the flip-flop section of the circuit. The second input of each NOR gate is fed by the output of the other NOR gate. As the levels on the S and R inputs change then so changes the output of the flip-flop. Flip-flop outputs are referred to as Q (the value equal to the true data input) and $\bar{Q}$ its complement. Now, what happens when the light turns red?

Applying a low level to the latch input changes things around considerably. Both AND gates now have a low on one of their inputs. No matter what other signals they may receive, their outputs will both be low and therefore the R and S inputs to the

flip-flop will be low. If the flip-flop is toggling back and forth, with the outputs alternately going high and low, when R and S both go low the toggling will stop. The outputs Q and $\bar{Q}$ will hold at the last value before the red light. If you study these diagrams for a few minutes then it will all become very clear.

Once you have learned how all these different logical circuits operate you will be able to work out some more complicated arrangements, and perhaps even spend some time researching the differences between TTL, CMOS and all those other little digital details.

TRANSISTOR LOGIC DEMONSTRATORS

Now that you fully understand the ins and outs of basic digital theory, (well, it made sense to us anyway) you're probably itching for a bit of hands-on experimenting to see if what we've said really works, and how it applies to the projects you're eagerly waiting to build. The following four quickie demonstrator projects can be assembled in a snap with parts you probably already have cluttering up the junk box. You might want to leave these demonstrators assembled as you build the IC projects, to serve as a logic guide for checking out and troubleshooting the projects in their final phases.

The size of these demonstrators also serves as an indicator of just how far the electronics industry has advanced in the space of just a few years, in terms of miniaturization of components, and component groups. Imagine what it would be like to build even the most rudimentary of our 99 Integrated Circuit projects, if each and every gate had to be hand-fabricated and wired point-to-point! By the time the builder got done with the making of the ersatz ICs, he or she wouldn't feel much like tackling the construction project for which they were intended. On this scale of construction, the Apollo spacecraft would have had to be as big as a Navy destroyer to contain all of the electronics necessary for the lunar voyage! While you may gripe about Detroit's shrinking cars, and your favorite restaurant's shrinking portions, be thankful for shrinking circuits!

Don't forget about the energy crisis either! Just

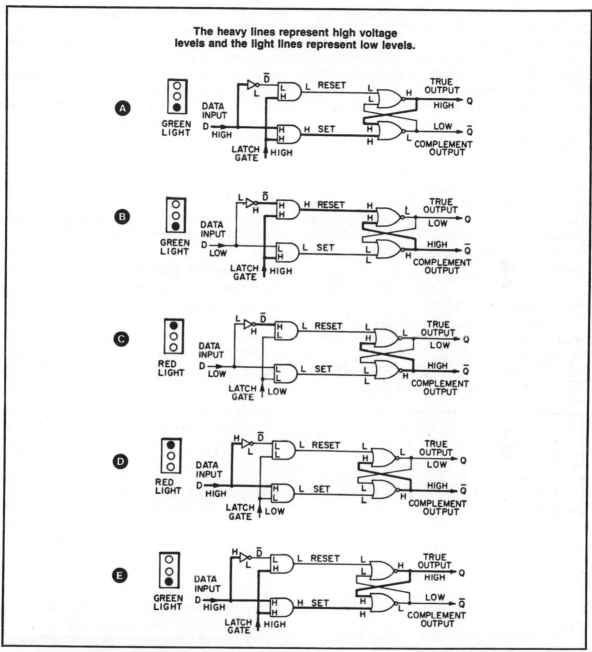

Fig. 4-7. (A) Under green-light (latch input high) conditions with a high data input, the set line is high and the reset low. The true output is high and it is fed back to reinforce the set line's data input. (B) A low data input will toggle the set and reset lines to their opposite levels. Now the complement output is high and it reinforces the reset line. (C) Changing the latch input of a low voltage level causes both AND gates to have a low output on set and reset. the complement output, however, still keeps a high on the reset NOR gate and the true output is still low. (D) If the data input now toggles to a high value it will have no effect on either the true or the complementary outputs. The flip-flop is now latched tight. (E) In the last diagram we return the high voltage level to the latch input. The circuit is now free to toggle back and forth with the incoming signal.

because you're not queueing up in mile-long lines for gasoline, don't think that electrical power is all that free and easy to come by. These circuits require the full output of a nine volt transistor battery to make them operable. Their equivalents in IC form use, in many cases, half the voltage, and only one-tenth the current. In practice, the efficient use of energy by the new types of integrated circuits can allow them to be powered by some of the less conventional, and ostensibly cheaper, sources of electricity, such as small photocells, thermochemical body-heat generators, and the like. In fact, if electrical consumption in industry was reduced the way it has been for and by the new ICs, we probably wouldn't need all of the new generating facilities currently being planned and fought over today!

AND Logic Demonstrator

In digital logic, an AND statement is true only if all parts of the logic leading to it (its inputs) are all true. If we take "true" to mean "on," a logic state we define as "1" (and not true = off = 0), we can see that a series switch configuration is a good way to illustrate the AND logical statement. See Fig. 4-8.

In integrated circuit logic, instead of actual mechanical switches, transistors are used as switches. Specifically, this circuit demonstrates the action on a "two-input AND gate." Only if both switches are on will the LED turn on. Similarly, you can expand the demonstrator to demonstrate as many inputs to an AND gate as you have switches to connect in series.

Once again, we present the "truth table" of this particular circuit which will tell you exactly what's happening and when. Truth tables are often used in digital design, and can be indispensable. Depending on the device, they can be quite long.

NAND Logic Demonstrator

NAND is logic shorthand for "Not And." So a NAND gate has an output of 1 only when an AND gate would not. Compare the right column (results, or output) of an AND gate truth table to that for the NAND gate above and you will see that they are exactly opposite. See Fig. 4-9.

Here, the LED will turn on only if the two

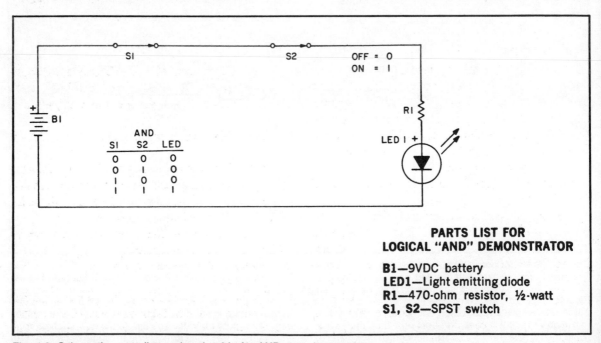

	AND	
S1	S2	LED
0	0	0
0	1	0
1	0	0
1	1	1

OFF = 0
ON = 1

PARTS LIST FOR LOGICAL "AND" DEMONSTRATOR

B1—9VDC battery
LED1—Light emitting diode
R1—470-ohm resistor, ½-watt
S1, S2—SPST switch

Fig. 4-8. Schematic, parts list, and truth table for AND gate demonstrator.

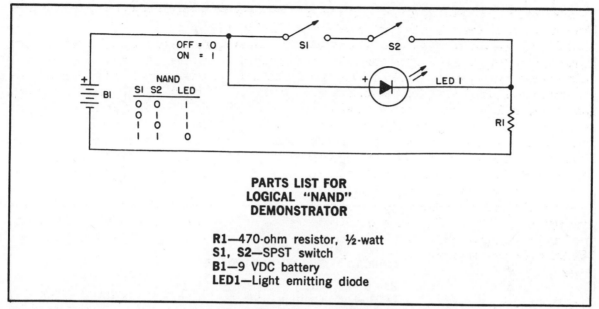

Fig. 4-9. Schematic, parts list, and truth table for NAND gate demonstrator.

switches are not both turned on. Be careful that the series combination of S1 and S2 can short out only the LED and not R1 as well or your battery will not last more than a few seconds. R1 limits the current drain on the battery to about 20 milliamps.

OR Logic Demonstrator

In digital logic, an OR statement is true if any one of the statements leading to it is true. Parallel switches are a good analogy for the OR logic function. If any of the parallel switches are on (=true="1"), the LED turns on. While the circuit in Fig. 4-10 demonstrates the operation of a "two-input OR gate," you may add as many parallel switches as you like to demonstrate the action of "wider" OR gates.

OR gates are very widely used in alarm circuits, for example, where an alarm should be sounded whenever anything occurs at any one of the several inputs. The chart of numbers is known as a "Truth Table." The columns at the left identify the states of the various inputs, the column at the right the state of the output. Compare the results (right column) of this Truth Table with the results of other types of logic and you will see why digital logic systems can be so versatile.

The nice thing about this circuit is that it's so visual. You'll find that it's so much easier to understand digital logic when you can watch what's happening rather than reading about it.

NOR Logic Demonstrator

Just as the output of a NAND gate is the opposite of that for an AND gate, this NOR gate produces results opposite those of an OR gate. See Fig. 4-11.

LED1 will turn on when neither S1 nor S2 are on.

A NOR gate is a good way to handle a failsafe system in which a circuit cannot operate unless all systems are "go;" in other words, if any of the inputs are on, the system cannot be.

This truth table compares the operation of different types of logic gates:

Think of 0 = off = not true,

1 = on = true

Digital logic is certainly in the forefront of modern electronics. Circuits such as this NOR Demonstrator can help to prepare you in understanding complex circuitry. The principles you learn remain

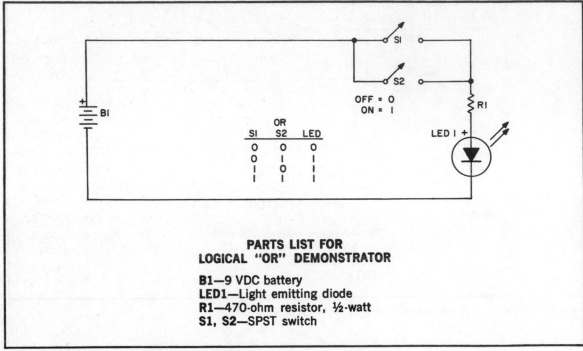

**PARTS LIST FOR
LOGICAL "OR" DEMONSTRATOR**

B1—9 VDC battery
LED1—Light emitting diode
R1—470-ohm resistor, ½-watt
S1, S2—SPST switch

Fig. 4-10. Schematic, parts list, and truth table for OR gate demonstrator.

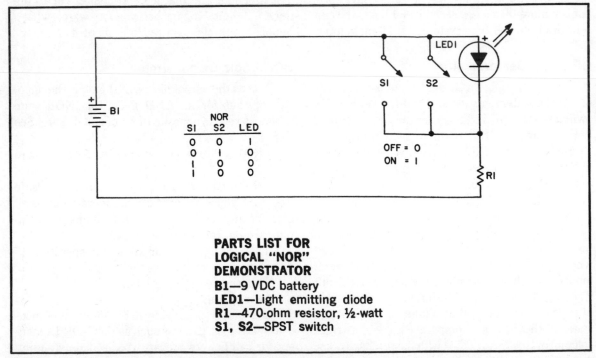

**PARTS LIST FOR
LOGICAL "NOR"
DEMONSTRATOR**
B1—9 VDC battery
LED1—Light emitting diode
R1—470-ohm resistor, ½-watt
S1, S2—SPST switch

Fig. 4-11. Schematic, parts list, and truth table for NOR gate demonstrator.

164

the same as in actual digital circuitry—only the method of achieving demonstrable results changes.

DIGITAL NUMBERING FOR THE HOBBYIST

Digital numbers—they are everywhere! The entire electronics world has been caught-up in the digital revolution—watches, radios, TVs, VOMs, frequency counters—the list is almost endless. But, have your construction projects been a part of the revolution or are you still back in the hobbyist stone age of meters and light bulbs? Do your projects look like 20th Century state-of-the-art or do they look more like a turn-of-the-century patent application?

If you think it is time to go digital but feel that the technology is beyond your grasp you are not alone. There is a mumbo jumbo that has grown up around digital electronics that makes people think they have to learn all about computers before they can do any kind of digital project. If you have ever made the mistake of asking a "computer know-it-all" how digital number displays work, you are sure to have received a two-hour lecture on binary numbers, Boolean algebra and assorted flip-flops, and come away knowing less than when you started.

Learn Backwards

All this hassle is unnecessary, however, if you learn digital electronics backwards!! Start with the familiar end result, a decimal number display, and work backwards into the circuitry that makes it possible.

Digital displays come in a number of different forms but all the circuits discussed here will use a common cathode, seven-segment LED (Light Emitting Diode) numeric display. These are cheap, easily obtainable and the circuitry can be adapted to other types—especially the liquid crystal type displays. The best way to learn about numeric displays is to put one together so you can physically see how it works and how the various components interact.

To simplify construction of the demonstration circuit accompanying this section a Continental Specialties Corporation PB-203 solderless breadboard was used. It allowed almost infinite experimentation with various circuit arrangements—experimentation that would have otherwise consumed a prohibitive amount of time. The parts are referred to by their common name since many parts with different numbers can perform the same tasks. The parts used in the demonstration circuit

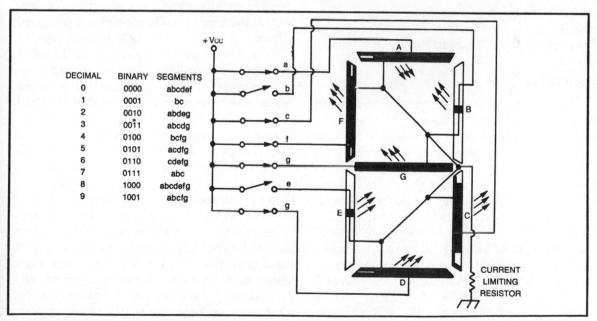

Fig. 4-12. Diagram of a seven-segment display.

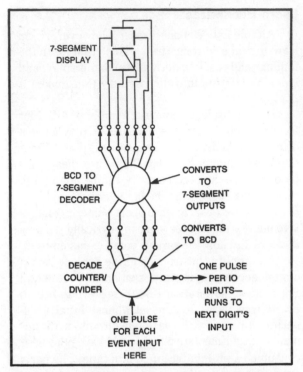

7-SEGMENT DISPLAY

BCD TO 7-SEGMENT DECODER — CONVERTS TO 7-SEGMENT OUTPUTS

CONVERTS TO BCD

DECADE COUNTER/ DIVIDER — ONE PULSE PER IO INPUTS— RUNS TO NEXT DIGIT'S INPUT

ONE PULSE FOR EACH EVENT INPUT HERE

Fig. 4-13. This block diagram shows how the sequence of pulses at the input are first translated to BCD and then to seven-segment coding.

are identified by their generic part number—most parts distributors will have a cross-reference from this number to the manufacturer's part number.

Translating

As you can see in the diagram of the seven-segment display, Fig. 4-12, any digit from zero to nine can be represented by a certain combination of lit LED segments. Each of these segments is an individual LED with its cathode tied to a common ground; hence the name common cathode (some have common anodes). Each segment can now be activated by a switch between the anode and a power source. Switching on segments a, c, d, f and g, for example will cause the digit five to be lit. (As a practical consideration be sure to use a current limiting resistor—110 ohms in the circuit shown.)

We can now represent any digit by various combinations of "on" or "off" of the seven switches. There is a potential for 49 different

character displays with this set-up—well beyond the needs of a numeric display.

So, by using a common integrated circuit chip we can reduce the number of switches to four. See Fig. 4-13. The internal circuitry of the BCD to seven-segment decoder (the name will make more sense later), as the chip is called, takes the combinations of the four "ons" and "offs" and applies power to the appropriate LED segments. This representation of a digit by four combinations of "on" and "off" is called Binary Coded Decimal or BCD for short. A binary number uses only zero and one rather than zero through nine. The one can be represented electronically by a high level voltage and the zero by a low level voltage. Figure 4-12 shows decimal numbers, their BCD equivalent and the segments that are lit on a numeric display.

We now have a circuit that can translate "computerese" BCD numbering into the decimal numbers we have used all our lives.

Learning to Count

Now we need to teach our circuit to count from zero to nine. We can do this by adding an integrated circuit chip called a decade counter. This integrated circuit has one input line and four outputs. The outputs, as you have probably guessed, are connected to the four input lines of the BCD to seven-segment decoder. The outputs are all at zero until a single pulse appears on the input line. Then one of the outputs changes to a "one" so that the BCD to Seven-Segment decoder receives the number 0001 and lights segments b and c. On the second pulse the decade counter sends out the number 0010 and a 2 lights up on the display. This continues until the decade counter gets to nine; it then recycles to zero.

You should congratulate yourself—you now have a practical event counter that will total (up to nine) the number of pulses generated by the occurrence of some event. A switch on a refrigerator door that will turn on once each time the door is opened might allow you to record how many times it has been opened. Unfortunately there is a phenomenon of mechanical switches called contact bounce, where one switch-closing can trigger 3 or 4 pulses. This can be eliminated by adding a one-shot multivibrator, or similar circuit, to clean up the unwanted pulses. For the demonstration circuit the event pulses were obtained from a free-running multivibrator signal generator for simplicity and freedom from unwanted pulses.

Extra Digits

Now it is time to add a few more digits. After all, how many useful things can be measured by a single digit? To do this we must add a second set of the three components already mentioned: a numeric display, a BCD to Seven-Segment Decoder and a Decade Counter. Everything is wired the same way except that the input for the second decade counter is attached to the "carry out" pin of the first counter. This pin gives off an output pulse each time the counter resets from nine to zero. So, after the first display gets to nine and then resets, the second display counts one so that the display reads ten. When the decade counter resets a second time the display clicks to 20. An almost infinite number of digits could be added that would count once each time the preceding stage reset to zero.

A counter such as this could be used for any sort of tallying operation where you have to keep a record of how many events have taken place. Most digital applications, however, involve rate operations—cycles-per-second, miles-per-hour, gallons-per-day or even dollars-per-week.

Rate Measurements

For the above counter to be converted to measure the number of events per unit of time a few additions have to be made. The first of these is called a clock. A clock gives you the seconds of miles-per-second or the hour of inches-per-hour. It sets the interval over which the number of events is counted. This is achieved by adding a simple

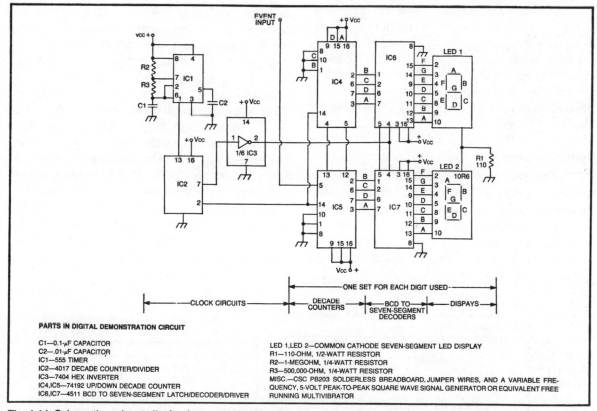

PARTS IN DIGITAL DEMONSTRATION CIRCUIT

C1—0.1-μF CAPACITOR
C2—.01-μF CAPACITOR
IC1—555 TIMER
IC2—4017 DECADE COUNTER/DIVIDER
IC3—7404 HEX INVERTER
IC4,IC5—74192 UP/DOWN DECADE COUNTER
IC6,IC7—4511 BCD TO SEVEN-SEGMENT LATCH/DECODER/DRIVER

LED 1,LED 2—COMMON CATHODE SEVEN-SEGMENT LED DISPLAY
R1—110-OHM, 1/2-WATT RESISTOR
R2—1-MEGOHM, 1/4-WATT RESISTOR
R3—500,000-OHM, 1/4-WATT RESISTOR
MISC—CSC PB203 SOLDERLESS BREADBOARD, JUMPER WIRES, AND A VARIABLE FREQUENCY, 5-VOLT PEAK-TO-PEAK SQUARE WAVE SIGNAL GENERATOR OR EQUIVALENT FREE RUNNING MULTIVIBRATOR

Fig. 4-14. Schematic and parts list for demonstration circuit.

freerunning multivibrator. In the case of the circuit shown it puts out five volts with momentary negative going pulses at regular intervals. Once calibrated to the proper rate this multivibrator remains at a constant frequency.

The clock has two main jobs: It must reset the entire counter circuit to zero at the appropriate time and it must freeze the display at the appropriate part of the counting cycle so that it is a readable and meaningful number rather than a blur of speeding digits.

This last task requires a device known as a latch. A latch is a circuit that freezes on whatever BCD number is in its register when a high voltage is applied to the "latch enable" pin. If your circuit is counting from zero to 1000 every 10 seconds and you put a high voltage on the "latch enable" pin at 6 seconds the display will hold at 600. If it is grounded at seven seconds the display will resume the count at 700. So the count doesn't stop—it is only the display that freezes. In the circuit shown in Fig. 4-14, the latch is incorporated in the BCD to Seven-segment decoder IC chip.

By carefully coordinating the counter "reset-to-zero" pulse and the latch pulse so that the latch freezes the count display a moment before the counter resets, we have an event per unit time display.

Synchronizing

To get this proper synchronization of clock, latch and reset, a Johnson counter or decade counter/divider is used. In this chip there are 10 output pins that go high (puts out a 5-volt pulse) in a repeating sequence. So for every 10 input pulses each pin goes high once, one after the other. If we control the latch with the pin that goes high on the first input pulse to the counter and then reset with the pin that goes high on the third input pulse we can control the display so that it will latch and reset at the proper time. The pin that goes high on the second pulse isn't used because of pulse overlapping. See Fig. 4-15.

One slight problem with the output to the latch is that it needs to be inverted. This is accomplished by sending the pulse by way of an inverter. You can use a common inverter. An inverter is a device that produces a high output with a low input and a low output from a high input.

Putting It All to Work

You have now finished your basic rate measuring device. Now it's up to you to incorporate all of this into your pet project. All you have to do is convert your project's output into series' of pulses of high and low voltage—high being about five volts and low about zero volts. A high-frequency of pulses will give a high numeric readout and a low frequency of pulses a low readout.

If your project gives a variable voltage readout you can buy a chip called an analog to digital converter—this puts out a higher frequency of pulses in proportion to an increase in voltage.

The chips used in this project were referred to by their general name rather than number since the attached schematic is only an example of a typical digital numbering circuit. There are hundreds of other combinations of similar integrated circuit chips. After you have worked with these circuits for a while you will begin to understand the system better and will find yourself designing more and more complex circuits.

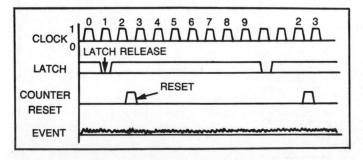

Fig. 4-15. The clock sets the timing of the latch and reset. In this circuit the latch holds the count eight clock pulses after the clock has reset so that the number on the display is only proportional to the number of events per cycle rather than a total of the events.

If you want to extend the number of digits much beyond two or three this technique starts to get very expensive and you should consider multiplexing the circuitry, but that is another article altogether. To describe it as simply as possible, multiplexing is the running of many displays off a single BCD to seven-segment decoder. Power goes to the display digit only when that digit is being decoded. Multiple digits are decoded in sequence so rapidly that they appear to be all lit at once.

THE DIGITAL MULTIMETER

In the past, measurement of voltage, current, and resistance have utilized analog devices; however, with the advent of large scale integration semiconductor chips, a new generation of digital sampling techniques has been developed that allows accuracy to laboratory standards with moderately priced equipment. Full appreciation of the flexibility and advantages of the newer digital devices is apparent when comparison is made with analog equipment.

The relationship between current and voltage for steady state linear direct current applications is called Ohm's law. This "law," the most basic concept of electronics, is written

$$E = IR$$

The basic unit of voltage (E) or electromotive force is the volt. The basic unit of current (I) or time rate of change of charge is the ampere. Resistance (R) is measured in ohms.

Impedance

Things become more complex when steady state ac circuits are investigated. The units of voltage and current do not change; however, there is now a dynamic relationship between voltage and current which must take into consideration the phase angle between these two parameters. Simple dc resistance becomes a complex impedance. Impedance by definition is voltage divided by current and is the sum of the resistive plus reactive components of the circuit. Coils and capacitors determine the magnitude of the reactance of a given circuit. See Fig. 4-16.

The dc resistance of an ideal capacitor is infinity. Actual capacitors have leakage dependent upon their composition, e.g., electrolytics will have much more leakage than ceramic or mica capacitors. An ideal inductor has zero resistance. Actual inductors have a series resistance which is a func-

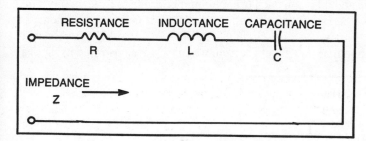

Fig. 4-16. Components affecting impedance.

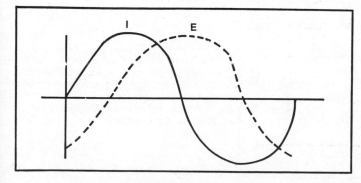

Fig. 4-17. Inductor current/voltage phasing.

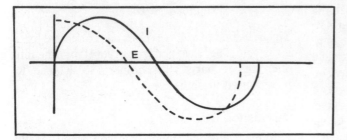

Fig. 4-18. Capacitor current/voltage phasing.

tion of diameter, temperature, length, and composition of the wire used in their windings.

Under transient and ac conditions, the current flow in an inductor always lags the voltage flow, whereas the current in a capacitor always leads the voltage. See Figs. 4-17 and 4-18.

Design Criteria

Certain criteria can be formulated concerning the equipment used to measure direct or alternating currents or voltages. First, the device should be accurate and capable of measuring both ac and dc currents or voltages. Second, linearity should be present over a wide range of readings. Third, the impedance of the device should be sufficiently high so as not to "load down" the circuit being measured. Fourth, measurements of resistance should be taken at low voltages so as not to alter the resistance of complex circuits that consist of active and passive elements. Last, the readings should be reproducible and not a function of the temperature, humidity, or the supply voltages necessary to power the measuring device.

The Stone Age

In the past, several methods were used to accomplish these goals. For ac, high frequency, and transient measurements, the oscilloscope provided the "gold standard" for a reproducible, high quality, high impedance device that had reasonable linearity. See Fig. 4-19. If the device was well calibrated, and had gain stability, measurements to two significant figures could be made over a wide range of voltages and frequencies. By use of suitable coupling devices, measurements of current could also be made. With appropriate attenuators, an oscilloscope could be made to have an input impedance of 10-megohms which was sufficient for most circuits. The phase relationship between voltage and current was easily demonstrated using dual

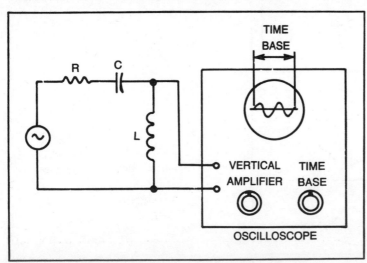

Fig. 4-19. Oscilloscope measurements.

sweep or chopped-beam oscilloscopes. Difficulties were commonly encountered with dc and very high frequency ac measurements, and with obtaining an accurate time base for the horizontal sweep circuit. Finally, the oscilloscope was not portable and proved to be a fragile device that was tied to a service bench.

Most measurements of voltage, current, and resistance not done on an oscilloscope were obtained with portable devices using D'Arsonval galvanometers called "meters." See Fig. 4-20. These devices, like the oscilloscope, suffered from several major faults. First, because of distortion in the magnetic field, true linearity was never achieved over the entire range of readings. Second, accuracies of only two or perhaps three significant places were available. Third, as with the oscilloscope, under certain conditions parallax (difference in reading that is dependent on the position of the observer) was a major problem. Fourth, the basic resistance of the galvanometer was low, on the order of 20,000-40,000-ohms-per-volt for expensive equipment and 5,000-10,000-ohms-per-volt for less costly gear. Impedances, when ac voltages were measured, were commensurately lower—on the order

of 1,000-5,000 ohms. Lastly, the devices were basically fragile and easy to burn out. In spite of these shortcomings, the analog volt ohmmeter was and is a popular, inexpensive device that sells for prices ranging from approximately $10 to $150, depending upon the accuracy, ranges, functions, and input resistance.

True laboratory standard accuracy—voltage readings to three and four significant places—could be obtained using D'Arsonval-type devices that operated over very narrow ranges and were used in bridge circuits that compared the unknown voltage to a known standard voltage. Unfortunately, this equipment was expensive, difficult to use, and not portable.

In another class of devices, the low basic input resistance of the galvanometer was improved by using vacuum tubes (VTVM) or semiconductor devices (e.g., FET). Unfortunately, this was done at the expense of doubling the price of the equipment and adding the problem of gain stability and input offset voltages.

Digital Designs

With the advent of large scale integrated cir-

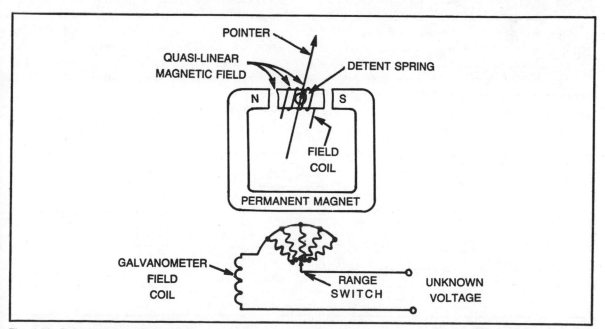

Fig. 4-20. Galvanometer construction.

cuits, an alternate means of measuring voltage, current, and resistance became available. This class of devices converted the analog signal, e.g., the current, voltage, or resistance, and displayed it in digital form. Higher accuracies were obtained by expanding the scale of measurement and eliminating meter reading errors—parallax and nonlinearity. Therefore an order of magnitude advantage was obtained. For example, if a high quality volt-ohmmeter had an accuracy to 1 percent of a given reading, similar quality digital devices could be made to read to 0.1 percent accuracy. Such an advantage is obvious when analyzing complex circuitry using semiconductor components. Furthermore, the ohmmeter function of these new generation digital devices uses very low currents when compared to the standard volt-ohm meter. Lastly, the input impedance of these devices is in the 10-megohm range, shunted by a small capacitor of approximately 50 pF.

Digital volt-ohmmeters are only as good as their amplifier stability and linearity, internal voltage and time references, and method of eliminating offset voltages. Various schemes have been devised to provide automatic zeroing, programmable or long term stability, and minimal offset voltages. See Fig. 4-21. Input signals are converted into a scaled dc voltage, which is then transformed into a digital readout by integration, logic, and display circuits. Dc voltages to be measured are applied across a voltage divider. A decade fraction of this voltage is selected by the range switch. The signal is then passed into a dc voltmeter which consists of an automatic offset correction (auto zero) circuit, a dual slope integrator, and a digital processing and multiplexing device. The reference voltage is derived from a highly stable Zener diode.

Ac Measurements

Ac voltages are measured in a similar manner, except a full wave bridge is used to yield a dc voltage equivalent to the RMS of the unknown ac signal. A high impedance buffer is used to isolate the bridge circuit. Resistance measurements are made by generating a precision known constant current which develops a dc voltage across the unknown resistor. The signal is then applied to the buffer amplifier and processed in a manner similar to the voltage measurements. Current measurements are made by passing the unknown current through a precision shunt-resistor which develops an ac or dc voltage proportional to the current in the shunt resistor. This voltage is again applied through the bridge (for ac currents), buffer, and integrator circuits. Various degrees of auto ranging are available depending upon the design and price of the instrument. This auto ranging refinement allows wide ranges of voltage to be measured with one setting of the range selector without internal overload. Some manufacturers offer a high/low ohm feature that permits in-circuit resistance measurements at voltage levels below the conduction threshold of semiconductor. The high ohm feature allows semiconductor junction tests by measurements of forward and reverse resistance ratios.

Accuracy

As mentioned earlier, the specifications of dig-

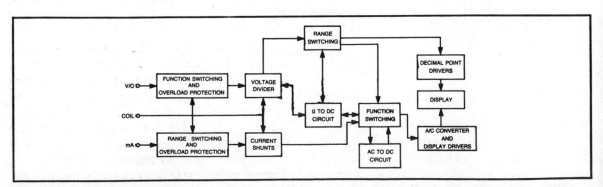

Fig. 4-21. Typical function diagram.

ital multimeters are normally in the range of 0.5 percent of the reading, plus 0.1 percent of the range ± one count for dc voltages. A display reading of 1.00-volt dc from a low impedance source will have an uncertainty of ±0.0035 volts; a truly amazing feat. Because of the sampling nature of the device and the auto ranging features, response time is usually less than 3 seconds to within stated accuracy. Settling time for the semi-ranging devices (100 percent overvoltage) is typically 1/2 of a second.

Optimal performance can be obtained by observing a number of precautions when test measurements are made. Ground loops must be avoided since differences of ground potentials may set up loop currents and distort the measured value. Problems of this type can be almost completely eliminated by using battery operated equipment. Ground loops may be lessened by connecting the test source ground to true earth ground if possible. In floating dc or ac measurements, it is possible to introduce a common mode voltage by reactive coupling when the line cord is connected. Again, problems of this type can be almost entirely eliminated by using a battery operated meter. If only ac operation is available, this type of measurement should be made on the highest range possible consistent with usable measurement resolution. Most devices will handle up to a 100 percent full range over-voltage with meaningful readings.

The basic design features of the digital multimeter make it the ideal replacement for the existing analog multimeters and FET/VOMs or VTVMs. In addition to providing equivalent functions and range, the inherent accuracy and features of this type of instrument provide a significant margin of improved performance over comparably priced analog meters. Digital multimeters are priced from $60 to several hundred dollars and come in kit or assembled form.

Conclusion

In summation, the proven stability of dual-slope integration combined with precision, ratio-trimmed resistor networks and advanced LSI technology has generated a series of digital multimeters that pro-

vide extreme versatility and accuracy at an affordable price. They have virtually made the hand-held galvanometer-based analog volt-ohm meter obsolete. Their major drawback is in their time to settle on a given reading and the necessity of using sampling techniques. They are an exciting, accurate, and dependable way of making basic measurements of voltage, current, and resistance in modern electronic circuitry.

DASHBOARD DIGITAL TEMPERATURE GAUGE

No matter what time of year it may be, from the arctic blasts of a Buffalo winter to the swelter of St. Louis in August, you've probably had the unfortunate experience of having your car's engine overheat. Whether it's due to a malfunctioning water pump, a broken fan belt, frozen coolant, or a leaky radiator hose, the bottom line is that it's one All-American pain in the neck when it happens. Regular and thorough automotive maintenance will prevent this most of the time. However, when the unexpected happens, a temperature gauge can forewarn you of impending disaster—and possible engine damage, before the engine overheats.

It's unfortunate that most car manufacturers do not see fit to offer gauge packages (except at outrageous optional prices) on their vehicles. The few that do, offer mostly uncalibrated units which are no more helpful than a dummy light—they tell you only that you're in trouble, not that you're about to be. The following is our answer to this dilemma, the second in a series of digital automotive (and marine) instrumentation feature articles.

Features

This relatively simple and inexpensive temperature gauge offers three-place digital readout of Fahrenheit temperatures in the car's engine from a low of 0° to a high of about 250° (well above where your engine is likely to start melting). About the only type of engine with which this gauge may not work would be the small, 4-cylinder diesels found in Volkswagens and some other imports. These engines normally operate at higher temperatures than gasoline engines, and may have an effective heat range outside the limits of this gauge. Check with your dealer or manufacturer for the nominal operating temperatures of your car's engine just to make sure.

Use of our gauge will not interfere with factory-installed gauges or dummy lights, and we suggest that they be retained as a back-up system. In addition, our gauge is easy on energy, with a maximum current consumption of 160 mA or less.

Circuit Operation

Spike protection (spikes result from turning inductive devices on and off) for the LM340T-5 (U1) is provided by capacitor C1 and diodes D1 and D2. Transients ("noise") on the 5-volt line are suppressed by capacitor C2 and the LM340T-5. Refer to Fig. 4-22.

A positive potential between pins 11 (+) and 10 (−) of U2 is converted by the CA3162E into a BCD (binary coded decimal) output which reflects that difference. The CA3161E is the control element that actuates the 7-segment display. For an example of a typical cycle of switching action, assume that the display is displaying "2." This is the 1's place or least significant digit. The instant pin 5 activates the pnp switching transistor of the least significant digit, the BCD for "2" is generated in the CA3162E. The BCD code leaves pins 2, 1, 15, and 16, and enters pins 7, 1, 2, and 6 of the CA3161E decoder driver (U3). The CA3161E then takes that BCD code and activates (lights) those segments of the 7-segment display forming a "2." In reality, an optical illusion is being created for the eye. At any given time, only one display (digit) is actually on. Because of the brain's image retention of the eye's sensing capacity, all displays appear to be on simultaneously. The same cyclic sequence occurs with the two remaining displays.

As a final note on operations, we should touch on the matter of cyclic conversions or comparisons made each second (note the point marked OPTION on the schematic). With the OPTION point left disconnected, the comparison (or display update rate) is set at 4 Hz. We feel that this is probably the most pleasing to the eye and the least distracting. With the OPTION point grounded, the comparison rate

goes up to 96 Hz. The result of this is that the display will appear to be unstable as the numbers fluctuate at the more rapid rate. As a result, and depending upon where in the line of the driver's vision the gauge is mounted, it may tend to be a distraction. This is the common bugaboo with all digital gauges, especially tachometers and speedometers, which can undergo rapid changes in readout as data input from the engine changes. Experiment yourself, but you'll probably agree that the 4 Hz rate is decidedly the most attractive of the two choices.

Sensing Probe Operation

The response to temperature change of a silicon diode is linear as it reflects a rise or fall. As the temperature rises across the diode's pn junction, the forward voltage developed across it drops. This would make it seem that diodes could be interchanged with no effect on readings. Unfortunately, such is not the case. While the rise and fall responses to temperature changes are for all practical purposes uniformly linear, the *base starting points are not.* Because of this, *calibration must be repeated* if the sensing probe diode is replaced.

Note that resistors R1 and R2 form a voltage divider network that has a one-volt (approximate) drop across R2. The one-volt is dropped across R3 and R7 in series with the temperature-sensing diode (the probe). The latter two resistors limit the current to the temperature-sensing diode. The forward voltage drop that is developed across the temperature-sensing diode is now applied to the negative input terminal, pin 10 of U2. As the temperature rises, the forward voltage drops linearly. The inversion resulting from the rise or fall is compensated for by applying the forward voltage to the negative input, which is pin 10 of U2.

Let's illustrate the action described in the preceding paragraph. Assume for each degree of Fahrenheit change there is a corresponding 1.0 mV change. Assume, also, that at 32° F, there is a 0.55-volt or 550 mV forward voltage drop. The CA3162E (U2) "looks" at the positive input (pin 11) and the negative input (pin 10), and then generates a BCD code reflecting that difference, transmitting

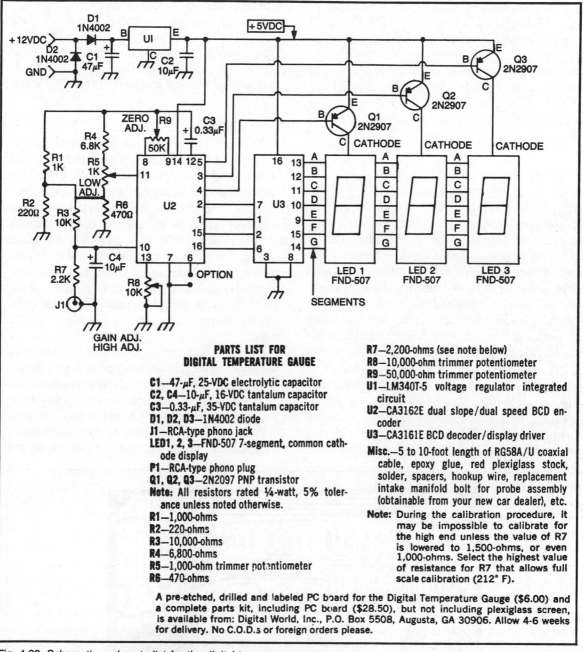

PARTS LIST FOR DIGITAL TEMPERATURE GAUGE

C1—47-μF, 25-VDC electrolytic capacitor
C2, C4—10-μF, 16-VDC tantalum capacitor
C3—0.33-μF, 35-VDC tantalum capacitor
D1, D2, D3—1N4002 diode
J1—RCA-type phono jack
LED1, 2, 3—FND-507 7-segment, common cathode display
P1—RCA-type phono plug
Q1, Q2, Q3—2N2097 PNP transistor
Note: All resistors rated ¼-watt, 5% tolerance unless noted otherwise.
R1—1,000-ohms
R2—220-ohms
R3—10,000-ohms
R4—6,800-ohms
R5—1,000-ohm trimmer potentiometer
R6—470-ohms

R7—2,200-ohms (see note below)
R8—10,000-ohm trimmer potentiometer
R9—50,000-ohm trimmer potentiometer
U1—LM340T-5 voltage regulator integrated circuit
U2—CA3162E dual slope/dual speed BCD encoder
U3—CA3161E BCD decoder/display driver
Misc.—5 to 10-foot length of RG58A/U coaxial cable, epoxy glue, red plexiglass stock, solder, spacers, hookup wire, replacement intake manifold bolt for probe assembly (obtainable from your new car dealer), etc.
Note: During the calibration procedure, it may be impossible to calibrate for the high end unless the value of R7 is lowered to 1,500-ohms, or even 1,000-ohms. Select the highest value of resistance for R7 that allows full scale calibration (212° F).

A pre-etched, drilled and labeled PC board for the Digital Temperature Gauge ($6.00) and a complete parts kit, including PC board ($28.50), but not including plexiglass screen, is available from: Digital World, Inc., P.O. Box 5508, Augusta, GA 30906. Allow 4-6 weeks for delivery. No C.O.D.s or foreign orders please.

Fig. 4-22. Schematic and parts list for the digital temperature gauge.

this to the display by means of the CA3161E (U3). If the positive input, pin 11, is 32 mV greater than the negative input, pin 10, or reads a total of 582 mV, then the CA3162E will "see" a difference of 32 mV and the 7-segment displays will display "032." As the temperature increases, the difference becomes wider. At 212° F, the voltage at the negative input would be 370 mV. Therefore, the voltage difference between pin 11 (positive) and pin 10 (negative) would be 212 (582 mV − 370 mV = 212° F). Since the tolerances of diodes tend to vary somewhat, we have only stated an approximate maximum reading range for our temperature gauge. The temperature at which your gauge will cease to function linearly will be determined by the quality of the individual diode used in the construction of the probe.

Assembly

After etching your PC board (see Fig. 4-23), check the finished product for foil bridges and other imperfections which might create difficulty during assembly and calibration. Leaving installation of U2 and U3 for later, install all other components on the board, following the component placement guide in Fig. 4-24. Be sure to observe polarity with respect to diodes, electrolytic and tantalum capacitors and the LED displays. Make sure that when J1 is installed, the outer shell is given a good ground by soldering it to the large foil area on the board.

We strongly suggest that you make use of IC sockets when installing U2 and U3. These two chips are highly sensitive to static electrical damage caused by handling without insulated tweezers. In addition, stray ac from the tip of your soldering iron (not to mention excessive heat) can also cause

irreparable damage to the chips.

With all components installed, make a final check of the board against the component layout diagram as a precaution. If the final check is positive, proceed to wire in the 2 leads for the 12-volt power source. The unit is now ready for calibration.

Probe Assembly

As mentioned earlier, the probe itself is simply a 1N4002 diode which is wired across one end of a length of RG58A/U coaxial cable. Check the diagram to obtain proper diode polarity and for details on its construction. Be certain that you have a length of cable that is sufficient to pass through the firewall and reach the point at which you are planning to install the gauge. You should avoid having to splice the coax at any point to add length. Moisture entering under the outer insulator of the coax will cause rapid deterioration and result in inaccurate or erratic temperature readings from the gauge.

Obtain a new intake manifold bolt (or stud) from your automotive dealer or parts supply house. Placing the bolt carefully in a bench vise (take care not to damage the threads), drill a 5/16-inch diameter hole down the center of the bolt, stopping 1/8-inch from the bottom. Solder the diode's anode to the center conductor, and the cathode to the

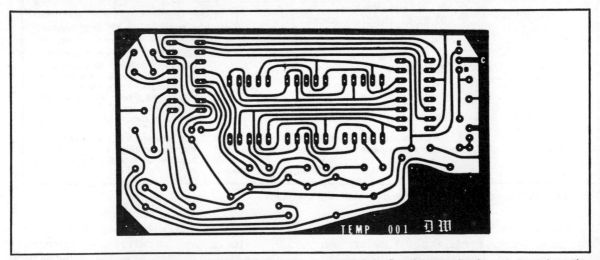

Fig. 4-23. Here is the full-scale etching template for the printed circuit board. See the parts list for ordering information on a ready-to-go board if you don't etch your own.

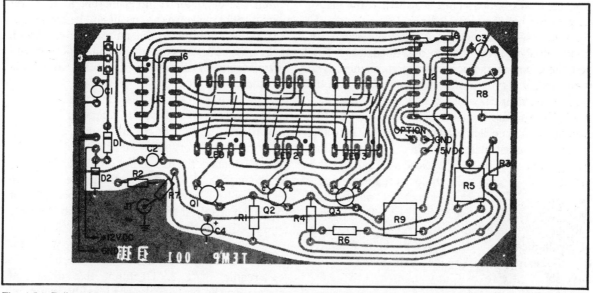

Fig. 4-24. Follow this component layout guide when assembling the PC board. Note that in this diagram, U1 is installed on top of the board. Depending upon your space requirements, it can go on top or bottom, but be careful not to reverse the pin connections.

braided shield (see Fig. 4-25). Now, mix the epoxy that will be used to anchor the probe in the hole. Use of a slow-setting type will allow you more time in setting the depth of the probe.

Now attach one terminal of an ohmmeter to both the shield and the center conductor of the coax at the free (gauge) end. Ground the other ohmmeter terminal to the bolt. You will use the ohmmeter to make certain that the soldered diode connections do not contact the sides of the bolt hole, creating an unwanted short.

Fill the hole halfway with the epoxy mixture. Some of this will be forced out as the probe is inserted, but it can be wiped away easily. Force the probe all the way in until it stops. At this point, the ohmmeter should be showing a completed circuit. Gently begin withdrawing the probe until the ohmmeter shows that the circuit is broken. Secure the coax in this position until the epoxy sets, continuing to check to see that there is no reading on the ohmmeter. Let the assembly dry for a least 24-hours before checking once again to see that the probe is not in contact with the bolt. If the process is successful, you may now proceed with the installation of the probe on the manifold.

If, due to the design of your car's manifold (or a reluctance on your part to remove a manifold bolt) you do not wish to follow the recommended installation procedure, we can suggest an alternative. Simply secure the probe to the side of the engine block with the epoxy. Prepare the area first with a thorough cleansing before applying the epoxy.

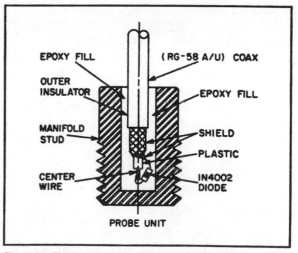

Fig. 4-25. This is a cutaway of the probe assembly mounted in the manifold stud.

Apply a coat of epoxy sufficient to coat the metal entirely within the intended installation area. Allow this to set until very tacky. Next, observing the same anti-short procedures as described above, embed the diode in the semi-hard epoxy, and cover with more epoxy to completely enclose the probe and coax end in it.

While this method is obviously the easier of the two, you will experience some loss of sensitivity and accuracy (we estimate somewhere between 5 and 10%, depending upon how close you can get the diode to the engine wall without creating electrical contact). Whether you accept the trade-off between accuracy and ease of installation is up to you, and should be determined primarily by your degree of mechanical expertise. If you doubt your ability to remove, modify and re-install the manifold bolt, have someone else do it for you, or else use the external attachment.

Troubleshooting

As an initial check prior to calibration, apply a dc voltage of between 10- and 16-volts (preferably 13.8-Vdc) to the power input of the gauge, after having connected the probe to the gauge via J1. You should obtain some reading on the displays, and all three should be lit. If this is not the case, and all displays are unlit, check the connections to the power source, and check to see that R9's wiper is centered. Furthermore, check to see that all components have been installed properly on the board with respect to polarity, especially D1 and D2. Improper orientation here will prevent power from reaching the rest of the circuit. If these steps fail to alleviate the problem, make a physical inspection of the printed circuit board for foil or solder bridges that might be creating shorts. Before removing any solder bridges in and around the ICs, remove the ICs from their sockets to avoid heat and ac current damage.

Calibration

Assuming that all bugs have been removed from the circuitry by means of the troubleshooting section (or by virtue of your expertise having obviated the need for troubleshooting in the first place), apply power to the circuit and begin the calibration procedures. At this point, we should note that the accuracy of your gauge will be determined by the degree of calibration exactness that you apply here. Take your time.

To zero the gauge (as you would with a mechanical meter movement), temporarily ground pins 10 and 11 of U2 to circuit ground, and adjust the wiper of R9 very slowly until all displays read zero. Disconnect the temporary ground on U2. Center the wiper of R8, and place the probe in ice water for a full five minutes (to compensate for thermal inertia). At the end of five minutes, slowly adjust R5 until the display is reading "032."

Next, immerse the probe in boiling water for five minutes, and at the end of this time, adjust R8 for a reading of "212." Of course, this adjustment is made on the basis of the sea level boiling point of water. Check the boiling point for your locality's altitude, and adjust R8 accordingly. Repeat the low and high end adjustments at least once more to compensate for any interaction among the two adjustments. Again, patience here will pay off in a more accurately operating instrument.

Installation

Select an appropriate position for the gauge, and install it by whatever convenient means suits your car and the position you have selected. Use a red Plexiglas screen across the opening in the cutout for the displays. Red, although it probably doesn't seem logical at first thought, will offer the highest contrast display background.

Next, install the modified manifold bolt (containing the probe) on the cylinder head. Obviously, in order to protect the coax at this point, it should be coiled into a tight loop to avoid putting undue stress on it during rotation. After the bolt has been properly retorqued, route the coax directly away from the engine towards the fender. This will avoid close contact with hot engine parts and high-voltage ignition leads, either of whose presence in close proximity to the coax could cause deleterious effects.

Locate a point in the firewall where accessory

wires are passed through grommets to the passenger compartment, and feed the coax through at this point. Should you be unable to locate or utilize existing holes, locate a point on the firewall clear of obstacles both in the engine compartment and passenger compartment (behind the dash) and drill a 3/8-inch hole through. After passing the coax through the hole, apply silicone cement to the area to provide a weatherproof seal. Water has a nasty habit of travelling along lines, through holes, and onto irreplaceable carpets and ruining them if sufficient precautions are not taken.

Trim any excess coax so that it runs to the gauge in as direct a manner as possible from the firewall, and install P1. Plug P1 into jack J1, and connect the power leads (preferably to the horn fuse for V+, and to a good chassis point for ground).

Conclusion

Some of you are no doubt questioning the wisdom of center-drilling so fragile a component as a manifold bolt, especially on older cars, where the original bolts may be either rust or heat-seized. If, when removing the original bolt to replace it with the probe-carrying bolt, you should happen to break the bolt off, do not become alarmed. This happens commonly during carburetor and gasket overhaul and replacement at car dealers and service stations. They are capable of drilling the remaining piece of the bolt out for you quite easily, leaving you free to install the new bolt.

We have selected this method of probe installation to insure the most accurate readings allowable. Other methods, such as insertion of the probe in the coolant itself, would tend to violate the pressure integrity of the car's systems, leaving open the possibility of leakage and fluid loss at a later time. Additionally, encasing the probe in the necessary waterproofing material would result in an unacceptable loss of sensitivity.

DASHBOARD DIGITAL VOLTMETER

You're making time down the interstate at three in the morning, and all of a sudden you become aware that the lights on the dash seem kind of dim, and that the headlights don't seem to be reaching out as far ahead to warn you of darkened semis parked on the shoulder. Are your eyes just playing tricks on you, or is there something the matter with your car's electrical system? A quick glance down at the three glowing LED numerals on the dash gives you the instant answer. Either you pull into a rest area and grab a few hours of shuteye, or you pull into a service area and have the battery, alternator and voltage regulator given a good scrutinizing by the mechanic.

In either case, your car's digital voltmeter has given you the information sought about the state of the electrical system, and maybe saved you either a headache, a smashup, or a king-sized repair and towing bill. Maybe all three.

Recent advances in the design and availability of industrial integrated circuits have opened up many doors to the electronics hobbyists. Analog-to-digital devices have become more complex internally, thus making the portions of the circuitry which have to be assembled by the hobbyist that much more simple. The Dashboard Digital Voltmeter takes advantage of these advances, utilizing three ICs and a small handful of discrete components to give you an instrument capable of better than ±1% accuracy in reading the voltage level delivered by your car's (or boat's) electrical system.

Two New ICs

The system is built about three ICs: the LM340T-5 (a 5-volt regulator now available for several years); a CA3162E; a CA3161E; and a support combination of diodes, resistors, and capacitors. It is the CA3161E and CA3162E that now open the door to new horizons in possible applications not only because of their unique capabilities, but also because they reduce substantially the numbers and types of formerly required support components. The heart of this system is the CA3162E, a dual-slope, dual-speed, A/D converter industrial chip. Its almost equally important companion, the CA3161E, is a BCD, 7-segment, decoder/driver chip. It is also unique in that it has a current-limiting feature. This eliminates the necessity of resistors

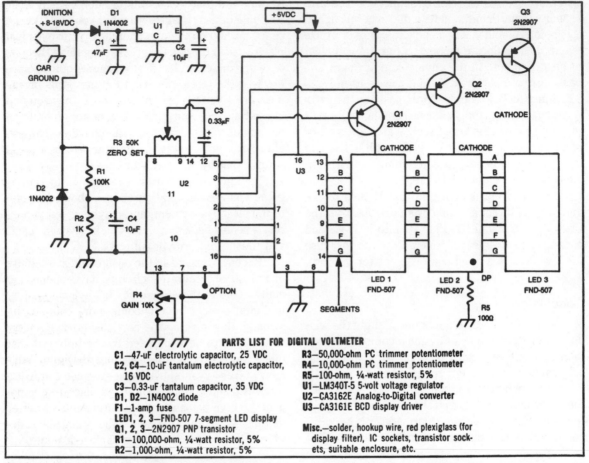

Fig. 4-26. Schematic and parts list for digital voltmeter.

PARTS LIST FOR DIGITAL VOLTMETER

C1—47-uF electrolytic capacitor, 25 VDC
C2, C4—10-uF tantalum electrolytic capacitor, 16 VDC
C3—0.33-uF tantalum capacitor, 35 VDC
D1, D2—1N4002 diode
F1—1-amp fuse
LED1, 2, 3—FND-507 7-segment LED display
Q1, 2, 3—2N2907 PNP transistor
R1—100,000-ohm, ¼-watt resistor, 5%
R2—1,000-ohm, ¼-watt resistor, 5%

R3—50,000-ohm PC trimmer potentiometer
R4—10,000-ohm PC trimmer potentiometer
R5—100-ohm, ¼-watt resistor, 5%
U1—LM340T-5 5-volt voltage regulator
U2—CA3162E Analog-to-Digital converter
U3—CA3161E BCD display driver

Misc.—solder, hookup wire, red plexiglass (for display filter), IC sockets, transistor sockets, suitable enclosure, etc.

in series with the 7-segment displays that were required in earlier designs.

The above feature not only reduces circuit board space requirements, but reduces the probability of component failure. Power required to operate this voltmeter is minimal (160 mA or less), a result of the multiplexing feature of the CA3162E. With that as a background, let's consider some of the more important operations of this simple, but very accurate digital instrument. Refer to Fig. 4-26.

Circuit Function

Analog voltage from 000 mV to 999 mV can be applied between pins 11 (+) and 10 (−) of the CA3162E (U2). That IC converts the voltage into a Binary Coded Decimal (BCD) equivalent. The BCD leaves pins 2, 1, 15, and 16 (the group represents the 1's, 2's, 4's, and 8's) and enters pins 7, 1, 2, and 6 respectively of the CA3161E (U3). The latter IC takes the BCD code, converts the output, then uses it (in conjunction with the 7-segment display) to generate (form) the number that correlates to the BCD input of the CA3161E. The multiplexing driver pins 5, 3, and 4 (5 being the least significant and 4 the most significant) turn on that display by means of the pnp switching transistors. Concurrently, the CA3162E is providing the BCD information to the CA3161E driver/decoder.

As indicated earlier, the system includes a combination of diodes and capacitors. These are required to control or minimize the voltage spikes (positive and negative) that result from turning inductive devices on and off; e.g., windshield wiper, air conditioner, and electric windows, etc.

The maximum input differential between pins 11 and 10 of CA3162E is 999 mV. A resistor network (R1, R2) is used to attenuate the applied 13.8-volts to 138 mV. An Ohm's law calculation would give a result of 136.6 mV. The gain-adjust potentiometer compensates for the slight drop. The FND 507s display this as 13.8-volts.

Note the point marked OPTION on the schematic. With pin 6 of the CA3162E grounded or disconnected, there are four conversions or comparisons made each second. Tying pin 6 to the 5-volt line will result in 96 conversions or comparisons per second. The 96/second rate moves with excessive rapidity, is not appealing to the eye, and usually results in the least significant digit appearing to be blurred. Of the two rates, the 4/second conversion (4 Hz) is by far the more pleasing to the eye, is easier for the eye to focus on quickly, and is the recommended rate. These rates could vary slightly because of capacitor difference and manufacturer variance from stated values.

Assembling the Voltmeter

Begin by making the printed circuit board. Figure 4-27 can be used as a template. Drill all holes before stripping.

Get the workbench ready for soldering. Use a low wattage, electrically-isolated, fine-tipped soldering tool and fine solder. A blunt-nosed tool could damage or destroy the ICs and create foil bridges between pins. This is both expensive and frustrating. If you have had limited experience in soldering in small areas, it may be wise to practice on something else before you start.

Now, locate all resistors and potentiometers on the circuit board and install them in their respective holes, as shown in Fig. 4-28. Next, do the same for all capacitors, observing polarity. Install the CA3161E and CA3162E. *Caution!* When inserting the ICs, be careful *not* to fold the pins under or bend them in any way.

IC *orientation* is critical. Be sure these chips (CA3162E and CA3161E) are aligned as shown on the diagram. Note the notch mark on the chips and the corresponding notch mark on the schematic, or the "1" on pin 1 on top of the plastic case. All manufacturers use one or both of these base reference directional indicators.

If you have doubts about your soldering ability or the type of solder tool you have (grounded or not grounded), place two 16-pin sockets in the chip holes. The ICs may then be placed (not soldered) in the sockets. Next, insert the three LEDs, noting the notch marks on the LEDs and the notch marks indicated on the diagram. For the final ac-

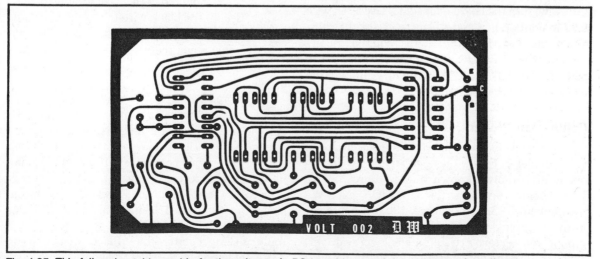

Fig. 4-27. This full-scale etching guide for the voltmeter's PC board is one of the trickiest we've offered.

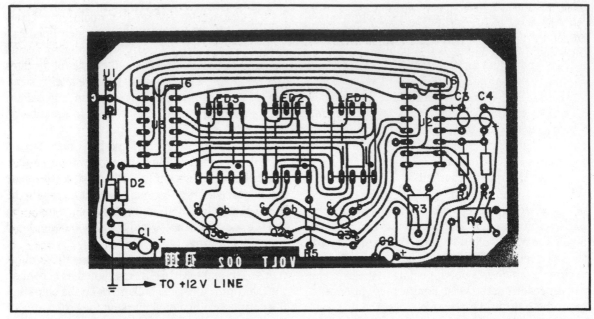

Fig. 4-28. The component placement diagram for the PC board shows all IC and capacitor polarities. Take special care to observe them during assembly phases of project.

tion on this side of the board, insert both diodes in their respective holes (observing cathode markings).

Reverse the circuit board and install the LM340T-5 regulator. Caution! This must be correctly placed or it will destroy your unit when power is applied. The metal side of the regulator must be facing the FND 507 pins. Recheck it to make sure.

Now, turn the board over again. Use a red wire for the ignition line and a black wire for the chassis ground. Determine the lengths required (usually three-feet is sufficient). Solder the red wire to the point marked IGNITION on the diagram and the black wire to the GROUND.

Calibration Procedure

Correct calibration determines the accuracy of your voltmeter. Follow these steps carefully and sequentially. Apply a known voltage source (above 10 and below 16-volts) to the IGNITION point. We recommend a 13.8-volt source. Next, for zero adjustment, ground pins 11 and 10 to the circuit board ground momentarily. Using a small screwdriver, slowly rotate the wiper arm on R3 until there is a

reading of 000. Remove the ground from pins 10 and 11. Set the gain control (R4) by rotating the wiper arm until the displays are displaying the same voltage as is being applied.

Installation

One final action is necessary before your unit is ready to be mounted in the dash location of your choice. Secure the black wire to the metal chassis ground and the red wire to any accessory line that is active only when the motor is running. Secure and mount the voltmeter in the location of your choice.

A colored Plexiglas facing (cover) is required and we recommend red for most display contrast. A location which is not usually exposed to the sunlight will make the displays easier to read during the brighter periods of the day. If the unit is going into an existing recess, the present glass cover may be used as a template for the Plexiglas cover dimensions. One-eighth or 1/16-inch thickness Plexiglas works well and is relatively easy to cut using a roofer's shingle cutter knife. Place two clamps on a straight line along the template edge, then cut one side at a time. Scribe it deeply with a dozen or more strokes, then break off the excess with a pliers. When drilling screw holes, use a small starter bit first, then the larger bit. This should prevent the larger bit from wandering across the Plexiglas.

The Plexiglas must be "spaced" away from the board by approximately 5/8-inch, using either spacers or the bolt/nut method. The latter method is to insert a bolt through the Plexiglas corner hole and put a nut on the reverse side. Put a second nut on the bolt, allowing a 1/2-inch inside space between the two nuts. Do this on all corners. Next, insert the bolts into the board corner holes and put on the final nuts. We recommend securing all four corners, rather than just two.

Troubleshooting

If the unit does not light up for the calibration procedure, first check that the wiper of R3 is centered. If it still does not light up, recheck your work. Carefully inspect for possible solder bridges and loose connections. If a solder bridge is discovered, remove it carefully. It is easy to destroy a chip during the removal process. If it still fails to light up, start a systematic test check to isolate possible faulty component(s).

If the unit does not function after installation, recheck for a good electrical connection on the line that supplies power from the car. Did you break or loosen the solder connections of the source wires during installation? If so, this will require removal and resoldering, plus a bit more care during installation the second time.

One Final Note

Some ICs, and quite possibly the ones used in this project, generate high frequency harmonics which might find their way into your car's radio. Try holding your LED readout pocket calculator next to the radio antenna with the radio tuned to a blank spot on the AM dial to see what we mean. If you experience any interference from the voltmeter circuit, try rerouting the antenna coax away from the voltmeter itself. A metal case around the voltmeter's PC board will also aid in the reduction

of RFI. We suggest that you avoid using the radio's power lead as the voltage source for your voltmeter. The power lead to the horn (or horn relay) or the hot lead of the windshield wiper switch (find it at the fuse box) is probably the best place to attach the voltmeter.

10 SECONDS AND COUNTING LAUNCH CONTROL

For years, thousands of people have been building and launching small scale model rockets that propel themselves with miniature solid-core propellant engines. But no matter how much time, money, and effort a person put into his (or her) rocket, the launch has always been pretty much the same; a switch, a battery, and perhaps a light bulb to check continuity.

A Breakthrough!

Thanks to lower Integrated Circuit (IC) prices, a handheld, computer-like launch controller is now practical even for a "model rocketeer" on a budget. The Rocket Computer consists of a display that—when ordered—counts down from 9 to 0 and then, thanks to a SCR (Silicon Controlled Rectifier), fires current through an igniter to start the propellant engine. Two LED's tell you if power is on and also give continuity verification. It's simple to operate with only three switches. The whole project can be assembled, even at retail prices, for only $5 or $20, less case.

Construction

The circuit is quite stable, so any method of construction can be used. IC sockets should be used to protect the "chips" from soldering heat, and facilitate easy replacement—if necessary. Refer to Fig. 4-29.

I built my Rocket Computer on perfboard, with IC sockets, and a wire-wrapping tool was used to wire it up. But, soldering the project with point-to-point wiring is just as easy and effective. Take care not to make any solder "bridges" between socket pins, as they are usually spaced pretty close together. The LED display pins must correspond with

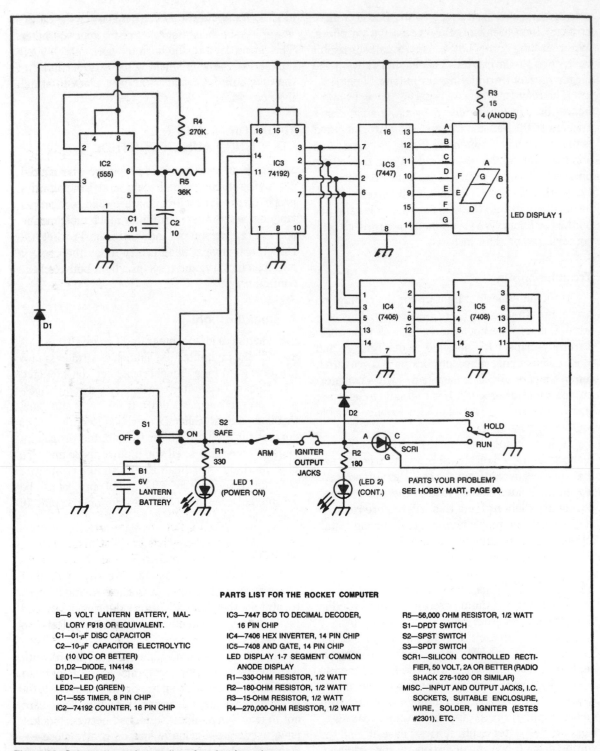

Fig. 4-29. Schematic and parts list of rocket launcher.

PARTS LIST FOR THE ROCKET COMPUTER

B—6 VOLT LANTERN BATTERY, MAL-
   LORY F918 OR EQUIVALENT.
C1—01-μF DISC CAPACITOR
C2—10-μF CAPACITOR ELECTROLYTIC
   (10 VDC OR BETTER)
D1,D2—DIODE, 1N4148
LED1—LED (RED)
LED2—LED (GREEN)
IC1—555 TIMER, 8 PIN CHIP
IC2—74192 COUNTER, 16 PIN CHIP

IC3—7447 BCD TO DECIMAL DECODER,
   16 PIN CHIP
IC4—7406 HEX INVERTER, 14 PIN CHIP
IC5—7408 AND GATE, 14 PIN CHIP
LED DISPLAY 1-7 SEGMENT COMMON
   ANODE DISPLAY
R1—330-OHM RESISTOR, 1/2 WATT
R2—180-OHM RESISTOR, 1/2 WATT
R3—15-OHM RESISTOR, 1/2 WATT
R4—270,000-OHM RESISTOR, 1/2 WATT

R5—56,000 OHM RESISTOR, 1/2 WATT
S1—DPDT SWITCH
S2—SPST SWITCH
S3—SPDT SWITCH
SCR1—SILICON CONTROLLED RECTI-
   FIER, 50 VOLT, 2A OR BETTER (RADIO
   SHACK 276-1020 OR SIMILAR)
MISC.—INPUT AND OUTPUT JACKS, I.C.
   SOCKETS, SUITABLE ENCLOSURE,
   WIRE, SOLDER, IGNITER (ESTES
   #2301), ETC.

IC 3's output pins. Most manufacturers of these displays give sufficient data to make this an easy task; simply match the A-G lines together. A 15-ohm resistor on the common anode lead should be rated at least at a half watt. (The common anode lead is easily identified on the LED display data also.) In the parts list, I recommend a Radio Shack RS-1020 SCR, but any SCR that can handle 2 amps or more of current with a low gate voltage can be used. Use spring clip terminals like I did to make igniter hook-up quick and easy. I mounted my terminals for the igniter on top of the case. Then, I mounted the power input jacks on the side. Once again, use spring clip or screw type connectors here. It is an excellent idea to use jacks for the power input and igniter output that do not look similar. This will avoid mistakes and possible damage. Finally, be sure to note polarity when wiring the input power jacks.

Testing and Blastoff!

Give the circuit a complete bench test before taking it out to your "launch pad." Use only a 6 volt lantern-type battery on this circuit. Only a small or large lantern battery can insure that there will be plenty of current available to drive both the circuitry and igniter. Test the circuit first without using an igniter hooked up. Attach your battery to the proper jacks. Now, turn switch S1 (off/on) to the on position. LED 1 should light. So should the display light up a 9. If the display did not light or a 9 is not observed, correct the error before going on. Everything OK? If so, continue. Turn S2 (safety/arm) up to arm. LED 2 will not light yet because no igniter is in. Now, take a low current igniter (Estes #2301) and hook it up to the igniter output jacks. LED 2 should now glow, proving continuity. (Polarity is not observed on an igniter.)

Now see if the unit can fire an igniter (not in an engine yet!!!) on your bench. Move the igniter away from anything inflammable as the igniter usually burns for a second at about the intensity of a match. Throw switch S3 (hold/run) to run. The display should count slowly down, and—get ready—at zero, the igniter should fire.

At all times, when using this unit, start your launching procedure with all switches in their "off," "safety," "HOLD" positions respectively. After the launch always pull S2 and S3 down to their safety and hold positions. Failure to do so can result in premature liftoff of the next rocket. Remember, safety in rocketry always comes first!

In the Firing Room

The heart of this circuit is the 74192 IC counter. This amazing little chip takes the clock pulses generated by the 555 timer IC and counts them in binary code. The 7447 IC receives the binary numbers and changes them into a form we can understand—decimal. The LED display counted. IC 7406 and IC7408 "watch" show us the numbers, and when they sense a zero, they send a pulse to the SCR, triggering it into conduction and thus firing the igniter.

MAXICLOCK

Time freeze! What's time freeze? To tell you the truth, nothing that great . . . we think it's everything else about this digital clock that's so great!

First of all, it's even simpler to build than our first clock project—a very popular one published over a year ago. Secondly, you'll find that even fewer parts do more jobs.

But today the best feature is one that is uppermost in everybody's mind—the major parts cost. In fact, the overall clock cost is just about half the price of our previous clock project. It's the least expensive electronic digital clock we could find—kit, project, or assembled—that has just about every feature you can think of in a line-powered digital clock.

It is a 6-digit clock. It is a calendar. It is a 24-hour alarm clock. It has a 10-minute snooze alarm. It has provision for internal battery power operation. It can be operated in either the 12- or 24-hour mode. It knows the days of the month (you update just once every four years at leap year). It is simple to build without a printed circuit board because there are no driver transistors for the display. It uses a standard low-cost "calculator" type display, and the display is internally wired—only 13 connections operate all 42 segments of the six-digit display. And all the display connections are made to an IC connector for ease of assembly.

It all adds up to one thing: You should be able to build this clock for a price considerably lower than digital clocks with fewer features. And, oh yes, about time freeze: It's the simple "seconds hold" feature you get with this clock. With it you set the time ahead a minute or two, wait for your time standard (WWV, local radio, Ma Bell, etc.) to count down to zero, flick the function switch, and watch your clock start counting from "00" seconds every time. A small feature, perhaps, but something everyone appreciates.

Other features of the clock are as follows: You can select between time, date, alarm "set" time, or time/date display (a time display for 8 seconds followed by a date display for 2 seconds). A 50 or 60 Hz switch and the time freeze feature let you set time with ease (in the 50 Hz position, the clock will run 20 percent faster on a 60 Hz line). You also have a "snooze" button to recycle the alarm by ten minutes. *There is only one switch for setting hours, minutes, days, and months!* Additional features are an "alarm is set" red LED indicator, leading zero blanking, and a green LED to indicate p.m. The clock also provides an optional 24-hour display, stand-by battery power, and display brightness control.

How Does It Work?

The brain of the clock is the Cal-Tex CT7001 integrated circuit consisting of thousands of transistors; it counts down the line frequency to seconds, minutes, days, and months. Refer to Fig. 4-30. Internal memories record the number of days in each month and the alarm settings. To avoid large numbers of wire leads, the display digits are multiplexed, which means that "gating" signals (digit turn-on signals) are applied in sequence to the "control" grid of each digit. But it happens so fast you "see" a continuous 6-digit display. The display segments of all digits are connected in parallel right inside the display case. It comes pre-wired that way in its compact enclosure.

The first transistor, Q1, turns the leading zero off when the "SF" segment (see schematic)

appears—this is the only segment not required to form digits 1 and 2. The second transistor, Q2, is a programmed unijunction transistor which drives the speaker to sound the alarm. You can change the sound of the alarm by making C1 smaller or larger as you desire.

Construction

To build the clock we used point-to-point wiring on a 3 × 4-in. perfboard. See Fig. 4-31. The clock fits into a 3 × 4 × 5-in. cabinet, but you may want to build it in a slightly larger cabinet with different styling. If your soldering skills are limited, we would recommend a 4 × 5 × 6-in. cabinet. All external connectors are brought out to push-in terminals at the edge of the perfboard.

Be careful handling the integrated circuit. A socket for the IC is a must. Install the IC in the socket only when you are finished with all the wiring to prevent a static charge from damaging it.

The display is quite sturdy, though dropping it on its edge on the concrete basement floor (as we did during construction) will definitely wipe it out! Cut a hole in the front of the cabinet for the display and attach it with a bracket, glue, or masking tape. All display connections are brought out on pins similar to a 14-pin dual in-line IC. The pins have to be bent slightly to fit into the IC socket. To improve visibility, we recommend putting a sheet of smoked or green-blue plastic or glass in front of the display.

Optional Features

You may want to drop some of the features provided in the basic clock to simplify its construction. You may also want to add a few extra features if you feel strongly about them. Mix and match; it's up to you.

- Leading or blanking zero in the 24-hour mode. If you prefer a leading 0 (05 15 45 instead of 5 15 45) leave out Q1 and R19 to R21.
- Display brightness. If you would like to control the intensity of the display, replace R24 with a 500-ohm potentiometer connected as a rheostat.
- Twenty-four hour display. You can choose the

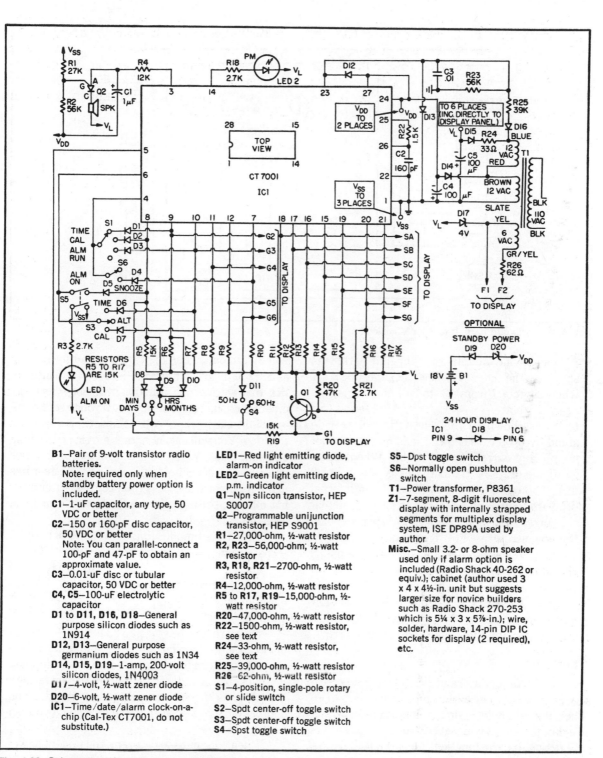

B1—Pair of 9-volt transistor radio batteries.
Note: required only when standby battery power option is included.

C1—1-uF capacitor, any type, 50 VDC or better

C2—150 or 160-pF disc capacitor, 50 VDC or better
Note: You can parallel-connect a 100-pF and 47-pF to obtain an approximate value.

C3—0.01-uF disc or tubular capacitor, 50 VDC or better

C4, C5—100-uF electrolytic capacitor

D1 to D11, D16, D18—General purpose silicon diodes such as 1N914

D12, D13—General purpose germanium diodes such as 1N34

D14, D15, D19—1-amp, 200-volt silicon diodes, 1N4003

D17—4-volt, ½-watt zener diode

D20—6-volt, ½-watt zener diode

IC1—Time/date/alarm clock-on-a-chip (Cal-Tex CT7001, do not substitute.)

LED1—Red light emitting diode, alarm-on indicator

LED2—Green light emitting diode, p.m. indicator

Q1—Npn silicon transistor, HEP S0007

Q2—Programmable unijunction transistor, HEP S9001

R1—27,000-ohm, ½-watt resistor

R2, R23—56,000-ohm; ½-watt resistor

R3, R18, R21—2700-ohm, ½-watt resistor

R4—12,000-ohm, ½-watt resistor

R5 to R17, R19—15,000-ohm, ½-watt resistor

R20—47,000-ohm, ½-watt resistor

R22—1500-ohm, ½-watt resistor, see text

R24—33-ohm, ½-watt resistor, see text

R25—39,000-ohm, ½-watt resistor

R26—62-ohm, ½-watt resistor

S1—4-position, single-pole rotary or slide switch

S2—Spdt center-off toggle switch

S3—Spdt center-off toggle switch

S4—Spst toggle switch

S5—Dpst toggle switch

S6—Normally open pushbutton switch

T1—Power transformer, P8361

Z1—7-segment, 8-digit fluorescent display with internally strapped segments for multiplex display system, ISE DP89A used by author

Misc.—Small 3.2- or 8-ohm speaker used only if alarm option is included (Radio Shack 40-262 or equiv.); cabinet (author used 3 x 4 x 4½-in. unit but suggests larger size for novice builders such as Radio Shack 270-253 which is 5¼ x 3 x 5⅞-in.); wire, solder, hardware, 14-pin DIP IC sockets for display (2 required), etc.

Fig. 4-30. Schematic and parts list for Maxiclock.

187

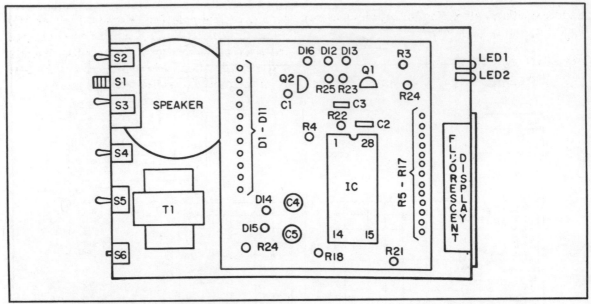

Fig. 4-31. Perfboard parts layout for Maxiclock.

24-hour mode simply by connecting D18 as shown on the schematic. The clock must be reset when switched from 12- to 24-hour display.

• Stand-by battery power. A couple of 9-volt batteries as shown on the schematic will provide stand-by power. When the ac is on they do not supply any current to the circuit. When the ac is off the drain on the batteries is only about 3 mA. Though the display will be off, an internal oscillator will keep the counters running so that the correct time and date will be displayed when the power returns. For this option, replace R22 with a 5000-ohm potentiometer connected as a rheostat. Adjust it by unplugging the clock for one minute at a time (with a stand-by battery installed). Then, check whether it is fast or slow when the ac power is again applied and adjust R22 in the direction which will reduce error.

Operation

Set the time, date, and alarm by turning S1 to the proper position (either time, date, or alarm). Then flip and hold S2 in the hour/months or minute/day position—whichever you wish to set. You will notice that the function you have elected to set will increment at one digit per second for as long as S2 is in the off-center position. You will also notice that setting one function will not affect any other function. This feature allows you to set February 29 in a leap year without upsetting any other function. You will also note that moving S1 to time stops the clock. When S2 is then actuated, seconds will reset to 00. These two imaginative features make for precise and easy time setting. After making all your settings, return S1 to its normal run setting.

The display mode, time-only, date-only or alternate (time and date), is selected with S3.

The alarm on switch S5 also turns on a red LED to make you aware that the alarm is set. The warning light may save you from being awakened at 7 a.m. on a weekend.

The alarm can be set up to 23 hours, 59 minutes in advance (let the alarm ring for a minute, or better still, just turn it off for a minute before flipping S5 back on for tomorrow morning's greeting). Switch S6 is the snooze button and will give you another ten minutes sleep in the morning if you can manage to give it a nudge.

When you set time or alarm, the p.m. light will

indicate whether your setting corresponds to a.m. (light off) or p.m. (light on).

The Wrap-Up

So that's it! A clock project that gives you more for less is e/e's style. Our supplier of hard-to-find items has promised to hold the line on prices (see the parts list), so we expect these optional features and useful functions to bring our readers the best clock their inflation-fighting dollars can buy.

Index

Index

Other Bestsellers from TAB

☐ **50 CMOS IC PROJECTS**—Delton T. Horn

Provides practical projects designed to use the popular CMOS family of integrated circuits. Horn presents a general introduction to CMOS ICs and technology . . . provides full schematics including working diagrams and parts lists . . . offers construction hints as well as suggestions for project variations and combinations. This book discusses: the basics of digital electronics, safe handling of CMOS devices, breadboarding, tips on experimenting with circuits, and more. You'll find signal generator and music-making projects, time-keeping circuits, game circuits, and a host of other miscellaneous circuits. 224 pp., 226 illus.

Paper $16.95   **Hard $25.95**
Book No. 2995

☐ **50 POWERFUL PRINTED CIRCUIT BOARDSPROJECTS**—Dave Prochnow

If you've ever experienced the frustration and disappointment of failed projects or are interested in finding practical, unique electronic devices, then you won't want to miss this book! Here, in a single reference, are 50 fully described, and detailed electronics projects, complete with schematic diagrams and instructions. More importantly, this book provides what few others on the market can. Each project in this book comes with its own computer generated photo image of the printed circuit board!

Paper $15.95   **Hard $23.95**
Book No. 2972

☐ **ENCYCLOPEDIA OF ELECTRONICS**—Stan Gibilisco

Here are more than 3,000 complete articles covering thousands of electronics terms and applications—each one Including all relevant formulas, charts, and tables. A must-have resource for anyone involved in any area of electronics or communications practice. Covers everything from basic electronics terms to state-of-the-art digital electronics theory and applications . . . from microcomputers to amateur radio and satellite TV! 1,024 pp., 1,300 illus. 8½″ × 11″ format.

Hard $60.00   **Book No. 2000**

☐ **THE ENCYCLOPEDIA OF ELECTRONIC CIRCUITS**—Rudolf F. Graf

Here Is every professional's dream treasury of analog and digital circuits—nearly 100 circuit categories . . . over 1,200 individual circuits designed for long-lasting applications potential. Adding even more to the value of this resource is the exhaustively thorough index which gives you instant access to exactly the circuits you need each and every time! 768 pp., 1,762 illus.

Paper $29.95   **Hard $60.00**
Book No. 1938

☐ **HOW TO DESIGN SOLID-STATE CIRCUITS**—2nd Edition—Mannie Horowitz and Delton T. Horn

Design and build useful electronic circuits from scratch! The authors provide the exact data you need on every aspect of semiconductor design . . . performance characteristics . . . applications potential . . . operating reliability . . . and more! Four major categories of semiconductors are examined: Diodes . . . Transistors . . . Integrated Circuits . . . Thyristors. This second edition is filled with procedures, advice, techniques, and background information. All the hands-on direction you need to understand and use semiconductors in all kinds of electronic devices is provided. Ranging from simple temperature-sensitive resistors to integrated circuit units composed of multiple microcircuits, this new edition describes a host of the latest in solid-state devices. 380 pp., 297 illus.

Paper $16.95   **Hard $24.95**
Book No. 2975

☐ **500 ELECTRONIC IC CIRCUITS WITH PRACTICAL APPLICATIONS**—James A. Whitson

More than just an electronics book that provides circuit schematics or step-by-step projects, this complete source-book provides both practical electronics circuits AND the additional information you need about specific components. You will be able to use this guide to improve your IC circuit-building skills as well as become more familiar with some of the popular ICs.336 pp., 600 illus.

Paper $18.95   **Hard $28.95**
Book No. 2920

☐ **55 EASY-TO-BUILD ELECTRONIC PROJECTS**—Editors of *Elementary Electronics*

If you're looking for a gold mine of exciting, fun-to-build, *and useful* electronics projects that are both easy and inexpensive to put together . . . here's where you'll hit pay dirt!! Here are more than 50 unique electronic projects selected from the best that have been published in *Elementary Electronics* Magazine . . . projects that have been tested and proven! 256 pp., 256 illus.

Paper $14.95   **Book No. 1999**

☐ **DESIGNING IC CIRCUITS . . . WITH EXPERIMENTS**—Delton T. Horn

With this excellent sourcebook as your guide, you'll be able to get started in the designing of your own practical circuits using op amps, 555 timers, voltage regulators, linear ICs, digital ICs, and other commonly available IC devices. It's crammed with practical design and construction tips and hints that are guaranteed to save you time and effort no matter what your IC application. 364 pp., 395 illus.

Paper $16.95   **Hard $24.95**
Book No. 1925

Other Bestsellers from TAB

☐ **BASIC ELECTRONICS THEORY—with projects and experiments**—2nd Edition—Delton T. Horn

If you're looking for an easy-to-follow introduction to modern electronics . . . or if you're an experienced hobbyist or technician in need of a quick-reference guide on the many facets of today's analog or digital electronics practice . . . there's simply no better sourcebook than *Basic Electronics Theory—with Projects and Experiments*! 672 pp., 645 illus.
Paper $18.95   **Book No. 1775**

☐ **MASTER HANDBOOK OF ELECTRONIC TABLES & FORMULAS**—4th Edition—Martin Clifford

Here's YOUR SOURCE for fast, accurate, easy-to-use solutions to all the common—and not so common—electronics and related math problems you encounter in your everyday electronics practice. It gives you instant access to all the formulas, nomographs, and vital component data you need including data on number systems, an EBCDIC table for graphic characters and much, much more! 392 pp., 246 illus.
Paper $16.95   **Book No. 1625**

☐ **POWER SUPPLIES, SWITCHING REGULATORS, INVERTERS AND CONVERTERS**—Irving M. Gottlieb

A comprehensive guide to operation power sources used in applications from computers and radio transmitters to TVs, and more! Contains the details and depth required by electronics professionals . . . the basic explanations and advice needed by hobbyists. This book offers a wide range of related technical data in a single format. 448 pp., 260 illus.
Paper $19.95   **Book No. 1665**

☐ **UNDERSTANDING DIGITAL ELECTRONICS**—R.H. Warring

Here in step-by-step format and easy-to-follow plain English, is an introduction, complete with clear, detailed drawings, to the principles and practices of digital electronics, arranged so that each topic can be referred to and studied separately. From the most basic principles of digital electronics, the author guides you smoothly through the implementation of working solutions using logic circuit devices. 154 pp., 140 illus.
Paper $8.95   **Hard $13.95**
Book No. 1593

(In PA, NY, and ME add applicable sales tax. Orders subject to credit approval. Orders outside U.S. must be prepaid with international money orders in U.S. dollars.)
*Prices subject to change without notice.

▬▬▬▬▬▬▬▬▬▬▬▬▬▬▬▬▬▬▬▬▬▬▬▬▬▬▬▬▬▬▬▬▬▬▬▬

To purchase these or any other books from TAB, visit your local bookstore, return this coupon, or call toll-free 1-800-233-1128 (In PA and AK call 1-717-794-2191).

Product No.	Hard or Paper	Title	Quantity	Price

☐ Check or money order enclosed made payable to TAB BOOKS Inc.

Charge my   ☐ VISA   ☐ MasterCard   ☐ American Express

Acct. No. _____ Exp. _____

Signature _____

Please Print
Name _____

Company _____

Address _____

City _____

State _____ Zip _____

Subtotal

Postage/Handling
($5.00 outside
U.S.A. and Canada) $2.50

In PA, NY, and ME
add applicable
sales tax

TOTAL

Mail coupon to:
TAB BOOKS Inc.
Blue Ridge Summit
PA 17294-0840

BC